All Aboard with E. M. Frimbo

Also by ROGERS E. M. WHITAKER

Decade of the Trains, the 1940s (with Don Ball, Jr.)

Also by TONY HISS

A Region at Risk: The Third Regional

Plan for the New York–New Jersey–Connecticut
Metropolitan Area (with Robert D. Yaro)

The Experience of Place

Henry Chung's Hunan Style Chinese Cookbook (editor)

Laughing Last: Alger Hiss by Tony Hiss

Know-How: A Fix-It Book for the Clumsy
but Pure of Heart (with Guy Alland and Miron Waskiw)

The Giant Panda Book

ALL ABOARD WITH E. M. FRIMBO

World's Greatest Railroad Buff

*by Rogers E. M. Whitaker
and Tony Hiss*

Greatly Expanded Edition
With a New Preface by Tony Hiss

*with additional Works of Engineering
by Barbara Vroom and Brendan Gill,
and Illustrations by Mark Livingston*

KODANSHA INTERNATIONAL
New York • Tokyo • London

Kodansha America, Inc.
114 Fifth Avenue, New York, New York 10011, U.S.A.

Kodansha International Ltd.
17-14 Otowa 1-chome, Bunkyo-ku, Tokyo 112, Japan

Published in 1997 by Kodansha America, Inc.
by arrangement with Tony Hiss and Francis Whitaker.

The first thirty-three chapters published in book form in 1974 by Grossman Publishers, a division of The Viking Press, New York.

This is a Kodansha Globe book.

Library of Congress Cataloging-in-Publication Data
Whitaker, Rogers E. M.
    All aboard with E. M. Frimbo: world's greatest railroad buff / by Rogers E. M. Whitaker and Tony Hiss; with additional works of engineering by Barbara Vroom and Brendan Gill; and illustrations by Mark Livingston.
        p.   cm. — (Kodansha globe)
    ISBN 1-56836-114-9 (pb)
    1. Railroads. 2. Whitaker, Rogers E. M.—Journeys. I. Hiss, Tony. II. Title.
III. Series.
TF20.W48 1996
385'.092—dc20
[B]   96-4356

Printed in the United States of America
    98 99 00   Q/FF   10 9 8 7 6 5 4 3 2

To Margaret Randall, as before.
And to ⟨F⟩, and two Hisses,
Alger and Jacob,
grandfather and grandson.

London, Feb. 22 (A.P.)—The world will run out of oil some time in the next century, and the only way to move goods and people across land probably will be by rail, Henry Sampson, editor of the authoritative *Jane's World Railways*, predicted today in a foreword to the 16th edition of the reference book.

        —New York Daily News,
        February 23, 1974

Contents

Previously Uncollected Chapters

Illustrations

XV

Preface to the Expanded Edition
Tony Hiss

Frimbo's back! And not a moment too soon. Only a year ago it looked, once again, as though all of America's passenger trains might shudder hopelessly to a permanent halt, just as it had looked thirty years ago, back in the bad, old, sour and moldering, mid-1960s, pre-Amtrak days, when Ernest Malcolm Frimbo burst into print. It was then that Frimbo's irresistible explorations into the remotest areas that parlor cars and cabooses could reach, and his increasingly dire, Paul Revere-on-an-iron-horse warnings of the railroad-less future that loomed ahead, became first a regular and then an eagerly awaited contribution to *The New Yorker*'s Talk of the Town section.

But ruin, once again, has ever so narrowly been averted. And it's instead becoming increasingly clear that, even if a Frimbonian millennium is not yet at hand, one of the lastingly important stories set to unfold during the first decade of the twenty-first century will be a massive shoring up of, an unprecedented pouring of money into, and a worldwide revival of interest in, Frimbo's favorite subject—train travel.

For me, it's greatly gratifying to be asked to write a new introduction officially announcing Frimbo's return—but I can't say it's a surprise. One secret of Frimbo's great and lasting charm has been that he was at heart a pacesetter and a trailblazer, although it pleased him to pose as an anachronism. He always understood that speed, efficiency, courtesy, and good cheer contributed every bit as much to the delightfulness of travel as a basket of freshly baked huckleberry muffins or a pitcher of freshly shaken brandies Alexander. Treating passengers like parcels, he correctly predicted, would have only calamitous results—it cheated people of an essential part of their humanity; it diminished and impoverished cities and travel corridors; and it degraded and corrupted transportation providers.

Practically nobody was making comments like these about passenger railroads back in the 1960s, but people caught on anyhow. Because Americans, as it turned out, hadn't given up on trains—only their leaders had, and their railroads. It's now been twenty-two years since the first publication of *All Aboard with E. M. Frimbo*, by this time a much-traveled travel book that collected some of the early *New Yorker* Frimbo pieces that Rogers Whitaker and I wrote about the wonders that railroads brought with them into the world. According to the letters that over the years have come my way as Frimbo's surviving junior partner, a generation of railroad lovers still manages to find room for the original *Frimbo* in their luggage, and likes to curl up with the book and its yarns. Some people just want to think about trains—but others take

All Aboard on board, perhaps on a narrow-gauge, glass-roofed observation car that's threading its way through the Alps, and some pore over it over second cups of coffee on a sunset-drenched, west coast Amtrak diner that, thanks to twisty seacoast tracks, occasionally seems to be leaning way out over the edge of the fading-to-purple Pacific Ocean.

These days many governments (national governments in Europe and Asia, and, increasingly, a number of state governments here in the States) have rediscovered passenger trains—helped along by a new system of accounting that makes it easier for politicians and bureaucrats to recognize that investments in railroads can create several kinds of highly positive payoffs simultaneously. The French government, for instance, calculates that its investments in high-speed rail on the new network of TGV, or Train à Grande Vitesse, lines pay a financial return of up to 17 percent, along with a "social return" of up to 33 percent. (The social return, as Marcia Lowe explains in her recent Worldwatch paper, *Back on Track: The Global Rail Revival,* is a way of putting a precise dollar value on all the lives, time, and oil the new trains have saved, and on all the pollution and congestion that, thanks to these trains, just don't exist.)

As a happy result of the long-heralded (by Frimbo) passenger train comeback, this new, greatly expanded, almost-twenty-first-century edition of *All Aboard with E. M. Frimbo* will very soon find its way on to some already-under-construction, twenty-first-century trains, such as Amtrak's 125-miles-an-hour electrified Metroliners between New York and Boston; or the 217-miles-an-hour third-generation TGV trains all across France; or the 300-plus-miles-an-hour, magnetically levitated German "ground planes" that will be streaking between Berlin and Hamburg by 2010; and some equally speedy trains down under, from Sydney to Melbourne.

Of course, in the summer of 1966, when Rogers Ernest Malcolm Whitaker and I first got to be friends, we weren't thinking about what still-to-be-born readers scooting around on as-yet-unperfected technologies might make of us thirty years later. I was twenty-five, bumptious, and oh-so-green, a *New Yorker* cub reporter looking around for stories. Whitaker, at sixty-six, was—someone not easily summed up, then or ever. For one thing, he pretended to be sixty-seven. He was born in a Boston suburb on January 15, 1900, but he always told people he had been born in 1899—perhaps so he could say, as Frimbo does in this book, "The railway was invented early in the nineteenth century and I was invented late in the nineteenth century."

A definitive account of Whitaker's life may finally emerge, once John L. Haber, the writer-director-producer who created *Frimbo,* a soon-to-be-revived musical comedy based on *All Aboard with E. M. Frimbo,* completes his massive and fascinating video documentary of Whitaker. Haber, in the meantime, has very generously allowed us to reproduce in this new edition some of the pictures from his incomparable Whitaker portrait collection.

Whitaker touched many lives, some of them quite free of any railroad connections, and Haber's still turning up new material. It's not easy, because Whitaker had a life that, like an old dreadnought, was built out of watertight compartments. His railroad friends might be astonished at a letter, dated more than twenty-five years ago, from Woody Allen to Whitaker that Haber faxed to me recently. Allen's letter is a thank-you note for some anonymous *New Yorker* reviews

Whitaker had written, many not much longer than *haiku,* of Allen's old stand-up comedy nightclub routines. "However it may sound," Allen wrote, "it is absolutely true that your interest in my work has been by far my most satisfying achievement in the entire night-club area, and your encouragement since my early days of performing sustained me through many, many nights when I truly doubted whether I had any real contribution to make as a comedian."

Today it's quite clear to me that the principal reason E. M. Frimbo still seems larger than life is that Rogers E. M. Whitaker, whose own railroad exploits we faithfully adapted for the semifictional Frimbo stories, led a life so ample that all of Frimbo's many to-ings and fro-ings accounted for only a small fraction of his own yearly activities. That's why there's plenty of previously uncollected Whitaker material in this expanded edition of *All Aboard with E. M. Frimbo,* including "Frimbo's Peak," a joint profile of two equally formidable Whitakers, Rogers and his kid brother, Francis, now eighty-nine, the dean of American artist blacksmiths, who still skis down two or three Rocky Mountains every winter, although he says that his knees are beginning to bother him. After Rogers' death in 1981, it was Francis who gathered a group of us together so we could scatter Rogers' ashes in Cumbres Pass, between New Mexico and Colorado, which at ten thousand feet, is the highest point in the United States traversed by passenger trains.

The present book, finally, is the compleat Frimbo. It spans six decades of *New Yorker* stories, from the 1940s through the 1990s, and brings together twenty-one additional Frimbo and Frimbo-inspired stories that came along after the original book was published. We've also found room for the ultimate accolade—a parody, and a good one, by Hendrik Hertzberg,

who's now *The New Yorker*'s executive editor. Then, for good
measure, we've thrown in an Old Curmudgeon story that
caused Whitaker no end of trouble. In the mid-1970s, in
order to squeeze more of Whitaker's life into the magazine,
we devised this second pseudonym, and the Curmudge, a
Manhattan-bounded figure who had a rather sharper tongue
than Frimbo, quickly built his own loyal following. (At one
point, we even briefly launched a third Whitaker character,
the Envoy Plenipotentiary. But that one was too hard to
pronounce.)

In the Old Curmudgeon piece we've included here, Whitaker recounted an old memory that still tugged at him: On a
cold, winter day when he was a young man, Rogers, at the
behest of his father, Charles Harris Whitaker (yet another
formidable Whitaker, the mentor of the two greatest regional
planners of the twentieth century, Lewis Mumford and Benton MacKaye), toured with the aged and ailing Louis Sullivan
around New York. Sullivan, the great American architect
whom Frank Lloyd Wright called *lieber Meister,* wanted a
last look at all the New York buildings he had worked on,
and when he found they'd all, save one, been demolished, he
burst into tears on the street.

When the piece was published, Whitaker's woes began.
Renowned architectural historians wrote and phoned *The New
Yorker* to complain that the magazine hadn't checked its facts,
and that, as everyone knew, Sullivan had only been responsible for one New York structure, the Bayard-Condict Building, which still stands on Bleecker Street. Whitaker replied
that his memory was far more reliable than their scholarship
could ever be. The matter has never been resolved.

It in no way diminishes Frimbo now to place him properly

in his true Whitakerian perspective. To be quite specific, or, as is said nowadays, in the interest of full disclosure:

Although Whitaker knew enough about railroading to have been commissioned a major in the United States Army Transportation Corps during the Second World War (a position that Harold Ross, the founding editor of *The New Yorker,* begged him in a hastily scribbled note not to accept —"Come up here and help us get out the magazine, which is more essential than 1,000,000 other jobs I know about"), and although during the last years of his life he was privately commissioned by Paul H. Reistrup, then Amtrak president, to ride the rails under assumed names and send in secret reports on what he saw and heard and how he was treated (Whitaker called these utterly frank memos to Reistrup "missiles," and they led to the reassignment of a number of Amtrak managers and train crew members), it may be helpful to remember that Whitaker did *all* his nearly 3,000,000 miles of train riding only on weekends and vacations.

He was much too busy for trains during the rest of the year; he spent most of his time at *The New Yorker,* where he was a sports columnist as well as the nightclub reviewer, and every week edited about a third of the magazine. He also had a private life, which included three marriages, although no children, and, between marriages, plenty of romances. And he was a dandy, specializing, long before Tom Wolfe discovered them, in double-breasted waistcoats with generous lapels. To me, he looked and sounded like a cross between Winston Churchill and W. C. Fields. And I didn't even have to think of a way to fit him into the Talk of the Town—Brendan Gill had already kindly done that for me.

The then-anonymous Talk department, which was always

Whitaker, watching one of his 3,000,000 miles flying by

trying to find the true voice of New York City, was already
full of *noms de plume* in those days, including "Our Man
Stanley" (really Philip Hamburger, still a *New Yorker* main-
stay) and the "long-winded lady" (the short story writer,
Maeve Brennan, daughter of a former Irish ambassador to
the United States). I'd even long-windedly invented one myself, "Our Man Stanley's teenage nephew, Hiram," as a way
of writing about a limo ride with Paul McCartney on the day
the Beatles arrived in New York. Brendan Gill (he was one
of the few established *New Yorker* writers who showed much
early kindness to the upstarts of my generation) told me that

back in the 1930s, when the original *New Yorker* crowd was still inseparable, one night after putting the magazine to bed they all went to a most unmemorable W.P.A. play that had as a leading character a frightening African witch doctor named Dr. Frimbo. Everyone present (except Whitaker) said that Frimbo looked *exactly* like Whitaker.

Almost ten years later, in 1945, when Gill was casting around for a story—in his early days he was a crackerjack Talk reporter—he hit on the idea of writing up some of Whitaker's more intricate weekend train jaunts, with multiple connections and frequent just-enough-time-for-a-quick-ride-between-trains trolley-car trips. Whitaker, then a mere mileage millionaire, was already famous among his colleagues, so Gill made an in-joke of it all by creating a character named E. M. Frimbo, reviving the witch doctor and pasting on the two middle names, Ernest Malcolm, that Whitaker gave himself when he arrived in New York after leaving Princeton (he was actually born without a middle name). This was supposed to be a one-shot deal, but in the mid-1950s, when John Frankenheimer made a movie called *The Train,* about sabotaging a Nazi attempt to take a trainload of stolen French art treasures off to Germany, Gill, by then the magazine's film critic, asked Whitaker to come along with him to a screening, and in his review made mention of how impressed Dr. Frimbo was by the technical accuracy of the wartime rolling stock used in the film.

And then came the barrage of pieces that Whitaker and I were jointly responsible for. For years, in our own quirky style, we saw to it that *The New Yorker* was the only national magazine that gave regular coverage to Amtrak, particularly its painful birth and many early trials. We were, of course, in no way responsible for the fact that Americans are consis-

The Cumbres & Toltec Scenic Railroad steaming toward Cumbres Pass

tently more committed to Amtrak's survival than their leaders realize—it's said, for instance, that every time Amtrak is threatened, Congress gets more angry letters than it does about any other subject, except Social Security. But we were the first journalists who showed that this abiding American passion for trains was newsworthy rather than quaint, because it was part of an ongoing grassroots effort, now finally coming into its own, to rebalance the growth of the country and calm its congestion and tame its sprawl.

There was a Frimbonian ring in Daniel Patrick Moynihan's voice a few years ago when he called on America to enter the post–interstate highway age. On the Senate floor he declared that "We have poured enough concrete." Ever since, the country has been experiencing an explosion of interest in greenways, scenic byways, traffic-calmed streets, rails-to-trails, rails-*with*-trails, and dozens of other concepts omitted from traditional highway engineering manuals that Frimbo would have applauded (from a well-upholstered train seat, of course). And Frimbo would certainly be actively championing several new post–interstate Amtrak innovations—you would frequently find him, for instance, at a candlelit table in the *Pacific Parlor,* a stylish, new, bring-'em-back-to-the-trains, double-decker, glass-topped, first-class lounge car that's just been added to the Seattle–Los Angeles run. (The *Pacific Parlor,* the first service upgrade on a long-distance American train in many years, stocks only highly delectable western fare, such as a dark and flinty Oregon beer that recently won a platinum medal among 150 microbreweries.)

And Amtrak, in partnership with the communities it serves, has started to fix up its front doors—restoring historic downtown depots; adding bistros and bookstalls; and replacing disgraceful, post-war, bus-shelter-barren "Amshacks," as they're often called, with the first passenger-worthy new railroad stations to be built in the country since the Depression. The result: Stations are starting to fill up—both with more people who want to get on trains, and with more people who don't at all want to get on trains but who want to stay downtown after dark. Train stations, because people all over the country have so much long-pent-up, longing-for-a-happy-ending affection for them, are proving to be perfect rallying points for downtowns desperate to bounce back. Frimbo would be greatly heartened.

A final note. There's one question I'm always asked—What can you tell me about the Contessa? People wonder if this mysterious figure, Frimbo's great flame, was real, or if we just added her for effect. I've always been discreet, because the Contessa's an intensely private person, but I don't think there's any harm now in saying that she is both real and beautiful. I met her only once, years ago, when she and her daughter visited Whitaker at his office. She was German, left her family before the war, and escaped to America with her adopted family, Jewish refugees who arrived in New York two days before Pearl Harbor. She and Major Whitaker met during the war, but she left the country in 1949 for Paris, and later married a Spanish count. She and Whitaker stayed in touch always, and occasionally took long trips together. But, in his watertight way, he never told her that this book is dedicated to her.

New York City
May 1996

Acknowledgments for the Expanded Edition

Thanks, first of all, to Philip S. Turner, editor-in-chief of Kodansha America, for both rediscovering and reinventing the book—bringing it back into print and at the same time insisting that it grow to its present size. That growth was also nobly assisted by *The New Yorker*'s tiptop library staff—including Christopher Shay, the librarian-in-chief, Ann Partrich, and Erin Overbey. You guys are aces!

Permissions proved to be complex, so many thanks go to Devereux Chatillon, Esq., *The New Yorker*'s editorial counsel, and to her expert assistant, Joy Weiner, who was a joy to work with; to Carbery O'Brien, of Workman Publishing's Permissions Department; to the wonderful Brendan Gill, who first thought of writing about Frimbo over fifty years ago; and to Nancy Wells, for ably representing the interests of her late niece, the marvelous Barbara Vroom, who wrote two chapters of the original book. And special thanks to a slew of people at ICM who worked overtime on this one, including John

B. De Laney, Sloan Harris, and the extraordinary Amanda Urban.

John L. Haber, the very gifted author and director of he musical *Frimbo*, gave invaluable help to the new edition, including pictures from his unrivaled collection of Frimboiana. Amtrak's Ronald J. Hartman, Scott Hercik, Brian Rosenwald, R. Clifford Black IV, and Bruce Heard all provided a torrent of information and insights, as did two remarkable Amtrak presidents: Tom Downs, the incumbent, and Paul Reistrup.

A large and ever helpful crew of people at the Rails-to-Trails Conservancy lent their most considerable expertise, including President David G. Burnett, Jenny Aley, Caroline Baker, Steve Emmett-Matox, Bob Patten, and Greg Smith.

I am also indebted to Robert G. Lewis for his unparalleled grasp of railroading; and to Alexandros Washburn, New York State director of Senator Daniel Patrick Moynihan's office; Ross Capon, executive director of the National Association of Railroad Passengers; G. W. Herkner Jr., director of Rail Contract Administration at New Jersey transit; William E. Loftus, president of the American Short Line Railroad Association; Gregory C. Kisloff, an intergovernmental relations consultant of renown; Dorothy Miner, Esq., a formidable expert on landmarks preservation law; Edward F. Graham, whose mileage totals rival even Frimbo's; and my wife, Lois Metzger, the novelist, whose superb editing skills transform any manuscript lucky enough to come her way.

Other heroes of this new edition are mentioned by name in the pages that follow.

Tony Hiss

Acknowledgments

The authors wish to thank the following for their kind, generous, and expert help in the making of this book: Lillian Ross, William Shawn, Susan Schlessinger, Charlie Number One of Charlies', 263 West 45th Street, New York, N.Y. 10036, and Johnnie of Frankie & Johnnie's Restaurant & Bar, 269 West 45th Street, New York, N. Y. 10036.

All Aboard with E. M. Frimbo

All for Love

We first met Ernest Malcolm Frimbo, the man who is regarded as the world's greatest railroad buff, in the little Alpine town of Zermatt, in Switzerland, in the summer of 1946. You can see the Matterhorn from Zermatt—it's that high up in the mountains. You reach Zermatt on a series of trains, the last of them a cog railway. By order of the Zermatt town council, there are no internal combustion engines on the premises, except for a few police cars and fire trucks and some delivery vans that are allowed about early in the morning. The Hôtel Mont Cervin, where, on doctor's orders, we were spending a couple of lazy weeks away from New York City and the weekly magazine we write for, sends a coach-and-two to the railroad station to meet incoming trains. "There are no stories in Zermatt," the doctor had told us. "And if there is one, anyway, you just look the other way. *Please.*"

But one morning—what can you do?—we noticed that the Mont Cervin coach-and-two seemed to be working overtime—trundling coach-load after coach-load of travelers to the hotel. And we noticed that on one of its trips the coach had only a single passenger, a tall, distinguished-looking man in a Homburg who looked around with the glance seen in portraits of Dr. Samuel Johnson. And then we noticed, on the way in to lunch, a discreetly small sign on the reception desk: BIENVENUS, LEXICOGRAPHES DU MONDE. And inside the hotel restaurant, which was full of newcomers, at a table by the window, all by himself, was a tall, distinguished-looking man who was staring at a menu with a dubious eye.

We stared ourselves. Presumably the man was a lexicographer. But the odd thing was, when we looked at him, we kept thinking, irresistibly, of—railroads. In the first place, he looked a lot like a conductor on a crack express. He had the same pink face. And the look he was giving the menu was certainly the look a conductor gives a small boy who is sitting right next to the emergency cord. He did not produce a pocket watch, but we knew he had one.

But there was more to it than this. As we watched him, a most vivid image sprang into our mind, and stayed there. We saw a steam engine. It was a Union Pacific 4-8-4, and it had stopped at a prairie village at five-forty in the morning. We could see steam curling up around the boiler, and then we could hear the driving rods clanking in the predawn stillness. Cinders settled down on the clover. The engineer was peering down miles of track silvered by a late-setting moon.

A story had appeared in Zermatt!

So we went to work, and asked a lot of questions, and finally secured an invitation to dine that night at the table by the window. The lexicographer who looked like a conductor and made us see a steam engine said, "Good evening.

My name is Frimbo. I can answer your questions. I have
taken the liberty of ordering—I assume you have no ob-
jections to veal Oscar and a bottle of Sion Fondant? We
lexicographers are having our first big get-together since
the war. We have a lot of work to catch up on. The war was
responsible for a lot of new words, you know. We are here
in Zermatt because I made a fuss and insisted we forgather
in a place where the loudest noises are made by trains. I
told everybody that nobody could get any work done with
a lot of automobiles in the neighborhood showering internal
combustion over everything in sight. Well, they finally gave
in, since I was only telling the truth.

"But it is also true that I am myself a rail buff, and that
I need to catch up on my traveling. During the war I've
only been able to get around at the rate of thirty or forty
thousand miles a year. Last year, for instance, I covered
only forty-one thousand miles, whereas in nineteen-forty-
one, my best year, I achieved a total of ninety thousand
seven hundred and fifty-six miles. Of course, I only travel
weekends and during my vacations—or when I am forced
to for professional reasons."

A rail buff! So that was the explanation. Of course. We
found ourselves warming to this man. Mr. Frimbo eyed us
disdainfully. "Most people think rail buffs are nuts," he
said. "I don't know why. If I rode around in a Buick all
weekend, no one would say a word. Furthermore, the government doesn't think we're nuts. After we got into the war,
the Army called me down to Washington and gave me a
majority, so the knowledge I've picked up wandering around
the countryside must be worth something."

We didn't want to get off on the wrong foot. "Major,"
we said, "please tell us more." And we asked him when he

had felt the first stirrings of his passion for trains. He said, "I understand that when I was a baby, living with my family in England, I used to make my nanny push me in my pram to a certain railroad bridge in Hadley Wood, on the outskirts of London, so I could watch the trains go by. When we had gone home to tea, I'm told, I was inconsolable. By the time my family moved back to the States, I was old enough to give my inclination full rein. Those were glorious days, because I had the whole world of trolleys as well as trains at my disposal. Young people nowadays don't know what could be done when trolleys were at their zenith. Why, out in Danville, Illinois, there was an interurban trolley line that had sleepers and dining cars! I knew that a number of these delights would not last the war—the rails would be used to keep mainline tracks in repair—so just before I became a major, I took six weeks off from work and rode and rode, carefully picking out lines like the Rapid City & Black Hills Western. I rode my seat off. God, how I rode! Day and night.

"But I am getting ahead of my story. When I came of age, I set myself a goal, like all young men. My ambition has been to ride over every single foot of passenger trackage in the United States. I think I can accomplish that in another ten years or so. I'm down to the hard bits now. Last month I added fifty miles of the Santa Fe Railroad in Texas to my list, but I had to take a taxi from Amarillo to Spearman, a distance of some ninety miles, to catch my train. It was bad enough to find myself in a car; to make matters worse, there was a frightful dust storm, and the hood of the car, an insubstantial quadricycle, kept blowing back and smashing against the windshield."

"You don't like cars, sir?"

Near Zermatt

"Cars and planes, sir, are the natural enemies of railroads. What is a car? A car is a rolling sneeze. A little slice of selfishness. As for planes, I have been trying to get the railroads to fight the airlines by adopting a slogan I have coined—'Go through Our Mountains, Not into Them.'"

A waiter now appeared with our veal Oscar, and Frimbo

attacked his portion as if it were one of the Wright brothers. He didn't speak to us again until he had finished eating. Then he said, "Now that was a dish worthy of the Swiss Restaurant Car Company—the people, you know, who prepare the meals in the dining cars on Swiss trains. Wonderful people! Have you ever drunk a Château Malessert? I thought not. It is a wine found only on Swiss restaurant cars. These remarkable cars are painted red, unlike most other Swiss railway cars, which are painted green. This very sound system allows *aficionados* to board trains at just the right place. I remember once suggesting to a congressman that much the same thing could be done with money—different denominations of bills could be printed up in different colors. But the congressman said, 'But that wouldn't help blind people,' and the matter died there, because I couldn't think up an answer to that.

"But to continue. My traveling companions and I observe only one ritual. Whenever we pass through the Swiss town of Olten—it's the town where the Swiss Restaurant Car Company has its headquarters—we rise in our first-class compartment and stand with our hats over our hearts."

"Do you always travel first class, sir?"

"Yes, sir. My father told me—and I think it was the only thing he ever told me—'A gentleman always rides in the Pullman.' Any more questions?"

We told Frimbo we'd like to know more about his methods and procedures. What was his last train trip before coming to Zermatt for the lexicographers' meeting? Had it covered any new trackage? Frimbo then described a three-day jaunt he had taken the previous weekend. He said it had been one day longer but no more devious than usual.

It immediately struck us as being a classic of its kind, and we set it down here as a significant social document, urging our students to bear in mind that the trip was undertaken all for love.

At eleven-thirty on Friday night, Frimbo caught the Baltimore & Ohio train bus at Rockefeller Center, in New York City. This bus took him to Jersey City, where he had reserved a lower berth on the one-oh-two A.M. Washington express. He reached Washington at seven-oh-five A.M. His sleeper was then attached to a Washington-to-St. Louis train, the *Metropolitan Special*, which left at seven-fifty-five A.M. He reached St. Louis at seven-forty Sunday morning. Drawing a deep breath, he caught the eight-fifteen train for Evansville, Indiana, reached Evansville at one-fifteen P.M., and there boarded the one-thirty-five local for Louisville. He reached Louisville at five-thirty-five and, presumably with some regret, took a cab to New Albany, Indiana. "There's an old trolley line between New Albany and Louisville," he told us. "I wanted to ride this one before some smelly bus takes its place."

Frimbo got the six-thirty trolley from New Albany, re-entered Louisville at seven-oh-five, and departed for Indianapolis at seven-thirty. He ate, shaved, and changed his shirt aboard the train, and disembarked at ten-thirty. He enjoyed a trolley ride of six or seven miles around the city, got back to the station at twelve-twelve Monday morning, and boarded a twelve-fifteen A.M. train for Danville, Illinois. He arrived at Danville at two-thirty A.M. and walked down the street to the station of the Illinois Terminal Railway, the interurban trolley company that once had sleepers and still, after the war, had observation-dining cars. The first trolley left at four-thirty A.M., and Frimbo rode it as far as Decatur Junction, where, at seven-oh-eight A.M., he boarded an interurban to Bloomington. He reached Bloomington at eight-forty-two A.M. and at nine-ten boarded a train called the *Alton Hummer* for Chicago. He arrived in Chicago at eleven-fifty-nine and made a quick run out to LaGrange on the Burlington. He returned by a Chicago & West Towns Railway Company trolley and then a Chicago Surface Lines trolley, reaching the La Salle Street station at two-fifty-seven P.M. and there engaged a bedroom on the *Twentieth Century.* "I always wear a black Homburg when I travel," Frimbo told us, "and I'm taken for a troubled businessman." The *Century* left Chicago at three-thirty P.M. Having been without sleep for thirty-nine hours, Frimbo went to bed early. He reached New York at nine-thirty A.M. Tuesday and was at his New York desk before ten.

"I covered about twenty-eight hundred miles," Frimbo said. "Three hundred and sixty-six of them were new. The New Albany-to-Louisville and Chicago & West Towns trolleys were the real gems. Naturally, a trip like that takes advance planning. People say, 'What do you do while you're on a train, especially now that they're so crowded and uncomfortable?' I say, 'Why, I just watch people in cars tied up in traffic jams on the highways, dragging along at three miles an hour.'

"I hope that we may meet again. At the moment I must go preside, as Temporary Chairman, over this evening's first plenary session of the lexicographers' conference. And then I have to get to bed early, because tomorrow I am taking some lexicographers who are fellow buffs on a narrow-gauge railroad to a point which affords an excellent view of the Matterhorn. I am planning a lunch at a little hostelry at the end of the line. Right now, you may ask just one more question."

Our question was: what further goal would Frimbo set himself when he had polished off all the passenger trackage in the U.S.A.?

"The world," he answered.

We Shall Overcome

*(Excerpts from the
Autobiography of
Ernest M. Frimbo)*

The railway was invented early in the nineteenth century and I was invented late in that century, so
the railway must have precedence. Because hardly anyone
was really migratory then, the railway began by hauling
timber and stone and coal and ore at a most leisurely speed,
inasmuch as horses were the motive power, but when someone proved that pent-up steam could be released to drive a
piston that could impart motion to a wheel, the age of overland travel was in hand. The journeyer on horseback and
the stagecoach fell, literally, by the wayside, and goods that
had been the prerogative of the canal started to move by rail.

The canals still survive, and thrive, but some of them
freeze over in the winter. The railway, it was soon learned,
did not freeze over; so the railway, it came to be under-
stood, was at last the most nearly perfect way of moving
from one place to another.

The precisely named Railway Mania that ensued had odd
effects. Following upon the reports of observers who had

noted the ease with which large bodies of troops and large consignments of materiel were moved about during the course of our Civil War, railways were built in Europe and in Russia not so much for the benefit of industry as for the benefit of the military. In England, the true birthplace of the railway, the Mania took the form of venomous competition and thus produced somewhat too much railway. In the United States, it was decided—after the Civil War had come to a close—that the Great West could not, if only for military reasons, be allowed to remain in its splendid isolation, and so the building of a railway to the Pacific became inevitable. But the venomous competition engendered by the Mania in this country also produced a great deal too much railway. And the long, largely arbitrary boundary line that divides us from Canada brought about, because of customs barriers, the need for eastern Canada to trade—for the most part—with western Canada and with then-Mother England, and so there was also a proliferation of railways in that country.

Well, all this is an enormous simplification of the matter, and I am indisposed to argue it. The First World War, though it demonstrated the absolute indispensability of the railway in a time of emergency, commenced the deflowering of that necessity. The engineering industries of the nations concerned in that war brought the internal-combustion engine to such a state of efficiency that self-propelled military vehicles (the tank comes quickly to mind) became nearly as valuable as the railway in the field of combat. After the war, the civilian equivalents of these vehicles attained so great a state of efficiency that they could often move people and goods quicker and cheaper than most branch-line, and not a few main-line, railways could. And this even before the highway lobbyists developed the Freeway Mania.

So began the slow suffocation not only of the railway but of those eminently nonpolluting means of transport called electric interurban railways and electric street cars. A great many of the interurban lines and street railways in this country died a most untimely death, as a finding by a recent congressional committee* has belatedly revealed, because years ago General Motors and sundry gasoline purveyors, tire makers, and bus builders set up an enterprise whose sole aim was to replace these railways and cars with internal-combustion (known in the trade as infernal-combustion) vehicles, in order that our national pollution could be expedited. This enterprise, National City Lines, bought up quite a few trolley lines that were earning a profit, converted them to bus lines that operated at a loss, and then sold them off to the cities they—so to speak—served.

The arrival of the airplane—which benefited no end from the man-hours expended upon its improvement in the interest of the wartime military establishment—removed travelers and many other sorts of commodities from the railway; today we fly more than just letters, strawberries, pompano, orchids—we fly men's suits, furniture, cattle. At what expenditure of energy, and at what premium cost to the user, one would rather not think.

It is not the Man on Horseback who gives us pause today. It is the Man in the Automobile. As we admit what we have known for a long time—that there is a finite limit to the world's mass of energy—we contemplate a scene of planned disorder: railways in bankruptcy and eager to expire; airlines in debt for a shortage of customers and the high cost of fuel; big bus companies dropping this run and that run;

* Report by Bradford C. Snell, assistant counsel to the Senate Antitrust Subcommittee, 1974.

small bus companies ceasing to exist; city transit lines on a deficit arrangement for lack of trade. Oh, and perhaps we should also consider the new supermanagements of railways. A few of these hierarchies have devoted themselves to prying the assets and the cash flow out of the systems they are in charge of and putting the stuff in other activities, even while they proclaim the need for government assistance to keep the railways in health.

Lately, it is true, people who have been accustomed to moving everywhere in their automobiles have thought about going back to the buses, the rapid-transit lines, the railways. They have discovered that, mostly, all these are in a poor state of repair. But the reversion to old habits must, nevertheless, be called progress: officialdom has announced that, because fewer journeys are being made by road, only 55,600 travelers died last year in highway accidents.

Whatever the faults of the society and the industrial system we have contrived, mobility is its essence. For me, mobility is not only a pastime but—sometimes—a way of earning a living. (We'll get to that later on.) Through the long illness of my favorite invalid, the railway, I have maintained my bedside manners and my temper. The railway, undernourished and often undermanaged, must, it does seem, be compelled to survive.

To do that, it does also seem, it must learn once again how to deal satisfactorily with its labor, its passengers, and its shippers of freight. The Congress, paying scant attention to the firmly expressed wishes of the current Administration, has applied one or two poultices to the wounds. One of the poultices was the bill that invented Amtrak. Amtrak has laid out (with the not especially noticeable assistance of a dozen railways) what remains to us of a system of long-distance passenger trains. Amtrak has diminished the disorder that had previously prevailed, but it has been rather thwarted by neatly phrased passages in the law that created it—phrases that, for instance, have inserted into its management several men whose displeasure with the whole scheme has frequently been made public.

However, no matter! We shall overcome.

And so, back to the time when the railway was in a buoyant mood, and to the days and nights I spent on it.

If I had it to do all over again, I would do the same. But I can't, for most of those many trains I rode from the beginning of the twentieth century were long ago annulled forever, and many of the rails on which they moved have been torn up. In New England, which is my part of the world, son follows father in the choice of profession; and I came upon my lifework by inheritance—my father was a born traveler. At the age of nine I was not outdoors playing baseball with boys my own age, and I was not indoors reading about the unlikely adventures of the Rover Boys. I was in my father's study, doing not my homework but my father's: he was going to the Pacific Coast, stopping off in Toledo, Chicago, Kansas City, Albuquerque, and Los Angeles on his way to San Francisco; he was coming back through Seattle, Vancouver, and Banff. What, then, were the best trains (with parlor or sleeping cars, and with dining cars) between these cities, and which among the innumerable tariffs prevailing was the most inclusive and advantageous round-trip fare?

My rewards for all this information (which had to be letter perfect) were a gigantic collection of railway timetables, a copious assortment of railway postcards (collected by my father en route), and use of the stub ends of his mileage books. These books held a thousand coupons apiece, each one worth a mile of journeying—or two cents—and Father would always come home with twenty-one miles left in one book, thirty-eight in another, and so on. I thought the world would fall before his wrath when the price of a book went from twenty dollars to twenty-five dollars in a single jump. With these stubs and the assistance of amused conductors, I was soon taking small Saturday trips of my own. Vast was my elation when I discovered that the stubs could also be used for seats in parlor cars and for luncheons in diners; and vast was my shame when I found out that parlor-car porters and dining-car waiters customarily were presented with tips. I didn't have that kind of pin money—only the scrip. (Every Monday now I buy a roll of quarters at the bank.)

The North American continent was not enough for my father, though. I was born in the suburbs of Boston, but as a babe in arms I made my very first railway journey on a slip carriage of a Great Western Railway express out of London's Paddington Station. (Sixty-three years later, in June 1965, Paddington said farewell to its last steam locomotive.) The carriage was slipped, i.e., dropped off, at Reading, through which the express rolled nonstop on its way to Bristol; and after a guard had handbraked the carriage into the station, a local carried us on to Goring, where my family lived in a house on the Thames. After I'd grown a bit older, I commuted—to the theater, the dentist, the analyst—on the Great Northern Railway from our house in Hadley Wood to King's Cross Station in London. (When I am in England in the summer I can still see, as I roll north on the magnificent all-parlor train called the *Yorkshire Pullman,* the grassy slope directly above the tunnel near Hadley Wood where as a little fellow I watched the great steam-hauled expresses dive into and shoot out of that hole in the hill.)

Much too soon, my father bundled us aboard a boat train to Dover, then a cross-channel steamer to Belgium, and into the center of the big Belgian industrial city of Liège. There I had my first tramcar journey, and became an instant and permanent devotee of electric traction. In the winter there were trips by rail back and forth between Liège and Brussels; in the summer came the annual sojourn to a seaside house near Ostend (Ostend had, and still has, tramways).

It was not until 1908, after arriving in Boston on the Cunard liner *Ivernia,* that I began what has become a lifetime career of commuting on the railways of the United States. I first lived in Boston, Arlington, Jamaica Plain, Waban, New Bedford, and Brookfield, Massachusetts—and I was hauled here and there by locomotives of the Boston & Maine, the New Haven, the Boston & Albany, the Old Colony, and—best of all—the narrow-gauge Boston, Revere Beach & Lynn, reached from Boston by the Atlantic Avenue steam ferry. If there wasn't a railway train to wherever I wanted to go, there was a ferry or a trolley car. New Bedford offered expresses by two routes to Boston; trolleys in every direction for miles and miles; a night steamer to New York; and a ferry, owned by the New Haven, across the harbor to Fairhaven—whence, from a one-platform station, New Haven locals wandered out onto Cape Cod.

The ferry fare was three cents and was collected aboard ship by a man who walked the length of the vessel and back. I walked ahead of him and voyaged without paying. (I realize in my old and repentant years that it was I who began the bankruptcy of the New Haven.) Some of the expresses from

A New England interurban

Boston—after stopping at the New Bedford station, to which, in the good old tradition, a trolley car ran to meet all the trains—went on to the wharf of the steamers for the islands.

I had just finished off covering all the trolley and steamer routes thereabouts when I was shipped by my family to Manchester, New Hampshire—but not with regrets, for Manchester had a prideful trolley system, an incline railway up Mount Uncanoonuc, and fourteen expresses a day to Boston. Manchester was not the biggest city in the world, but it was on the route of the first transcontinental sleeping car. Every Thursday the morning Boston & Maine-Canadian Pacific train from Boston to Montreal carried a tourist Pullman that went all the way to Vancouver, British Columbia. Later on, we summered in Brandon and Burlington, Vermont, which were both on the Rutland, a noble railway, although it was tumbledown even in those days. The northbound morning mail-and-milk-can local would run three and four hours late, but it did have a Pullman on the rear.

Ah! The *Green Mountain Flyer,* with its three parlor cars, its Rutland diner (half coach, half tables with black leather chairs), and its dingy coaches in which I journeyed between the two towns. And the *Mount Royal,* with its five or six Pullmans, one of which ran between Rutland and Burlington on the milk-can job, so that every village had its overnight sleeper service to New York. The Burlington trolleys that ran down to where the Shelburne Museum is now, standing in part on what was my great-great-grandfather's farm. And the new Union Station in Burlington (the Vermont Power Company has preserved it—platforms, trainshed, and all—as an office building), from which the Rutland and Central Vermont offered trains to Montreal and New York. And the steamboats on Lake Champlain—some of them operated by the Delaware & Hudson—which served the great railway hotel at Bluff Point.

Then came New Jersey. I commuted from Montclair to New York on the Lackawanna; from Somerville and Bound Brook on the Jersey Central; from Bound Brook to school in New Brunswick on a fine old hourly wooden interurban along the Raritan River; and from New Brunswick to New York on the Pennsylvania. In the District of Columbia came more years of schooling, and more weekends on the interurbans to Rockville, Great Falls, Mount Vernon, and Alexandria. (I often thought about the line to Alexandria when, in the middle of the Second World War, I was stationed in the Pentagon as a minute part of the Transportation Corps. While the Army was wondering how to get the thousands of people in the Pentagon to and from work, men were lifting the double track of the Alexandria line which ran inches away from the Pentagon on its way south. Is this not the history of transportation in this country?)

Other weekends there were chartered day coaches over the Baltimore & Ohio and the Pennsylvania for school basketball or track meets or football in Baltimore; or excursions to Norfolk on the Old Bay Line steamers, with return by the Chesapeake & Ohio's ferry and train to Richmond, then by the first train back to Washington. Afterward there was long-distance commuting: on the Pennsy or the B & O in combination with the Philadelphia & Reading to Trenton, and from there by one of the two interurbans to Princeton for my college years and my term in the Army for the First World War. Then off to New York to earn my keep.

Being lexicographical consultant to *The New York Times* was all right, for the *Times* gave me Thursday or Friday off, when commuter service (and there was an incredible amount of it at that time) was in full flow—satisfactory indeed for someone who likes to do his exploring by railway. I was still following in my father's routine—he was first the traveler, second the lexicographer. Later I graduated to being consultant to a publishing house whose printing was done on Staten Island; this required an occasional journey on the elevated to Battery Park, an excursion on a steam ferry to St. George, and a ride on the wooden cars of the B & O to Richmond (today this is the electrified Staten Island Rapid Transit) behind tiny tank steam locomotives.

Even better was a publishing house which asked me to visit its printer in Albany (night boat up the Hudson, New York Central afternoon train down) and its printer in Harrisburg (Reading's *Queen of the Valley* and *Harrisburg Special*, with their diners and open-platform observation cars, were my favorite carriers). The head of the publishing house lived far out in New Jersey, and a great many weekends I went to Hackettstown—burdened with my reports—on Lackawanna locals that were never in a hurry.

Plenty of traveling, and all expenses paid; but after a while, a lack of variety. So I opened my own shop, E. M. Frimbo, Ltd., and started selling lexicographical advice to all comers—university departments, advertising executives, publishers, magazine editors, and other downtrodden word users. My traveling only increased. My goal was to ride over every mile of passenger trackage, and on every passenger train in the United States—and my early years of study served me well. By the time I was nine I was studying timetables; by the time I was twenty I had discovered the *Official Guide*—that monthly compilation of all the railroad schedules in the country—which revealed to me the existence of railways and passenger trains of which I had never heard; by the time I was twenty-five I had discovered employee timetables—those specialized mines of information that railways distribute only to their own employees. Employee timetables revealed such special information as the fact that certain Wabash freights would on certain days carry passengers between certain stations. And the race was on.

It was still too early to discover that great American institution, the fan club, and the chartered trains it ran; but as soon as the fan clubs came into existence I began joining them and riding their chartered trains. Wishing to explore lines I had never seen, I chartered trains myself and drummed up customers—those who wanted to examine the Wilkes-Barre & Eastern, the Southern New Jersey, the Delaware & Northern, and other railways that are no longer even memories. I helped set up a national correspondence school. "The Santa Fe is going to pull off its mixed" (i.e., part-freight, part-passenger) "into Pampa," someone at the University of New Mexico would write in; and thus alerted, a group of us would converge upon that train before it ceased to exist.

There were other devices. I developed a side line as a journalist and wrote commentary on sports events in the Ivy League colleges (most of which can still be reached by railway today). I even took to the air at times, I regret to say. In the midst of the football season, word came that the Stockton Terminal & Eastern was running a steam excursion train the following Sunday. The weekend went like this: The P.R.R.'s *Midday Congressional* at eleven Saturday morning to Philadelphia for the Princeton-Pennsylvania football game; the *Representative* at five-oh-nine that afternoon back to New York; an evening at a newspaper office composing an account of the game; a taxi to the airport; an overnight flight to San Francisco; a cab into town; a bus to the Western Pacific station; a dome car on the *California Zephyr* to Stockton; a cab east into the country to a crossing where I could flag down the S T & E special, which had left Stockton ahead of me; this train back to Stockton that afternoon; the Santa Fe's *Golden Gate* to San Francisco in the evening; and a plane back to New York Sunday night.

And one more device (others are chronicled elsewhere):
through John Barriger, while he was president of the Pittsburgh & Lake Erie, I was able to travel over some rather
special bits of rail in his domain, using his inspection car—an
automobile with a set of flanged wheels at railway gauge.

Well, that was my life in North America until the extent
of my travels and the extinction of trains suddenly met head-
on. In June 1957 a chartered cab arrived in Hannah, North
Dakota, as I arrived in a Great Northern gas-powered rail-
car—and suddenly my goal was achieved. I rode back to the
main line in that chartered cab, wondering what to do next:
there were no more passenger trains in the United States for
me to ride.

It was Everett L. Thompson of the B & O passenger department who got me started on my next goal—the world—
in 1958 when he showed me that a strategy which had worked
in the States could be employed successfully abroad. What
he did was collect a group of determined buffs like me and
haul us off to Europe for a month in the care of Spanish,
Swiss, Italian, and British railway officials. I entered my second childhood. I saw Liège again (our house, and indeed the
neighborhood, had been demolished by the great wars, but
the trams were still there), and I saw Brussels, and London,
and Goring, and the tunnel near Hadley Wood all over again.
At Swindon I saw being erected England's last steam locomotive, so aptly named *Evening Star*. I met Alan Pegler, the
leading railway buff of the British Isles, who owned and
operated the 4-6-2 engine called *Flying Scotsman;* and I was
allowed to drive a Fairlie locomotive on the two-foot gauge
Festiniog Railway in Wales.

So I opened a London office to offer myself a legitimate

excuse to make Europe my second home—at least a summer home—where there is a lifetime of railway travel to be done. Oh, mine is still a tale of two continents—of any number of continents, actually. In this country I keep riding the Metroliners, the *Broadway Limited,* the *Southern Crescent.* In 1965 —a representative recent year—I covered 104,745 miles by rail, 7812 by air, and about 3000 by ship. (Automobile miles don't count.) So it goes, and so it will keep on going as long as there are passenger trains to ride, here or anywhere else in the world.

Frimbo Arrested

Needless to say, our first meeting with Ernest Frimbo was not our last. We have kept in touch ever since —intermittently, of course, because Frimbo is almost always going somewhere. But even when we don't get to see him, we hear from him. A postcard from Moscow of steam engines moving through birch forests. A cable from Ceylon, a night letter from Nicaragua, a telegram from Tiflis. Once he sent us a set of New York, New Haven & Hartford R.R. cuff links. And once he sent us a copy of a letter he had written someone else, back in July of 1941.

That letter went like this:

On Monday of this week, I left Ogden, Utah, bound west, on a secondary train of the Southern Pacific. My destination was a desolate, tiny town called Cobre, and the point of getting off there on a blazing hot day was to travel on the only passenger train run by the Nevada Northern Railway, a railway which is basically a mining operation—

ore of some sort. It is not particularly interested in passengers at all, but it operates one passenger train to pick up mail and express and the occasional revenue customer for the town of Ely, which is the headquarters of the mining company that owns the Nevada Northern.

The Nevada Northern passenger train is a gem, even in these days when there are plenty of gems still riding the rails in the United States: a very small steam locomotive and a single passenger car which looks as though it was once either a dining car or the business car of some railway official. Beautiful inlaid mahogany work all through the car, a tiny compartment at one end for baggage and mail—and myself, the sole customer; in fact, the only customer, I was told, to turn up in the last two months.

The line runs almost due south from Cobre through some of the most beautiful desert country in America. A high range of mountains flanks the tracks to the west. To the east the unceasing desert rolls and steams and boils. This country is so desolate that only the Japanese would consent to live along the railway, and the Nevada Northern is unique in that all the section hands—the men who do the track repairs—and the men who man the small stations along the line are Japanese. They do not seem to mind the heat.

The conductor told me that this heat had been unbroken for over three months—that even though they expected a drought every summer, nothing like this had ever been experienced. I told him that back East I was known as Frimbo the Rainmaker, because of my proclivity for bringing rain wherever I happen to visit. He laughed politely, but, sure enough, in less than an hour and a half, as we trundled on our way south to Ely, black clouds appeared over the range of mountains to the west. Fifteen minutes later, the landscape was rendered almost invisible by a cloudburst. The cloudburst went on for at least half an hour, and by that time the temperature must have dropped 30 or 40 degrees. It was, in fact, chilly.

"Now," I said to the conductor, "you see why I'm known as Frimbo the Rainmaker."

"Please," he said, "let us speak to the management and perhaps we can persuade you to live here."

The town of Ely is a real frontier town, and I arrived in the middle of the annual Old Timers' Week, for which everyone in town is supposed to turn up, not in Eastern-style business clothes, but dressed like a cow hand or a miner— and wearing a beard. Preparation for the Week begins a month in advance, when every man in town starts growing a beard.

I put myself in the hotel, went out on the street—and was promptly arrested for not being, so to speak, in uniform. I was handcuffed, hauled down a couple of side streets, and taken into a building where a group of men gayly proclaiming themselves to be a kangaroo court sentenced me to spend the next three weeks in Ely, ordered me to grow a beard in the meantime—and sent me back to the hotel under guard.

Well, I had a problem. You see, a hundred miles or more to the west of Ely, over the Panamint range, lies the railway called the Tonopah & Goldfield. As its name implies, this railway, soon to be abandoned, serves a gold-mining area —once one of the richest in the United States. The mines are now played out, but the town of Tonopah is still there, and the railway is still running a freight train two or three times a week. One of the two or three times was the day after my arrival in Ely. I had planned to take what is called in local parlance a mail car to Tonopah. What this means is: someone has a franchise with the U.S. Post Office to carry the mails back and forth by highway three times a week between Tonopah and Ely, and he is licensed to carry two or three passengers in his car.

But if I tried to blow town in the mail car, I might wind up in the slammer. What was I to do? Buy a beard? Looking through the telephone book, I found an interesting entry —"Air Nevada." I get on the phone, and a man identifies himself as Air Nevada. And I say I wish to know whether he's running any charter flights—that I want to fly as early as possible tomorrow morning to Tonopah to catch this morning freight train. He agrees to charter me the flight—and says, "We must leave no later than half past five in the morning, if you want to be sure to catch that eight-thirty train." I agree to be in the lobby at five-thirty, and he agrees to come in a car to meet me.

To our mutual chagrin, the man who arrived turned out to be one of the men from the kangaroo court. He looked a bit abashed. *I* looked a bit abashed. I said, "Is it all right for me to leave town?"

He said, "Since you are a cash customer, yes."

The plane turned out to be a two-seated (not side by side) open cockpit plane, and with my luggage I could barely work into the rear seat behind the pilot. In fact, when I got myself and all my luggage in, I discovered that the safety strap would not encompass both me and my impedimenta. The pilot agreed to fly very slowly.

And I could see why he agreed to fly very slowly. The minute we took off, we headed, rising minutely into thin air (Tonopah is several thousand feet above sea level) toward the Panamint range. "There is a pass through the Panamint range," said the pilot, "but I don't know whether we're go-ing to make it on the first try."

Well, we circled three or four times at the head of the pass before we had enough altitude, and then we flew through the thing—clearing the pines at the top by what seemed to me less than a hundred feet, and scaring a large herd of wild horses which was making its way across the

pass from east to west. In search of Lord knows what, since there was nothing but desert.

Not long after that, we spied what certainly looked to me like the town of Tonopah, sitting in the middle of the desert. I asked the pilot whether it was Tonopah, and he said, "I don't know, I haven't got a map."

So I fished in my side pocket and pulled out a Socony

In Nevada

road map of Nevada, and decided that, judging by our location between the town and the pass, it must indeed be
Tonopah.

"The airfield," the pilot said, "is on the east side of town.
I've never landed there, but I know where it is."

As we started our descent, and glided closer and closer
to what he said was the airport, I suddenly yelled at him,
"I've never seen an airport before with trees going across
it!"

"My God!" he yelled back. "We're aiming for the wrong
place. I guess the airport must be on the west side of town."

We went to the west side of the town, and there was no
airport to be seen. We circled around, came back to the
east side of Tonopah, and there, about a mile south of the
small forest we had attempted to land in, was the airport.
Unstaffed.

I got out of the plane, collected my luggage, paid my fee,
shook hands, walked to the edge of the airport, unhooked
the gate in the wire fence, and flagged down a family of
Okies who were going West—luggage, children, cats, dogs,
everything. "I'll give you two dollars to take me into town,"
I said. They seemed quite happy to have the extra business,
though I had to ride, along with my luggage, on the running board of the car.

After a search in the middle of town for the railway station for Goldfield, I arrived just ten minutes before my
freight train was to take off. I galloped up to the caboose
and spoke to the conductor. Said I wanted to ride north.
And he said, "Get aboard."

The conductor's a real friendly guy, and it turns out he
has been working for this railroad for many years. He is a

native of Brandon, Vermont, where my family and I had been in the habit of spending the summer for many years.

At the end of the run, in a town called Mina, the Tono- pah & Goldfield train pulls up alongside a Southern Pacific mixed train, which was to take me to Reno. Mina is near the end of a famous narrow-gauge railway called the Carson & Colorado, which once went all the way from Mina down through the mountains into the Owens Valley of California. This line is no longer in operation, much to my regret, but the track is still intact. And in the beautiful desert sunlight of that noontime—which was when we arrived at Mina—I could see the line of track going all the way to the foot of the mountains, which it would have to climb to get into Cali- fornia. I have a photograph of it on a camera plate.

The conductor and the rest of the train crew and I went to the hashhouse in Mina and had a colossal steak dinner along with the crew of the Southern Pacific mixed train (a mixed train, as you know, is a freight train, basically run- ning on an extremely relaxed schedule, but carrying some sort of passenger car—often half the caboose—for any local passengers who wish to brave the long, tedious, and often, in this climate, boiling hot journey across the desert).

I thought you'd like to know that this is how I made my rather circuitous way from Ogden to Reno, and why there has been such a lapse between the postcard I sent you from Ogden and the letter I am now writing you from my hotel in Reno tonight.

The Contessa

It was while we were yarning one night with E. M. Frimbo in the reading room of the Lexicographers' Club that we first heard about his travels with the Contessa. Ah, the Lexicographers' Club! If you've never heard of this cozy place, that's not surprising, because it's one of the best-kept secrets in New York. The club was founded in 1811 in a Dutch farmhouse on the East River, near where Thirty-seventh Street is today, by a group of seventy-five wise-acres. In 1847, the club was offered half a million dollars for the farm by a developer. This offer was immediately accepted, and the club moved to a small brownstone on Murray Hill, carefully transporting its magnificent wine cellar across town on a wagon whose wheels had been padded with felt. In 1958, another developer, great-grand-son to the first, offered the club twelve million dollars for the brownstone. This offer was accepted on the same day, and the club now occupies the fifty-second floor of a mid-town skyscraper. There is no name on the door. The wine cellar was moved to the new location only after Consolidated Edison agreed to reduce electrical power to the skyscraper by fifteen per cent for one hour, so that the elevators would move slowly enough not to jostle the bottles. Membership in the Lexicographers' Club has been strictly limited to seventy-five ever since 1811. Noah Webster was blackballed in 1828. Frimbo always stays there when he's in town.

The Contessa's name came up over a couple of brandies Alexander—Frimbo's favorite evening drink. It was a cold mid-winter night, and snowflakes drifted outside the reading-room windows. Frimbo had been telling a story about himself, a Maharani, and three Indian railways—the Darjeeling-Himalaya, the Great Indian Peninsular, and an outfit called His Highness the Nizam's Guaranteed State Railway. Then he paused, and a certain look came into his eyes.

He said, "One of my rather special traveling companions —I have not mentioned her before—was a young lady whom I shall call the Contessa, because that is what she is. She lives in Paris, and only occasionally comes to New York for a visit. On the occasion of her last visit to this city, while we were at dinner, we decided that it might be a nice idea to spend part of the ensuing winter together in northern Africa, instead of in her country house in Umbria—for that part of Italy is frigid indeed in January and February.

"Now, this would be a rather special operation for me, because the Contessa, like most Europeans who live in the world of art and fashion, is apt to travel by limousine and plane, and it was up to me to demonstrate that there were good times to be had on board trains. After some discussion, we hit upon Morocco as a suitable place for a holiday, and I explained my plan of operation: we would proceed by train from Paris to the Straits of Gibraltar, take ship from there to Morocco, and then proceed along the Moroccan coast by rail. We would go as far as we could toward the High Atlas mountains. It was agreed that we would make this an extremely leisurely journey; that is, we'd spend three or four days in each city we visited, and the rail journeys would be as short and as simple as possible. This in order to set up a scheme of life that would suit both our temperaments. Despite this amicable arrangement, I could see that the Contessa had some qualms: she told me that she would let me know after our first train trip whether we would proceed with the rest of my plan. I, of course, had no fears about *that*.

"A few months later, I was in London on business which I shan't go into. I telephoned the Contessa to say that in three weeks I would be arriving in Paris, and should we not then set off for Africa?

"My favorite way of traveling between London and Paris is, need I say, the train known rather ambiguously as the *Night Ferry*. It consists of a set of sleeping cars and a restaurant car, and it leaves London's Victoria Station at the extremely convenient hour of ten in the evening, proceeds to Dover, gets itself put aboard a train ferry, spends a comfortable or occasionally rather rocky few hours crossing the Channel to Dunkirk—where it is taken off the ferry, reassembled, and posted off to Paris, Nord Station. It arrives about breakfast time, depending upon the vagaries of the weather in England and Europe. These are sometimes simultaneously as bad as can be, but there's no possible way of beating the *Night Ferry* as a way of transportation. If you go by air, there's little likelihood either of being on time or even of being there on the right day.

"The Contessa was not used to being up and about at an

unearthly hour like nine in the morning, but she was indeed there—and only a couple of minutes late—at Nord Station to meet me. We set off for a few days romping in Paris, and then, on the appointed morning, the two of us assembled at the Austerlitz Station to board what was then one of the finest trains in all the world—the *Sud Express,* Paris to Madrid. The *Sud Express* has since been outmoded by a far faster, much more modern train called the *Puerta del Sol*— Gateway of the Sun, in plain English. The *Puerta del Sol* leaves Paris many hours later than the *Sud Express* and carries through sleeping cars from Paris to Madrid. At the Spanish border—this is what makes the train so modern— the running gear under these cars is changed while the passengers are still inside. You have to either change running gear or change trains at the border because Spanish and Portuguese main-line railroad track is broad-gauge track— five feet six inches wide, more than half a foot wider than the standard-gauge track of all the rest of the European railroads.

"The less up-to-date *Sud Express* consisted of two trains: a standard-gauge day train from Paris to the border, a broad-gauge night train from the border to Madrid. The day train carried at the rear end a magnificent heavy-weight Pullman—what we would call a parlor car. Such cars have now completely disappeared from the European scene. They represented a way of life that will never again be duplicated. Inlaid wood in the form of stylized flowers, a pleasing arrangement of metallic decoration, large comfortable armchairs, a small kitchen at one end where absolutely enchanting meals were prepared en route, a very decently thought-out wine cellar. In fact, all the perquisites of traveling in your own private railway car.

"The Contessa and I had a long, long lunch in this Pullman on our rapid progress toward Bordeaux and the Spanish border. After lunch I ordered a bottle of white wine and a siphon of fizzy water. We managed to consume the bottle of wine during the afternoon—and another half bottle as well. At Irún, the first large town across the border, we boarded our Spanish broad-gauge Wagon-Lits sleeping car and proceeded to a Spanish broad-gauge Wagon-Lits restaurant car. Or should I say 'dining car'? This restaurant car was of the old order, decorated in the manner of our French Pullman parlor car, and it was quite an experience. You were never quite sure what the devil you were eating, but it was all absolutely magnificent, especially when embellished with large drafts of Spanish wine."

Here Frimbo signaled the reading-room steward for another round of brandies Alexander, and ventured on a short digression. "I might add at this point," he said in a faraway tone of voice, "speaking of the glorious glories of the old Iberian Wagon-Lits sleeping cars, that one New Year's Eve I took a train from Lisbon, in Portugal, overnight to Madrid—a train with a really regional name: the *Lusitania Express*. In those joyous days the *Lusitania Express* was hauled by Portuguese and Spanish steam locomotives of enormous size, enormous noise and lung power. There was a mail car on that train, a baggage car, a first-class coach for sitting-up-at-night passengers, a Wagon-Lits restaurant car, and a single Wagon-Lits sleeping car. If business was really terrific, there might be as many as two or three sleeping cars, but rarely was the *Lusitania Express* more than five or six cars.

"On this New Year's Eve we trooped into dinner. It was not a large crowd, naturally—only Frimbos are abroad on

New Year's Eve. The conductor of the Wagon-Lits, having served dinner with his accomplices, struck a small gong at the front end of the restaurant car and said—I translate the Portuguese rather freely—'Ladies and gentlemen, on the occasion of New Year's Eve, the International Company of Wagon-Lits and Restaurant Cars wishes you welcome and presents to each and every one of you, with its compliments, a double shot of port wine.'

"He then proceeded down the length of the car with his accomplices, dishing out the port wine, whereupon we all drank a toast to him, retired quite happily to our berths, and literally floated into Madrid."

"But the Contessa," we said. "How did she take to all this? Did *she* float into Madrid? Was she favorably impressed?"

"Yes," said Frimbo offhandedly. (He was signing the steward's drink chit.) "Yes, she was favorably impressed. Yes, yes. The Contessa had never in all her life, it turned out, been aboard a Wagon-Lits sleeping car. And she had never had anything like the Pullman-car luncheon, not to mention the pleasure of an idle afternoon of sipping white wine and seltzer as we rolled across France at seventy-five miles an hour. As soon as we got to Madrid we posted off to the Hotel Wellington—one of the most estimable hostelries in the world—all the cab drivers in those days called it the Velling-tong—and upon our arrival her first words to me were, 'We shall continue the journey as you have planned it.'

"Well, now come two days in Madrid, which we spend doing the Contessa's bidding, namely, a picture-by-picture inspection of the entire Prado Museum. Not a blooming picture of a railway train anywhere! All right, I swallow hard and do my duty. The only relief is lunch at a lovely little

side-street restaurant the Contessa knows. Next day, more
wings of the Prado. Finally, early in the afternoon, she looks
at a catalogue and decides that we have, indeed, done the
Prado complete.

" 'Now,' she says, 'let us do something you want to do.'

" 'Would you mind,' say I, 'traveling on the Madrid Me-
tropolitano, as they call the Underground in this city? I have
not traveled the line that goes down to the Delicias Station
and on to a part of Madrid I'd like to explore.'

"So off we go, the Contessa gallantly surviving underground travel for the next two-and-a-half hours."

"The Contessa on the subway?" (A question from us.)

"Yes." (Frimbo.) "And the Contessa was highly regaled
by this rather unusual afterpiece to the Prado. That night
we went to one of the flamenco night clubs, which offer the
usual glorious Spanish mélange of music and dance. The
next day, after walking around the parks and experimenting
with a couple of other restaurants she knew, we boarded the
sleeping-car train to Algeciras for an all-night journey down
to the Straits of Gibraltar. This train had a rather peculiar
restaurant car. By no means was it elaborate. It consisted
of a cozy little counter and a small kitchen at one end of a
second-class coach. The staff seemed a little bit indolent,
but a few passages of the Contessa's choicest Spanish gal-
vanized them into action, and we soon had a rather plain-
spoken but extremely good dinner.

"I should say here that the Contessa speaks every civilized language in the most magnificent manner. Also a couple of uncivilized languages, one of which we will come to
presently. She said after dinner, as a parting shot to the
restaurant-car staff, 'We shall be in this car at eight o'clock

tomorrow morning, and we shall expect breakfast. Under-stood?'

"A great deal of bowing. 'Madame, madame, madame,' said the staff.

"We were back at eight o'clock, and breakfast was ready.

"The Contessa's Spanish came into full and good use again in Algeciras. She commandeered two taxi cabs—one for us, one for our luggage—and we rattled down to the pier. More Spanish there, and two tickets were produced for a rather fine top-deck cabin on a brand-new Spanish ship for our considerable journey to Tangier. And that night we dined in Tangier. We had a drawing-room sort of dinner in the restaurant of our French hotel. All the best hotels in Morocco are still French, you know. The tables in the restaurant seemed to be about twenty feet apart, and in one corner a musician seated at a grand piano was assiduously working his way through the entire repertory of Chopin.

"The next morning I told the Contessa that the following two days were hers, and asked her what she wished to do. 'As a matter of fact,' she said, 'one reason I picked Morocco for the winter holiday was that I had been commissioned by a Paris paper to do a piece about my impressions of Morocco. Your invitation is coming in extremely handy. We will make an inspection of the Casbah. The Casbahs in Morocco are extremely well run. Remember, this is a genteel dictatorship, and an extremely well-managed one. With my French and my Spanish—Tangier is both French and Spanish, you know—we will have no difficulty.'

"Indeed, we did not. Going into the Casbah is like going into the tanglewild in a fairy story. There are miles and miles and miles and miles of passageways, all roofed in, or all so covered with foliage that rarely do you see the sun. So you have very little way of orienting yourself, and you have to sort of feel your way toward an exit. The Casbah contains restaurants, shops of every kind, Spanish and various dialects of Arabic, French popping out of everyone's mouth, and, of course, as everywhere, the one curse—the little boy touts. The touts want you to patronize a certain draper, a certain embroiderer, a certain jeweler, a certain restaurant. Two of the touts kept pestering the Contessa. Finally, she turned to one of them and said, in French, 'We are not interested. We are not American. We are not English. We are not German. We are Japanese.'

" *'Japonais,'* said the boys. *'Ah, ha, ha!'*

" *'Oui, Japonais,'* said the Contessa. *'Allez-vous en!'*

"Abashed, they withdrew. We went to a restaurant of our own choice."

"Genius!" we exclaimed.

"The next day," Frimbo continued, "borrowing a typewriter from the manager of the hotel, the Contessa typed her story for the Paris newspaper. Then we had another splendid dinner, and prepared ourselves for our trip to Casablanca. The next morning found us on the train. Service on the Royal Moroccan Railways is extremely infrequent, but the trains themselves are delectable—absolutely delectable. Some of the older rolling stock has lace curtains in the first-class compartments, as well as all sorts of elaborate upholstery and brasswork. There is a little bar and a little restaurant at the end of every first-class coach, under the charge of a Wagon-Lits staff, which provides drinks and lunch en route.

"The trains gallop along at quite a leisurely pace—it

seems never to exceed forty miles an hour—and we had ample time to view Morocco—which is, indeed, a scene on which to feast the eyes. Morocco, along the shore, is not desert but rolling agricultural country. The mountains are far in the distance. On a very clear day, when the train climbs a little hill, you can see the famous High Atlas mountains a hundred and fifty or two hundred miles inland.

"The hotel in Casablanca was a repeat of the hotel in Tangier: deluxe, deluxe, deluxe, rooftop restaurant, shops. The Contessa, though she has few of the weaknesses of other women, does like to shop. A day was set aside for her to shop, and for me to wander around practicing my French. In another day, we were back on the train. 'Contessa,' I said, 'we are off to Marrakesh—the end of the railways in Morocco, as far inland as we can go by train.'

"We traveled on another delightful parlor-car-type coach with a good restaurant and a good bar, and spent a few nights in Marrakesh in another elaborate French hotel— gambling casino, swimming pool, shops, restaurant, music.

"The one drawback, really, about traveling in Morocco, even with the Contessa, is that Morocco, like other North African countries, seems to be almost entirely populated by Arabs. Apparently they have no use for each other, and certainly they have no use for foreigners—except in respect to how much money can be extracted from them, or each other, with the least amount of effort. We wished to visit the Casbah in Marrakesh, and we asked the doorman of our hotel to summon a cab driver. Four drivers answered this summons. Now, an Arab cab driver has already made up his mind where you are going to go. You are not going to the Casbah—or the telegraph office or the post office or the office of the Royal Maroc Airlines. You are going to the shops

from which he extracts a commission. Or you are going on
a grisly tour of a few rat-race operations just outside the
Casbah. The four drivers told us we did not want to go to
the Casbah. 'No, no, no,' they kept saying. 'You don't want
to go there. We take you, we take you on a tour.'

"The Contessa broke into one of her less civilized
tongues—namely, Arabic—and did a thorough cursing out
of the cab drivers. Whereupon there was dead silence for a
moment. Then, one of them, shuddering, stepped forward,
opened the rear door of his cab, and bowed to the Contessa.

"We went to the Casbah."

We told Frimbo we thought we had fallen hopelessly in
love with this woman. He said he had seen it happen before.
Then he laughed. "I'm going to push you out into the snow
now," he said, "because I want to go to bed. But I was just
thinking about our second day in Marrakesh—so you can
stay one more minute. We were having difficulties with the
assistant manager of the hotel there. The rooms assigned to
us were not quite right, and there had been a couple of other
bits of nonsense, such as careless handling of mail addressed
to both of us.

"So the Contessa advanced upon the assistant manager
in his office and told him what needed to be done. His re-
sponse suggested disinterest and no will to take action. The
Contessa addressed him again. 'Ah, yes, M. Quarrié,' she
said. 'Now I remember you. You were the assistant manager
at the Al Mounia Hotel three years ago, were you not?'

" 'Yes, madame, I was.'

" 'And you were fired from that job, were you not? And
that is why you are here now?'

"Dead silence on the part of M. Quarrié.

"The Contessa resumed. 'As I was saying, I've brought

these matters to your attention. I expect something to be done about them immediately. Am I correct?'

" 'At once, madame,' said M. Quarrié. And he bowed her out of his office."

Iron Horses

People in the movie business like to consult Mr. Frimbo's expertise. Once he got a call from a Hollywood script writer who wanted to know whether he could have a man on top of a train in a cowboy-and-Indians flick fire a rifle shot that would turn an old-fashioned stub switch in the nick of time and save the train from derailment. Frimbo said he thought the movie could get away with it. Another time two Hollywood men wanted to know whether they could put diesels in a documentary about the Twenties. Frimbo said NO. He is currently helping Al Maysles (one of the men who made *Gimme Shelter*) plan a documentary about people on trains.

In March 1965, Brendan Gill, who was then reviewing movies for *The New Yorker*, took Frimbo to the première of *The Train* to get his critique. Here's Gill's review of that movie:

Being nothing if not conscientious, I took care to attend *The Train* in the company of Mr. Ernest M. Frimbo, one of the world's leading railroad authorities. Mr. Frimbo, a lexicographer whose lifelong passion for trains has been dealt with more than once in the Talk of the Town department of this magazine, particularly enjoys such things as hopping over to Ireland for a long weekend's browse among that country's hither-and-thithering little railway lines. (Thanks to the saint whom we honor this week, there are no snakes in Ireland, but there are rail lines that wind like snakes, and trains move on them at so cautious a speed that it requires a long weekend to cover even a comparatively short distance between two points, or pints, as the word is pronounced over there.) Mr. Frimbo was beside himself with pleasure at *The Train,* and so was I, though our reasons for being pleased were very different. Knowing scarcely more about trains than how to get on and off them, I was satisfied to enjoy the movie as a model thriller, filled with marvelous feats of derring-do and boasting excellent performances by Burt Lancaster, in the role of a gallant and gloriously acrobatic French railroad man, and Paul Scofield, in the role of a sinister and aloof Nazi officer. Mr. Frimbo, on the other hand, enjoyed the movie as a sort of celebration of the locomotive way of life; not since Buster Keaton's perfect comedy *The General* has the camera surrendered itself more eagerly to the steamy, sooty, black-and-silver, hissing-and-hooting world of rolling stock, signal towers, yards, shops, cranes, tunnels, bridges, and track. Normally rather taciturn, Mr. Frimbo was downright effusive in his praise of the movie's director, John Frankenheimer. "That young man knows a subject when he sees one," he said. "Young as he is, he has the proper respect for trains. This is the only railroad picture I've ever seen that wasn't spoiled with silly technical errors. Oh, the sound track occasionally indicates a train speed somewhat in excess of the speed actually depicted, but otherwise I would pronounce this an ideal picture for every member of the family."

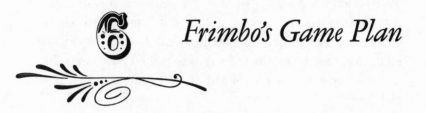

6   *Frimbo's Game Plan*

The small engraved card that came in the mail said:

MR. ERNEST M. FRIMBO WILL DELIVER TWO LEC-
TURES BEFORE THE LEXICOGRAPHERS' CLUB EN-
TITLED "DEVIOUS SCHEMES FOR WORLD-WIDE
TRAVEL." HE HOPES YOU CAN ATTEND. NO SLIDES,
NO MOVIES. BLACK TIE.

We went to both lectures. They were held in the club's Great Hall—the room that holds the club's Johnson *Dictionary*, its *Oxford English Dictionary* (first edition), its Gutenberg Bible. Having secured permission to take with us our SONY cassette-corder, we now have in our possession the only transcript of the proceedings.

The first lecture:

"Good evening, ladies and gentlemen. What I'd like to talk about tonight is what today would be called the Game Plan. The object that I and some of our fellow members had in better railway days was to go every weekend by train, either singly or in groups of up to a dozen, to a place we had never been before. I think you will agree we had things nicely worked out when I tell you that at one time we had on our books plans for the next one hundred and fifty-three weekends. Three years in advance! Of course, everything was subject to change in case one of us discovered, say, that a certain railway was to be closed, meaning that we ought to move weekend one-fifty-three up to weekend four.

"All right. Now, how do you go about making plans for one hundred and fifty-three weekends on lines you—and often any passengers at all—have never been on before? Obviously, you have to be devious. You have to be brash and beard authority for special permission to do things. But how? The answer was the long-distance telephone call.

"In the days I'm speaking of, railway officials were railway officials. They were not transplanted lawyers, they were not finance men, they were not—how would you say it?—conglomerate men; they were men whose sole interest in life was—pure and simple—the best way of operating railroads. And to them, anyone who felt the way they did was automatically a boon companion. I would get on the blower in New York and call one of these men out in the wilds of, let's say, Pennsylvania. This particular man was the president of a railroad that's still in existence—though few people outside of the coal-mining industry have ever heard of it—called the Pittsburgh & Shawmut, and it hasn't hauled passengers in years.

"His secretary would answer, and there would be none of this nonsense about what are you calling in reference to, or some such ugly phrase, and no one to put you on hold.

The operator would say, 'This is a long-distance call,' and then Mr. So-and-So would get on the phone instantly. Why? Curiosity, my friends. Someone had actually paid for this phone call, and he wanted to see who the hell it was. Now, I had ascertained through surveillance that the Pittsburgh & Shawmut was to have an office outing by train, an outing, naturally, not open to the public. I would tell the president that I'd heard about the outing and wanted to invite myself.

"He would immediately answer, 'Well, as a matter of fact, I'm putting my private car on that train and we're serving a buffet lunch for me and some of my vice presidents. Now, uh, that car would be car Number Seventy-Three. The train will leave the junction with the Pennsylvania Railroad north of Pittsburgh at nine-forty-five Sunday morning. You just come up to the car—I'll give the porter your name—and we will take you aboard.' You see, brashness pays off!

"Now, there's a railway in Canada that once bore the glorious name of Temiskaming & Northern Ontario. After enough people had complained that the railway was a fraud because it did not go anywhere near Temiskaming, it became the Ontario Northland. It runs from North Bay, Ontario, up to the lower tip of James Bay through what is, indeed, wild country. There are very few trains to the northern end of the line, and when you get there the train waits two or three days before it comes back. What to do? I called up the president long distance and said, 'You run the train called the *Polar Bear* up to Moosonee every so often, but there's no hotel up there.' 'Yes,' the president says, 'it *is* rather difficult. As a matter of fact, the rule is that no one can buy a ticket for Moosonee unless he has a confirmed reservation at someone's house or a hotel—and, as you say, there aren't any hotels. But if you've called me all the way from New York, I'll let you in on something: our railway has a very small but comfortable pine-log lodge up there. I'll have our sled meet the *Polar Bear,* and then you can stay in the lodge until the train goes back, or whatever you like.'

"Well, off we go on the *Polar Bear,* a marvelous old train full of all sorts of real backwoods Canadians. Moosonee itself was a town not reached by any roads. It had a flying-doctor service—he landed his pontoon plane on rivers and lakes. When they got a message that somebody had appendicitis in a small Eskimo community, the flying doctor went in his pontoon plane and fetched the patient back to Moosonee. The only way of talking with the outside world was the local weather station, and you could use that service only from ten to noon in the morning, and from one to two in the afternoon. The Hudson's Bay Company had a factory there—meaning a place run by a Hudson's Bay Company factor—where Eskimos and white men brought their furs to exchange them for flour, bullets, leather goods, and all that sort of thing. Well, how many days can you look at just flour and bullets? So after a day I decided not to wait for the return train but to move on, and I went to the radio shack at the weather station and asked the Eskimo girl working there to put me in touch with Austin Airways, an Ontario outfit that charters pontoon planes. She went to the wall of her little shack, cranked an old-fashioned telephone. A vast amount of crackling occurred, and she said—I'll try to repeat her exact words—'This is Bluie West, Bluie West calling Oval Brown. Oval Brown, do you read me?' *Crackle, crackle, crackle.* 'Oval Brown reads Bluie West, what is it?' 'There is a Mr. Frimbo here who wants

to ask Austin Airways to come pick him up. . . . O.K.?
. . . Yes, I'll tell him two hundred dollars.'

"So three hours later, a pontoon plane drops on the river,
and a couple of Eskimos with a canoe paddle me and my
baggage out to the plane. I climb aboard and fly to a town
with the enchanting name of South Porcupine, and I—yes,
young man?"

Small Voice from Back of Room: "Is it hard to get out
of a canoe and into a pontoon plane?"

Frimbo: "With luggage, yes. But I was in boys' camp
in Vermont in the summertime. I learned to handle canoes
in all kinds of weather.

"Going to Alaska to ride the Alaska Railway presented
a slightly different problem. The Alaska Railway, as you
may know, is nationalized—a province of the United States
Department of the Interior. It is there for strategic military
reasons, as well as to handle commerce, and it usually, of
necessity, operates at a loss. It had a great deal of freight
at the time I decided to ride on it but very little passenger
service.

"The man in charge of the Alaska Railway was, naturally, a civil servant, but I do a little background reading
and discover that he had been a divisional superintendent on
the St. Louis Southwestern—a railway known to us in the
trade as the Cotton Belt. Then I remember the names of
a few other divisional superintendents on the Cotton Belt.
When I get to Anchorage—the headquarters of the Alaska
Railway—and call up the man, I identify myself and tell
him I happen to be in town and mention that I'm very
interested in the line from Anchorage down to Seward, a
long line, without any passenger trains, down the Seward
Peninsula which runs within inches of a live, moving glacier

through spectacular scenery indeed. Then I say, 'Mr. Moore' —or whatever his name is—'I hear you're an old Cotton Belt man. Do you remember Joe Connors, who used to be divisional superintendent down at Pine Bluffs, Arkansas?'

" 'Why, yes, indeed,' he says. 'Do you know him?'

There aren't any hotels

" 'Yes, I do,' say I. 'I worked with him during the war.'
" 'Well,' says he, 'come on in.'
"So the next morning we have a fine chat, and then I say, 'What about that line down to Seward?' And he says, 'Well, there's nothing going from here for a couple of days,

but there'll be a freight going out from Seward at seven-thirty tomorrow morning. I'll have a man pick you up at your hotel at about three o'clock.'

"At a quarter to three Sunday morning, the receptionist in my hotel rings me up and says, in some alarm, 'Sir, the Chief of Police is downstairs waiting for you.' I go downstairs, and he says, 'I've been asked to drive you down to Seward.' He was a man of about forty-five, a very jolly chap, interested in my project, and quite unwilling to take any money for his services. He said that Anchorage likes to look after strangers, and he drove me a hundred and thirty-five miles through pitch darkness to Seward. The conductor of the freight train was standing on the steps of his caboose. 'Well,' he said, 'we're all set to go.'

"We set off. Moose came down to inspect our leisurely progress. I got to see the glacier, and moose got to see E. M. Frimbo. So I added Seward to my roster of railway trackage.

"You see, you make use of every devious device. For a while I dealt in railway stocks for my family account and came to know a number of what are known as rail specialists, men in Wall Street houses who deal only in railway stocks and bonds. I went to the Security Analysts' luncheons on Tuesday to hear railway officials addressing these specialists and either telling them the truth or lying, as the case might be. The rail specialists asked some pretty pertinent questions, a few of which produced stammering by the guests of honor.

"After one session, a rail specialist said to me, 'The Consolidated Railways of Cuba wish to float a bond issue of fifty million dollars for re-equipment, and my firm, which may underwrite the project, is sending me down there for

a firsthand opinion. Come along and be my assistant expert! You ask knowing questions of the English-speaking
officials, I'll deal with the others, and I think we'll be able
to promote a little special travel for ourselves.'

" 'Done and done,' I said, and there followed some de-
lirious days on the railways of Cuba. A narrow-gauge line
through sugar-cane fields in a little open car behind a fine
old American-built steam engine hauling a quarter of a mile
of sugar-cane cars. Hospitality in a hacienda, and a trip
back to Havana in the private car of the general manager
of the Cuban Northern Railway, a luxurious old wooden
rolling palace with a servant who washed my socks and
underwear and pressed my trousers (so that I would be
presentable in the capital) and who, asked for a brandy
Alexander, returned with a quart container in a bowl of
cracked ice and a plateful of cookies, sliced pineapple,
guava, and other goodies. That sort of thing. My Wall
Streeter was devious in his own right: instead of coming
straight back, we returned to New York via Yucatán, riding
the now-vanished narrow-gauge steam railway from Mérida
to Campeche on our way. That was a train! It was filled
with tens of thousands of Yucatánians and their accompanying luggage—bales of fruit, clothing, live chickens, and what
not. Some of the towns we passed through had no streets at
all—the passageways between the houses had been hewn out
of the living rock. No bond issue was involved in this side
trip. We simply rode this railway because it was *there!*"

Frimbo's Frolic

In the early winter of—oh, 1966, it must have been—we spent a happy day riding the rails with Ernest M. Frimbo. We hadn't seen much of the old gent for a while, although he had been dropping us a line from time to time, usually choosing to write on gaudy special stationery run up for expresses now long gone. His latest arrived one morning in December, and it was an invitation. The notepaper had a colored picture of a columbine in the upper left-hand corner. Just below the flower the words "The Columbine" were printed in a tasteful script. The columbine is the state flower of Colorado, and *The Columbine* was a train that used to run from Chicago to Denver. It was discontinued twenty-five years ago.

> I am inviting you to accompany me on an excursion arranged by the Electric Railroaders' Association [Frimbo wrote]. The train will go up the Harlem Division tracks of the New York Central to North White Plains, then over the Hudson Division tracks to Harmon, where there

will be a tour of the shops and the repair facilities, and
then down over the Spuyten Duyvil Bridge and on the
West Side freight-line tracks in Manhattan down to
Thirtieth Street. This last is a magnificent experience.
We will be using an S Class electric locomotive, built in
1906. Of course, that is not quite so grand as a steam
locomotive—my first love—but at least it is not a diesel.
We will cross the Grand Central Loop and the New
York & Harlem wye. There will also be a surprise! Meet
me on the upper level of G.C.T. at nine sharp.

Yrs.,

E. M. FRIMBO

P.S.: I know you like to be informed of my totals,
and I have done some adding, and the figure as of the
week before Labor Day, 1966, is 1,906,781 miles. I don't
expect it will get much bigger before I see you.

The day we met Frimbo at Grand Central Terminal was
perfect—cold and clear and cloudless. We arrived on the
upper level at the stroke of nine, and found our friend waiting for us. He was looking extraordinarily fit. His skin was
pink and firm, his eyes were clear, and his step was springy.
Frimbo professes to prefer bad weather, because, he says,
then he can think of all the hundreds of grounded planes,
and all the thousands of people who are sitting in airports
listening to bad music and not getting where they want to
go, but he obviously enjoys good days when they come
along. The last time we had seen him, seven or eight months
earlier, he looked a little depressed. He had been hoping to
go to Yugoslavia and Turkey in the summer and ride on
some of the steam trains along the Adriatic and in Anatolia,
but his plans had fallen through. A friend of ours who was
with us at the time tried to cheer him up, saying, "Why
don't you go to Greece instead?" Frimbo stopped looking

depressed and started looking angry. "Greece is mostly diesel," he said.

Frimbo was wearing an old gray tweed suit with blue stripes, which he keeps for such occasions, and he was standing at the front of our train and surveying its engine, a large black electric locomotive. "That is Engine Number 110," he said as soon as he caught sight of us. "She'll be pulling us today. Sixty years old and still pulling a train! That's more than I can say about most people I know. When I first came to New York, in nineteen-twelve, it was in a train with an engine about like that one, as I recall. Grand Central was being built—it was in very much the same shape that Penn Station is in right now—and the tracks on Park Avenue were an open cut."

A number of boys with cameras began to cluster around Number 110, and one of them politely asked Frimbo to step back so that he could get a better shot. Frimbo looked disgusted. "There are two kinds of railroad buffs," he said. "Class A is strictly utilitarian and informational. Class B, which I am afraid is what this person is, is what we call a nudge." Then his face brightened. "Well, it's a good turnout, at least. And I was almost forgetting the surprise I promised you. Look down the train and tell me what you see."

We did so, and said that we saw seven coaches and a diner.

"Exactly," Frimbo said. "A diner. I can't remember that there ever was a dining car on any train on the West Side line. Years ago, there was passenger service on the West Side, but that was only the *Dolly Varden*, which was a train that consisted of one coach and ran in the middle of the night. It ran at all only because the railroad was legally obliged to maintain passenger service. The franchises given to the railroads in the old days often included requirements like that. My stepmother's grandfather sold a large tract of land to the Pennsy outside Cincinnati with the proviso that the railroad erect a small flag stop on his land. The station wasn't any bigger than a rabbit hutch, but when the old man felt like boarding a train, it had to stop, even if it was the *Cincinnati Limited*. Those delightful days are gone, but today we will consume a meal, or part of one, as we roll down the West Side of Manhattan. My friends will be beside themselves with jealousy."

Frimbo consulted his watch. It is a pocket watch, modern and small, which he likes because it keeps good time and because whenever he opens its case—an alligator one—it automatically winds up. "Time to get aboard," he said. "You may have noticed that the engine is facing due south, into

Some buffs on the celebrated Virginia & Truckee Railway

the heart of Grand Central Terminal. That's because we are about to swing around one of the loops—semicircular pieces of track right under the station. Then we'll be headed in the right direction. They put in two loop tracks when they built the station, so commuter trains wouldn't have to back and foul everything up, and this will be only the second time I have ever ridden over this loop. The first was in the forties."

We followed Frimbo aboard the train and through the coaches to the one next to the diner. The coach was full of noisy and happy buffs, and many of them recognized him.

"Why, hello, Ernest!" one buff said. "Haven't seen you since Richmond." The National Railway Historical Society had held a meeting in Richmond over the Labor Day weekend.

"A fruitful weekend," Frimbo said. "Bad Southern cooking but good Southern steam locomotives."

At one end of the coach, two young men had set up a bookstall, and Frimbo went straight to it. They were offering about thirty titles, and Frimbo bought twenty-four books and pamphlets and whatnot, including "Articulated Cars of North America," "Rapid Transit Lines in Boston," and "The Steam Railroad Calendar for 1967." While he was paying for his purchases, the train started, passed around the loop, and headed for North White Plains.

Frimbo settled down in a seat, and so did we. Across the aisle from him was a serious-looking young man wearing a Cavalier EE Auto 35 camera. The young man looked shy, but he also looked as though he very much wanted to say something to Frimbo, and pretty soon he plucked up courage. "Mr. Frimbo," he said formally, "I must tell you that you left a serious impression on me last year when you spoke before the Railroad Enthusiasts. I wonder if I might ask you: What is your favorite train?"

Frimbo considered. "I guess the *Twentieth Century Limited*," he replied.

The young man ventured another question. "Mr. Frimbo, I am faced with a tough decision," he said. "I am more of a passenger-coach fan than anything else, and I, with some other fellows, have the opportunity to buy one. On the other hand, I could spend that money riding around the country on trains. Would you give me your advice?"

"It's a tough choice, all right," Frimbo said. "But the answer is plain. Ride. Do the U.S. Cover as much ground as you can. In five years, you won't be able to go from coast to coast by train. I have traveled one million nine hundred and fourteen thousand seven hundred and eight miles, by my latest reckoning, and I have never regretted a single mile."

"Mr. Frimbo, I will take your advice," the young man said firmly. "I admire you. You are like an encyclopedia. I would just love to copy some of your life, if at all possible. I have traveled ten thousand two hundred and ninety-two miles this year."

He paused, and Frimbo said, "Good."

The young man said, "Thank you, sir. I think I will step into the dining car."

Frimbo turned to us, trying to look displeased. "You see how I am forced to act as housemaster," he said in a whisper. Suddenly his eye was caught by a small spur of track on our right. "Ah, we have reached Melrose," he said, in his usual voice. "That little branch line over there was always used when F.D.R. was President to transfer his train from the New Haven route coming out of Penn Station from Washington onto the Central line, to take him up to Hyde Park. A friend of mine had to work out the Presidential route and always accompanied that train, which ran at night and carried his special armor-plated car. Everything was kept very secret." He laughed. "For anyone who knew anything about trains, it wasn't much of a secret. That branch line is the only piece of track connecting the New York Central and the New Haven run out of Penn Station, and, short of floating the President across the Hudson River on a car barge, it was the only conceivable route his train could use."

Our train reached North White Plains a few minutes later and stopped for a while, so that the nudges could get a few snapshots. Then it started back toward the New York & Harlem wye, which comes at the junction of the Harlem Division and the Hudson Division. The wye is a short, curved piece of track connecting the two divisions, and even Frimbo had never been on it before. It is normally used only by freight trains. He was much pleased when the train stopped briefly on the wye, waiting for an all-clear signal on the main-line tracks of the Hudson Division, and he got to talking about railroad language. "It's a good language, and etymologically sound, and it gets me irritated when ignorant people start miscalling things," he said. "Take that station of my stepmother's grandfather. It was a flag stop, because you put up a flag when you wanted the train to stop, but most people, not knowing any better, would call it a whistle stop. A lot of good it would do to blow a whistle at a thundering express train. And take milk trains. Over and over again I've heard people say, 'Sorry we're so late. We had to catch the milk train,' meaning they had to take a local. They just don't think. If a milk train stopped at every flag stop, the milk would be sour before it got near the city. The milk train is often the fastest train there is. And another thing. I remember once watching a long freight roll by out in New Mexico with a friend of mine and his young son. 'Look, Son, here comes the caboose,' this dumb friend of mine said to his kid. 'You can always tell the rear end of the train by the caboose, because "caboose" means "rear end." ' That got me boiling. The caboose, I told him, is the end of the train, but it certainly doesn't *mean* the end of the train, because it is the office of the conductor, who is the head of the train, and it is his car—he can fix it up the way he wants. The word is derived from the Spanish word '*cabeza*,' which means 'head.' At least, that's what every railroader believes."

At Harmon, Frimbo joined the tour of the railroad sheds, but he didn't say much. He remembers the days when the sheds were used to repair steam engines, and the sight of a lot of disabled diesels clearly gave him no pleasure. But he perked up when we got back on the train and headed for the Spuyten Duyvil Bridge—the little drawbridge under the Henry Hudson Bridge that leads to the West Side freight-line tracks. "We will now proceed to the diner and participate in a historic event," he announced. The diner was offering sandwiches, and Frimbo ordered a hamburger and ate it with great enjoyment. At a table across the aisle a heavy-set man with an air of authority, and a watch chain going from pocket to pocket across his waistcoat, was finishing a hamburger of his own. On his head sat a well-worn, slumping fedora. He nodded to Frimbo, got up, and walked out. "That had to be a railroad official," Frimbo said. "Sent along to keep an eye on a special train like this, in case anything

unprogramed happens. An old custom, mostly honored in
the breech now. Always, he wears a hat like that—never
takes it off indoors, maybe not even in the shower bath. It's
the badge of a good, old-school official."

The train crossed the drawbridge and made its way
through Inwood Hill Park, Fort Tryon Park, Fort Washington Park, and Riverside Park, staying close to the Hudson.
All around it were bare trees, and, try as we could, we were
unable to make out a single house, except the Little Red
Lighthouse under the George Washington Bridge. We saw
very few people, too; the tennis courts just below the lighthouse were occupied, and one woman and one dog were taking the air. Frimbo looked contented. "I call this the Invisible Manhattan," he said. "If an outsider were to approach this city for the first time on these tracks, he would
think Manhattan was a small hill town. Soon we'll leave
the country and enter a tunnel, and go downtown in darkness behind all those funny broken windows you can see
from the West Side Drive, but for the moment we can enjoy a railroad-preserved rusticity. Roads bring filling stations
and pizza parlors, but a railroad likes trees."

Below Seventy-second Street, the train emerged from the
tunnel and headed south through an open cut between Tenth
and Eleventh Avenues. Before the cut was constructed, in
1929 and 1930, the trains had used tracks on those avenues.
They were allowed to go no faster than four miles an hour,
and each train was preceded by a man on horseback, known
as a Tenth Avenue cowboy, who cleared the way. Frimbo
likes the cut because from it it is possible to see—in the
block above the Jost Brothers Jewelry Mfg. Co., at 514
West Forty-eighth Street—a small and battered grape arbor
in a back yard. Upon leaving the cut, the train entered the

Thirtieth Street Freight Yards, which railroad men call the St. John's Park Freight Station—the name of the original terminal of the line, south of Canal Street, a building that was torn down years ago. Here we stopped, on a steel viaduct overlooking the yard, and Frimbo descended from the dining car to get a better view.

This was the penultimate stop of the excursion, and the engine moved to the northern end of the train in order to take us back uptown. It was getting dark, and a few clouds, the first of the day, glowed pinkly over the rooftops of Weehawken and Hoboken. Frimbo led us back to the coach, where he began rummaging in a briefcase. "I look forward to nineteen-sixty-seven," he said. "I expect to ride on trains in Australia and Czechoslovakia, among other places, and by this time next year I'll be into my third million." He paused to examine a small blueprint of a passenger coach, which he had come across in his briefcase. We noticed that the polite young man who had promised to take Frimbo's advice had resumed his seat across the aisle and was also examining Frimbo's blueprint. After a while, Frimbo looked up and saw him. "Would you like to have this?" he asked. It was obvious that the young man would, but he was too shy to say so, and so he said, "No, thank you." The youth busied himself with a briefcase of his own, and then said that he had forgotten his cap in the dining car, and left his seat. Frimbo didn't say anything, but pretty soon he got up and tiptoed over to the young man's seat. He glanced around, slipped the blueprint into the young man's briefcase, and tiptoed back to his own seat, sitting down with a sigh. "A frolicsome trip," Frimbo said.

Mr. McGregor's Garden

8

Frimbo's second lecture before the Lexicographers' Club was delivered several weeks after the first. Again he played to a packed house. Here is a transcript:

"Good evening, ladies and gentlemen. This lecture is about South America, and it is entitled 'Mr. McGregor's Garden.' After I and my steady traveling companions had really got into the business of organizing our tours, one of them, an extremely successful businessman named Harry Dodge, one of the most famous rail buffs in the United States, came up with the idea of thoroughly doing South America. Dodge lived near Washington, and the first thing he did was to visit the South American embassies in Washington. There he collected a sheaf of letters. They all began like this:

> His Excellency President So-and-So of the National
> Railways of Uruguay [or whatever]
>
> My dear Horatio:
>   It is with the most extreme pleasure that I introduce
> to you three of my most intimate American friends

[only one of whom the Ambassador had ever met in his life]. Every courtesy you extend to them will, my dear fellow, be deemed a courtesy to me.

With affectionate regards,
etc., etc., etc.

"Our party of three had the usual trouble with travel agencies, which in South America are even less able to cope with railway travelers than our own are. In spite of the agencies, we arrived by air in Buenos Aires and were met by an agency courier. This was extremely necessary because the amount of paper work involved in getting a foreigner into or out of a South American country was incredible. There were many documents. For Costa Rica I had to have, in addition to my passport, a letter from the Chief of Police in the City of New York saying that I was not wanted for any crime, a letter from a business house saying I was in its employ, a letter from a travel agency saying I had a certain amount of funds with me and would not become a dependency of the country I was visiting. About half a pound of papers, all in the native language. And eight photographs. The paper could have damn near covered the entire acreage of the country.

"The courier carted us off to the absolutely magnificent old pile known as the Plaza Hotel on the grand square in Buenos Aires and let us rest for a day. Before he departed we gave him one of the 'Dear Horatio' letters.

"The following morning a chap with a real Oxbridge accent called me and said, 'My dear sir, what hour would be convenient for you and your companions to take coffee with El Presidente of the national railways to discuss the purpose of your journey? I will send a limousine to pick you up.'

"All South American railway Presidentes have a magnificent desk and magnificent manners and excellent English. We are served morning coffee amidst a discussion of how pleasant it is and how good it is for relations between our two great sister republics to have important gentlemen like yourselves coming to inspect our railway system, of which we are very proud, and we hope you will be able to give a good report of it to your government when you return.

"Then El Presidente would clear his throat and say, 'Now, about what you wish to do?'

"And we would clear our throats and tell him exactly what we wished to do. Argentina has a railway system of probably thirty thousand miles—this sounds incredible, but it is true of many countries who overrailroaded in the days of private ownership, when railroads were often built just to kill off other railroads. But we knew just what we wanted. My two companions were photographers, and they wanted permission to go to whatever roundhouses still had steam locomotives and to see the switch engines in the Retiro station in Buenos Aires, for a few of these were wood-burners —yes, sparks and all, and the lovely fragrance of burning wood. It was like sitting by your own fireplace at home.

"None of these requests fazed our Argentine El Presidente. 'Yes,' he said, 'the roundhouses. The best of them is twenty-five miles away.' Then, pressing a button, he said into a telephone, 'Would you ask Mr. McGregor to step in for a moment?' Mr. McGregor, a Scot, would enter and be introduced. El Presidente would tell him what we wanted and ask him to make arrangements.

"I had better explain Mr. McGregor. It is a generic name—he occurs all over South America. Many South American railways were built by British capital, and they had British engines, British officials, British engineers, British signaling, and British rolling stock. When the railways were nationalized, the governments, which usually appointed high-ranking Army officers to head up the systems, and sent home packs of Britishers, cannily kept a Mr. McGregor— of Glasgow, say, or Edinburgh—on hand, just in case. All the Mr. McGregors we met—under whatever names they had—had the same story. They'd been working for a British railway that had been nationalized. They had married a charming South American girl. Their children went to South American schools. They belonged to the local clubs. And they wouldn't live through another winter in Glasgow for a million pounds. Officially, they were retired, but each McGregor had an office in the back of the building. There was no lettering on the door of this office, but it always had a direct line to El Presidente's office. And whenever anything called for special dealing, Mr. McGregor was summoned. There had been a slightly embarrassing wreck on one of the railways—I won't name the country—so when we arrived to have morning coffee with one El Presidente, Mr. McGregor was already there, and El Presidente was saying to McGregor, 'Well, run down the line and see what you can do.'

"Wherever we went, it was always explained that Mr. McGregor is not on the staff, he is retired, he simply potters about, he drops in now and then because he's lonesome, but we came to realize that he was the Mr. Fixit all over South America. What the Penn Central needs is a few Mr. Mc-Gregors.

"We took the train twenty-five miles out to a magnificent roundhouse, which seemed to have several thousand locomotives all being stoked up. A representative designated by Mr. McGregor introduced us to the superintendent. Again, 'What would you like?' and we cleared our throats and picked out forty locomotives and said, 'Bring them out one by one on the turntable and set them so that the sun strikes them just the right way for photographing them.' Well, all right. It took four hours and all the employees were happy as larks, running around, stoking up, and the superintendent very proud to show off what he had.

"In Brazil, morning coffee with El Presidente in Rio. We wished to go to the nineteenth-century capital, Petropolis, reached by an extraordinary railway, part of it so steep that the locomotives have to be hooked on to a cable running uphill—called, for some reason, a 'rope-worked incline' —which pulls an engine and one or two cars for several miles until they reach the top, pulls up another locomotive and two more cars, and so on. The train is then reassembled, and trundles off on more feasible territory.

"El Presidente told us what we already knew, because we had been able to acquire a few timetables: that service to Petropolis was next to nothing now, because of a new highway. Getting timetables in South America is, by the way, a prodigious task. Mostly they are printed on broadsheets and posted on the walls of the stations; a pocket timetable is practically unheard of. El Presidente said, 'I regret the service is so inconvenient. My only suggestion— I hope it will be acceptable—is that we run a special train, with our compliments—a steam locomotive pushing one of our inspection cars.'

"Well, indeed it was acceptable. 'Mr. McGregor, will you arrange for an equerry to accompany our esteemed guests?' In the morning, to the amazement of all the people in the railway station, we set off in a car pushed by an antique tea kettle of a steam locomotive. In Petropolis, after ascending the rope-worked incline, as advertised—at, I may say, a speed that was literally pedestrian—we proceeded again to a roundhouse, where we found an incredible old sleeping car that I wanted to take home with me. It was built with two compartments, each of which slept twelve and had one nickel-plated wash basin in the middle.

"In Chile we ran into further trouble with travel agencies. Chile is a million miles long and two feet wide. A splendid railway system runs almost the entire length of the country, right down alongside the spine of South America, from real tropical country practically to Tierra del Fuego and Cape Horn. I wanted to spend the night in one of their very, very, very old wooden German sleeping cars, whose unique interiors I had seen only in photographs. The German influence, you know, had been very strong down there. I had a completely Latin friend in Concepción with the un-Latin name of Pablo Springmuller, and the German sleeping cars ran between Santiago, where we were barracked, and Concepción.

"But the travel agencies were cavalier. They said, 'Ah, the tourist season, it is impossible, nothing can be arranged, too crowded.' So I walked down to the railway station and in my broken Spanish got in touch with a man whose name I'd been given in New York. I told him two of us wished to go all the way down to Concepción—it's several hundred miles from Santiago—on a daytime train and then return, only an hour and a quarter later, in one of those German sleeping cars. He instantly perked up. 'Ah, you know about those cars? Yes, yes, yes. Come back after lunch.'

"After lunch I got the tickets, shook hands, and walked

back to the travel agency to see whether any mail had come in from New York. 'Ah,' they said, 'now you have found out that what we told you is the truth, eh? You are prepared to fly to Concepción, no?' 'No,' I said. 'I think we'll take the train. We have tickets.' They studied them. 'Ah,' they said. 'That cannot be. These are forgeries.'

"The explanation? The travel agencies got commissions from airlines that were a great deal better than the commissions paid by the government railways.

"The Antofagasta & Bolivia runs from the large port of Antofagasta, toward the northern end of Chile, to La Paz, the capital of Bolivia, through what looks like the country of the moon. From sea level it climbs thousands of feet into the Andes, and then drops down precipitously to La Paz, which is itself something like eleven thousand feet above sea level. We had discovered through our international connections that this railway had only one through train a week —the *Rapido*. It was still steam-hauled, a complete 'deluxe' train with wooden sleeping cars, a wooden restaurant car, and a few of the amenities. We had written from New York to the manager of the Antofagasta & Bolivia—this was still a British railway—asking him to be good enough to set aside two compartments on the *Rapido*.

" 'And how are you getting from Antofagasta to La Paz?' asked the travel agency in Santiago. 'There is no railway there, you know.' I produced a letter from the manager and said, 'Two compartments are reserved for us. Will you arrange for us to fly to Antofagasta so we can proceed by train?'

" 'Ah!' they said. 'Another forgery. You'll see when you get to Antofagasta. You will go to our agency, and they will tell you that there is no train.' 'Give me the address of your agency,' I said. After we'd been parked in a splendid hotel overlooking the ocean just outside Antofagasta, we walked into town to the address given by the travel agency in Santiago. It was a vacant lot.

"The lot was quite near the railroad station, as it turned out. There the general manager was expecting us, and our tickets were ready. The journey to La Paz was, naturally, incredible—that climb through those bleak mountains: up, up, up, up for thirty-six hours—then across a vast plain, and then across a great depression, thirty-five miles wide, which, because it was the end of the rainy season, had become a vast lake. And for thirty-five miles our little wooden train —or should I say boat?—with the little steam engine on the head of it trundled through this lake. The water came up almost to the floors of the cars. The wheels moved very, very slowly—we were shoving a thirty-five-mile lake ahead of us. The train crew seemed astonished that we were impressed, and we gathered that this sort of thing goes on all the time during certain seasons of the year.

"La Paz, whose altitude gave us all earaches, is built on a slope of the Andes even more precipitate than the slope on which San Francisco and its cable cars are built. Of course we wanted to hop on the La Paz trams at once. To our distress we saw trolley tracks completely covered with rust in a number of streets, and, heavy-hearted, we repaired to the offices of the La Paz tramway system armed only with a 'To-Whom-It-May-Concern' letter from the Bolivian ambassador. The secretary of the tramline, an Englishman, told us the rust was genuine—trams had ceased running six months ago. Drawing as long faces as we possibly could, we said, 'We came these thousands of miles from the United States to ride on your tramline, and it is not running.'

" 'Well,' he said, 'I wouldn't say it's not *running*—we've kept two of the cars working to do repair work on the line. After all, we do have a certain freight business.' And the upshot was that we were given the use of one of these cars, with a motorman and a conductor who spoke a bit of English, for four hours early the next morning. These men were instructed to take us wherever we wished. And so we set off up a magnificent slope—the tramline climbed right out of La Paz. It was like going up the wall of a house, twisting and turning for perhaps ten miles, and then roaring back into La Paz, buckety buckety, so that we could return the car at the promised hour.

"Next came a train ride up over the top of the Andes from La Paz to the shores of that celebrated international lake, Titicaca, the highest body of water in the world. And there, twelve thousand, five hundred and seven feet above sea level, we embarked on a steamship for Peru. This ship had been built in Glasgow in eighteen-seventy-nine, unbolted, shipped to South America, taken by mule train up to Lake Titicaca, then rebolted together on the shores of the lake by various McGregors, and put into international service. We spent the night aboard and I will leave you with a description of this fantastic voyage. The other passengers were: six Knights of Malta who refused to say why they were on board, a bunch of incredibly vigorous Irish monks off to indoctrinate the outlying peasants of Peru with their brand of Christianity, several Chinese who refused to say why they were there, too, and some obnoxious German businessmen. We dined at a common table, and the conversation was rapid-fire and dizzying and amusing, except for the Germans. They, thinking they were smarter than everybody else, were trying to exchange Bolivian currency for real money.

"Now, Bolivian currency is the only currency in the world that is not even worth papering your bathroom with —in fact, South American banks, which change money all the time because people are constantly crossing the borders, refuse to have anything to do with it. But these Germans were trying to trade off large quantities of the stuff to a bunch of wiseacres—namely, the rest of the passenger list. The Germans were also operating under the assumption— erroneous, of course—that nobody aboard ship could understand German. When we wouldn't bite, they began discussing among themselves the *verdampt*ness of these obtuse peasants—until one of the Knights of Malta dressed them down properly in German.

"Thank you, ladies and gentlemen."

Last Run

On Saturday, December 2, 1967, the *Twentieth Century Limited,* one of the most famous trains in the world, made its final run from New York to Chicago. We were aboard. We wouldn't have been if we hadn't received an agitated phone call the previous day from Ernest M. Frimbo. "Nobody knows it," Frimbo told us over the telephone, "but the *Century* is coming to an end tomorrow night." We said something, and he said, "Yes, yes, very funny. I am talking trains, not apocalyptics. I am telling you this because nobody is supposed to know. The New York Central is too embarrassed to admit that it's yanking the train. And it should be embarrassed. I find it impossible to speak about that railroad calmly. But I want to tell you that if you're quick about it, you can get a bedroom on that last run. You're bound to be the only members of the press making the trip, because your colleagues have been hoodwinked by Central flapdoodle."

We said that we had been hoping for some time to find an excuse to take the *Century*.

Frimbo went on, "It isn't what it was, you know, but I must have ridden on the *Century* maybe fifty times over the years, and it's still better than what will replace it. Wish I could be with you on that run, but I've got an unbreakable date with a train in Arizona. Don't forget—the *Century* leaves at six on Track 34. Make a note for me of what a railroad man would call its consist—the number and variety and order of its cars. Oh, yes. Lucius Beebe wrote a book about the *Century*, which you had better take along. It's fascinating and somewhat unreliable. Full steam ahead!"

Our friend rang off, and we steamed over to Grand Central Terminal, where we booked Bedroom B in Car 253 for the following night from a pleasant ticket agent, who said, "You're just in time—that's the last run. I guess a lot of people will be very sorry," and then looked abashed.

The next afternoon, just after five-thirty, we made our way back to Grand Central, baggage and the Beebe in hand. A small crowd of rail fans and reporters and news photographers had gathered around the check-in counters at Track 34. The rail fans, standing on the famous red carpet that said "20TH CENTURY LIMITED," were taking pictures of the observation car at the end of the *Century*, and the newsmen were taking pictures of the rail fans taking pictures, and talking with the passengers checking in. The passengers all said, in effect, that they had had no idea that this was the last run of the *Twentieth Century Limited,* and wasn't it a shame?

We had our tickets taken and our pictures taken, and climbed aboard. Car 253 proved to be the second car from the observation car, and named *Missouri Valley*. We started making notes for Frimbo. The observation car was *Wingate Brook*, and the sleeping car between it and us was *Port Clinton*. Ahead of us were another sleeping car (*Peach Valley*), a dining car, a car that was half club car and half galley for the diner, a day coach that displayed reproductions of two paintings by Cézanne, a sleeper coach, a dormitory car (which is used by the dining-car staff and has triple-decker bunks), and an electric engine. Our bedroom was a comfortable room that showed signs of wear. It had metal walls painted gray, a large brown armchair with an antimacassar, a smaller brown armchair without an antimacassar, a red rug with a faded floral design, a small separate bathroom, an even smaller closet, and a picture window, which needed washing. On the seat of the large armchair was a brochure informing us that we would receive complimentary champagne with our dinner and complimentary newspapers and boutonnieres with our breakfast, that we could have our shoes shined and our suits pressed, and that, if we wanted them, a typewriter and an electric shaver were available.

At six o'clock precisely, the *Century* pulled out. We decided that Frimbo would expect us to settle down in the observation car, so we made our way back to *Wingate Brook*, carrying the Beebe with us. At the end of our sleeping car, two *Century* porters were saying good-by to two Grand Central redcaps, who were leaning on their pushcarts. The redcaps waved, and one of them looked as though he thought he ought to make a few appropriate remarks, but then he just grinned and waved again and said, "Well, see you, boys."

We liked the lounge in the observation car. It was outfitted with sofas, armchairs, a table and a lamp or two, three bunches of fresh yellow and white chrysanthemums, including a grand branch in the rear window. The lounge wasn't very full, so we chose chairs near the window with the chrysanthemums, and opened up the Beebe. Outside, there were flashes of light as the rail fans took their final pictures, and we waved to them. Mr. Beebe told us that he had unearthed a New York Central publicity release about the consist of the first run of the *Twentieth Century Limited*, on June 15, 1902:

> The trains [he quoted] will be composed of buffet, smoking, and library composite cars *Decius, Cyrus,* observation cars *Alroy* and *Sappho,* 12 section drawing-room state-room cars *Petruchio, Philario, Gonzalo* and *Benvolio. . . .* The exterior of the car is painted Pullman standard color, the ornamentation in gold being simple, but very artistic.

Mr. Beebe said that the interiors of the cars were particularly noticeable for, in the railroad's words, an "absence of all heavy carvings, ornate grilles and metal work, stuffy hangings, etc."

After we had been reading for a while, the car filled up, and we fell into conversation with the man who had been standing in front of us in the check-in line and with a well-dressed young man who was carrying a camera. The man from the check-in line said that he was a dermatologist. "Heading for a convention at the Palmer House," he told the young man and us. "Held there every year at this time. I always start my Christmas shopping at that convention. Don't know why. Live in New York but always start my shopping in Chicago. Have a drink."

The young man said that he was a railroad buff, and that he would love a drink as soon as he had taken a picture of the observation-car porter. "I have over five hundred pictures of this train," he said. "I have been taking one a week since nineteen-fifty-nine. At home, I have over twenty-two thousand railroad pictures."

The porter brought us all a drink, and said, "Would you gentlemens like some hors d'oeuvres?"

The dermatologist said, "Just 'cause you asked me to."

The porter looked pleased. "I didn't have to twist *your* arm," he said.

The young man said he had heard that the New Haven Railroad had bought the observation car from the New York Central.

The porter grinned. "I wonder whatever *they'll* do with it," he said.

We asked the young man if, by any chance, he had ever met Ernest Frimbo.

He said, "I certainly have. He is the foremost rail fan there is. I'm a Frimbo disciple. In the days when the *Century* had a barbershop on board, he and his friends would get on and ride as far as Albany just to get a shave and a haircut."

Our two new friends went off to dinner, and the conductor of the *Century* came around checking tickets. He noticed a boy with long, fair hair, who had been sitting quietly in the observation car for some time, and went over to talk with him. The boy said that he hoped the conductor remembered him—that he was the person who had come down to the station to see a friend off, and then had decided he just had to take the final run of the *Century*. He said that the conductor had said he would accept a check.

The conductor looked very solemn, then said, "Well, it *is* the last run. You give me your check and I'll give you a receipt." The boy wrote out a check, and the conductor took a receipt form out of his pocket and punched it with his ticket punch. "That's my punch mark," he said as he handed the receipt to the boy. "Everybody in the country knows that punch mark."

After the conductor had left, we walked over to the boy and asked if we might see the conductor's punch mark. It was shaped like a tiny map of the United States and had a slightly exaggerated bulge in the region of Texas.

Around about Albany, we headed for the diner. The steward, a good-humored man in a dinner jacket and gold-rimmed spectacles, handed us a menu printed in gold and black. The menu said:

WELCOME TO
THE CENTURY ROOM
offering the ultimate in
dining car cuisine and service

We both ordered Spiced Apple Rings, Queen Olives, Rosetted Radishes, Stuffed Celery N.Y.C., Carrot Sticks, Bisque of New Asparagus, Roast Prime Ribs of Beef au Jus, with Baked Hubbard Squash and Camille Potatoes, Orange-Pecan Sticks and Dinner Rolls, Hearts of Lettuce with Thousand Island Dressing, Old-Fashioned Strawberry Shortcake with Whipped Cream, and Coffee. We drank our complimentary champagne with the roast beef, and the whole meal was fine. The steward told us that he would give us some after-dinner mints when we had finished our coffee, and an apple and an orange that we could take to our bedroom.

The *Century* stopped in Buffalo to pick up some cars from the *New England States*, a train that originated in Boston, and to change some of its crew. There was a delay. The

New England States had had a fire in one of its sleepers and was running behind time. We climbed down onto the platform. Our new conductor, who was going as far as Toledo, was standing a few feet away from us, carrying a black dispatch box and talking with an elderly rail fan. The rail fan was carrying a copy of Beebe's book, and he asked the conductor to autograph it. The conductor looked as though he were about to say no. Instead, he said, "Well, it *is* the last run," and reached for the book. The rail fan said, "I came all the way from Niagara Falls to see the *Century* for the last time. That's about twenty-five miles. It used to be a great train."

The conductor agreed. "This was a train," he said. "Why, I've carried Jim Farley, Joe Louis, a lot of famous people on this train." He reached down and opened his dispatch box and took out two postcards. One showed a train with an old steam engine and was printed in brown ink on a gold background. "That was a long time ago," he said. He turned the card over. "See? It's even got that old green George Washington penny stamp on it." He held up the other card. The other card showed a train with a more modern steam engine. The train was thundering through hills that were orange because it was autumn, under a pale-blue sky with some fleecy white clouds in it. A great deal of gray smoke was pouring out of the engine's stack.

The rail fan referred to the *Century* by its official name, Train Number 25, and said he supposed the *Century* would lose that number as soon as it reached Chicago.

The conductor said it would lose the number sooner than that, because the new schedule went into effect at four o'clock in the morning. Officially, the *Century* would expire somewhere near Ashtabula. "We're Twenty-Five until four," he said. "Then we become Twenty-Seven, and that's the end of the *Century*." He put his postcards back in his dispatch box and closed it.

We returned to our bedroom, which was now made up, with two beds where the large armchair had been, and decided to sleep for a couple of hours but to be awake at four, if we could manage it. We woke up sometime later. The train was standing still. We looked out the window and couldn't see anything. We checked our watches, and they said five minutes to four. It seemed like a good idea to go back to sleep, but we decided that Frimbo would have got up and investigated, so we put overcoats on over our pajamas and walked up the train, looking for the conductor. We found him sitting in the dining car working on some papers. He heard us coming and looked at his watch. It was now a few minutes after four. "Well, she's dead," he said. "But we're sitting here in Harbor Creek, Pennsylvania, only because an express train has been derailed up ahead. Looks like we'll have to detour around it over the Norfolk & Western tracks. I guess we may be late enough so that you'll get a free breakfast." He picked up his papers, and said, "There's a little good in every bad."

When we woke up again, our watches said twelve-forty-five, and the sky outside our window was bright gray, above flat brown fields. The train was moving. It had been due in Chicago at nine-forty. We had slept through the free morning papers and the free boutonnieres, and we were afraid we might have slept right through Chicago. We put on overcoats again. Outside the bedroom we found the conductor in conference with our porter. The porter said to us, "We're not into Cleveland yet," and the conductor said, "She sure is dying hard, isn't she? I'm afraid we'll be almost nine

hours late into Chicago, and that will make the last run of
the *Century* six hours longer than the first run. We got
caught behind a slow freight on the Norfolk & Western
tracks and did sixty miles in seven hours. When we finally
got back on the Central track, at Madison, Ohio, we were
still almost fifty miles east of Cleveland. I didn't get to
church this morning."

The porter said, "Soon as we get to Cleveland, the dining
car will take on some water, and they can serve lunch."

We went back to bed and ate the apple and the orange,
and took another pull at the Beebe:

> In times of crisis [Mr. Beebe said] . . . the entire
> collective will power of the New York Central System
> seemed to focus on getting *The Century* through with
> the least possible delay. High priority freight might
> freeze to the tracks at Buffalo and other ranking trains
> go into the hole all the way from Cleveland to Elkhart,
> but extra gangs and flangers, wedge plows and helper
> engines diverted from other runs combined to get the
> line's crack varnish over the road with the least possible
> damage to its schedule.

Lunch, after Cleveland, was a quiet meal. The steward
was cheerful, and said, "Want to sit down? Here's a seat
right here. Things aren't so bad." The passengers were glum.
We had some more asparagus soup and a mushroom ome-
lette. There was no liquor, because there are laws in Ohio
and Indiana about Sunday drinking. Afterward, we went
back to the observation car, along with a number of other
people, to look at Ohio, and by and by everyone cheered up.
Four sailors sat down with a pack of cards and started to
play poker. The sun came out. A woman who told us she
was from Milwaukee said, "When we were stopped in those

fields in the middle of the night, I felt just like that Dr. Zhivago." And a woman wearing a mink hat said, "Everyone seems placid, and I'm glad. I guess maybe it's because it's the last run there will ever be of the *Twentieth Century Limited.*"

We reached Chicago that night, at a quarter to seven, Central time.

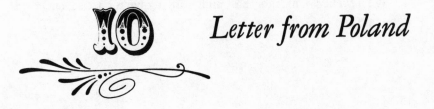

Letter from Poland

My dear Contessa: I write you from the Grand, in Warsaw—a hotel whose rooms could not accommodate luggage of the quantity you are accustomed to but whose restaurant you could not fault. As to that, I have not, in the course of our fortnight in Poland, had to fault any restaurant at all, though the restaurant cars in the trains we have traveled have been at times slapdash, a circumstance excusable, I suppose, when one contemplates the number of passengers clamoring to be fed.

You were correct in your prediction that a helter-skelter journey such as ours might encounter difficulties, but I had not expected them to move in upon us at the very beginning —or even before the beginning, inasmuch as some of us had to stand in the corridors of our morning express from Berlin to Poznań, which was our entry this time into Poland. A few of the lovable narrow-gauge steam railways we have visited, enscribed on film, and journeyed upon are best reached by a chartered omnibus, and one had been laid on for us during the several days we spent in Poznań for this very purpose, but we learned, amid enormous dismay, as we lunched on our first day with our Polish government courier, that the official tourist agency had decided that we were to spend the *entire* fortnight in this vehicle. All of our party had moved into Poland on the understanding that we were to take part in a *railway* holiday.

Our first afternoon aboard this vehicle disclosed the fact that it was without any of what we shall call facilities for ladies and gentlemen, and I, being somewhat of a geographer, quickly calculated that one of the hops we were to encompass in it came to 190 miles, and another to 380 miles. Polish highways are pleasant; they follow the contour of the land without disturbing it, and they exert a magnetic attraction on farmers with horse-drawn wagons and horse-drawn hay rakes, and the highways are only two lanes wide.

In the circumstance, our progress was hardly royal, and once, when we were on our way to intercept a narrow-gauge train, our courier had to leap from our bus, race to a railway crossing on the highway just ahead, and, hands raised aloft, halt the train, the final one of the day, which had already left the station where we were to board it. So we had to scramble aboard without tickets, of course. All that remained to be done was to inform the driver of the bus where he was to rescue us at the end of our journey—a hamlet so small that it was invisible on even the detailed map our courier had produced. Ninety minutes later, arrived at the hamlet, we managed excellent photographs of the maneuvers the engine crew went through as they stowed coal and water aboard their tiny charge for the return run next morning, and—finally deciphering our hand-wavings—posed the locomotive for us in a pair of photogenic settings. And on the next day, debarking from our bus in the forecourt of a narrow-gauge railway station for which the word "picturesque" must have been invented, we discovered that the passenger train upon which we had planned to pass a cheery Sunday morning had been withdrawn months ago.

I should here explain that our courier, instructed by the Polish tourist bureau that we were to be bussing it around Poland, had not armed himself with a railway timetable, and we were working by dead (literally dead) reckoning, the timetable I had carted across the Atlantic being a year out of date. Most of the older men in Poland still speak German, which was a compulsory assignment in school during the Nazi occupation, and the chap in our group whose German was razor-sharp soon ascertained that the steam engine we could hear at that moment getting up its courage and its steam around the corner was to leave in a few minutes with the apparently weekly (or perhaps annual) freight train for who knew where. Attached to the rear of this train was a guard's van—what we in the States would call a caboose—and I leave it to your perspicacity, my dear Contessa, to divine the nature of the question our German spokesman now put to the guard. Our courier, to whom the official bus tour of Poland was beginning to look less and less like an official bus tour, seemed distraught indeed, as well he might: he had already transgressed the rules of the road by flagging down yesterday's narrow-gauge train. But we gave him a look, told him we expected to see him and his bus at the end of the run, and set off, in a tiny wooden-wheeled château—so small, in fact, that I had to bend double whenever I moved about it for a better view—across rural Poland. Mission accomplished! But I would not have wished, dear Contessa, that you had been my consort for any part of this five-day dusty vagabondage.

On the evening we reached the Baltic, at Szczecin (once the more pronounceable Stettin, under German rule), where we were to spend a brief night before setting off at 8:30 in the morning for Katowice, 380 miles distant, I, for one, was ready to take a busman's holiday (reversed), and announced as dinner ended that I was walking to the central railway station in order to make inquiry. "In what language?" everyone demanded, and it was then, Contessa, that you, prettily prattling your glib Polish, should have passed a miracle and stood at my side.

"In sign language," I replied, and noted with glee that the three bachelors in our entourage rose as one and followed me to the station.

It was not quite ten that evening as we arrived, but it could have been the commuter hour at Pennsylvania Station. I moved past a rank of grilled windows until I espied one behind which an unmistakable railway timetable book reposed, and then stood there clearing my throat until the young lady (all Polish ticket sellers appear to be young ladies) in residence looked up. Clasping my hands and then opening them, as if they were the covers of a book, I then pointed to the timetable, and in an instant it was in my hand. Ah! A fast train just before eleven in the morning all the way to Katowice, and the crossed knife and fork imprinted below the number of the train was, of course, the international European indication that a restaurant car would be provided, and a large black R inside a hollow square was, of course, the indication that seat reservations were advisable.

But a vertical wavy line down the column in which my train appeared was the indication that the train did not run every day, and the explanation of the wavy line, though couched in what I had to assume was the finest of Polish, didn't give me a clue. I approached my ticket seller, pointed to the wavy line, wrote in my notebook the days of the week —one through seven, in numerals—and passed it to her; she struck out the "2" and the "3"; ah, well, tomorrow was "5," a Friday, so that was all right, and off I posted to a window marked by a duplicate of the black R in the hollow square. In my notebook I inscribed the number and departure time of my train, the date and the month ("23 VII," or the twenty-third of July), the symbolic R followed by a plus sign and a "4," the arrival time at Katowice, and a venture-some "1 kl," the *German* abbreviation for "first class." The whole thing, it turned out, was to cost each of us a terrifying six dollars.

At breakfast, our courier gloomily inspected the tickets I had procured and pronounced them valid, and was in-formed that the four defectors from his long-distance sight-seeing bus would leave their luggage in his care. We set off for a tour of the city—by tram, naturally—as our fellow citizens got aboard their bus. Our final tram delivered us at the station plaza a quarter hour before train time, and we were ushered into a first-class compartment that, it turned out, was to be ours alone for the day. An hour after depar-ture, when my companions were beginning to doubt my as-sertion that we would be dining en route, a restaurant car was shunted aboard, and, fortified by broiled chicken, Polish ham, a matter-of-fact steak, and a quantity of beer, we managed (at two long sittings) to pass a most pleasant day. Our train was alternately diesel and electric (I have explained to you, my dove, what these harsh words mean), but as we approached Katowice, the central city of the enormous Silesian coal-and-iron complex, a satisfying array of steam locomotives began to present themselves. After we had alighted, we walked slowly through the city (I had been there a year or so earlier, and knew where our hotel was), admiring the trams, which were everywhere.

At six, we left our handbags in the hotel and set off on the trams. Back at eight, and still no courier, no companions. At nine they arrived, and when we told them about our restaurant car and our tram-riding, there was a great silence. After dinner, we escorted our fellow travelers (in a

A Polish 600-mm. gauge

sense) to the railway station; they would be bussing it out of town at eight in the morning, and this would be their one opportunity to view the station, which had just been magnificently rebuilt. There we espied what we had been hoping to find ever since we arrived in Poland—a timetable for sale. "I wonder," said one of us bachelors as he watched me studying it, "whether our courier knows he's not likely ever to see us again."

Mileage

On a Saturday in April 1968, we took a train from Pennsylvania Station in New York to Paoli. It was no ordinary trip for us, because we were in the company of E. M. Frimbo. It was a special occasion for Frimbo, too. "Before getting to Philadelphia, I will have reached my two-millionth mile of travel by railway," he said when he invited us along. "That's about eighty times around the equator."

At a little before five P.M. we met Frimbo outside Car 496 of the *Broadway Limited*—destination Chicago, departure five-oh-five P.M. "There's a stop at North Philadelphia, but we'll go on down the Main Line to Paoli and take a local back to town," Frimbo said. "That way, we don't have to rush dinner." The porter took our topcoats, and the conductor, who was wearing a fresh white carnation in his buttonhole, directed us to Double Bedroom K. For ourselves we chose peach-colored seats opposite the window, and Frimbo, looking comfortably at home, settled in the chair alongside the window. "You're looking straight ahead, but

From the two million miles—a South African Railways 4-8-4

I'm looking forward," he said. "These days, railroad people had *better* be forward-looking."

As the train pulled out, we asked Frimbo when he had celebrated his first million.

"Fifteen years ago, on a Baltimore & Ohio freight line," he told us. "I've included a lot of foreign railways. Last year, it was Australia, Japan, Czechoslovakia, and Hungary."

By now, we were looking out at a dingy body of water. "We're crossing the Hackensack River," said Frimbo, tak-

ing out his mileage notebook. "According to my calculations, I should reach the two-millionth just at Princeton Junction, about five minutes to six. Very satisfactory. I went to Princeton. Let's have dinner."

On the way to the dining car, we remarked that the train moved so smoothly that we felt none of the usual jolts.

"No jolts on the *Broadway*," said Frimbo. "Now that the *Twentieth Century* is gone, this is my favorite train in the East."

The dining steward said hello to Frimbo and showed us

to a table with a green cloth and a vase of fresh red carnations. "Haven't seen you since Monday," our waiter said to Frimbo. "How are you?"

"Fine," said Frimbo. "I'm celebrating my two-millionth mile."

"The three-millionth ought to be coming up before long," said the waiter.

We dined on steak, endive-and-watercress salad, peach Melba, and a bottle of Pommard. When the waiter brought finger bowls and dessert, Frimbo took out his watch. "Just a minute or two now," he said.

We looked out the window at a small station.

"Princeton Junction. That's it!" said Frimbo. "Right on time."

"*À votre santé!*" the steward proposed.

The waiter brought a tray of Pennsylvania Railroad chocolate mints.

"This staff can serve French toast at breakfast and propose a French toast at dinner," Frimbo said. "They're still proud of the train. Railways and ships are still the only civilized means of travel."

On the way back to No. 496, Frimbo said, "I hope you're noticing the names of the cars." We noted the *Harbor Rest*, which was the club car, and the *Imperial Vale* and the *Kaskaskia Rapids*. Number 496 was the *Crystal Creek*. "They aren't just pretty sounds," he went on. "The purpose is to describe the interior arrangements. Imperials are four compartments, four double bedrooms, and two drawing rooms. Rapids are six double bedrooms and ten roomettes. Creeks are double rooms and single duplex rooms."

From Double Bedroom K, the view looked like a picture postcard of trees. "We go mostly through the woods,"

Frimbo said. "It's the only way to see a New Jersey land-scape without gas stations."

Frimbo talked some more about the names of Pullmans. "At one time the Pullman company decided that business-men wanted single bedrooms, so they built a series of cars divided up into fourteen single bedrooms. Then it was time to get a series name. 'Well, let's get the word "night" in there,' said someone. ' "Nightingale," ' said someone else. ' "Nightshade," ' said a third, without looking it up in the dictionary. So there was almost a Pullman named *Night-shade,* but I think the idea was vetoed at the last minute.

"The Pennsylvania ordered such a colossal number of Pullmans built according to the Imperial design that even-tually invention flagged. I regret to say that there actually was a car called *Imperial Elf.* Finally someone ended the series by thinking up the name *Imperial Empire.*

"Sleeping cars on Southern railways had really regional names. One of them was *Deep South.* Another was *Rebel Yell.*"

We asked Frimbo to name his favorite American trains.

"The *Super Chief,* Chicago–Los Angeles; the *Panama Limited,* Chicago–New Orleans; the *Broadway Limited,*" he said. After a moment, he added, " 'Limited' means a lim-ited number of stops and accommodations. A name more honored in the breach today."

The train stopped briefly at North Philadelphia, near several cheerfully bright-yellow cars, which Frimbo said were living quarters for men working on the tracks, and con-tinued down the Main Line, past Wynnewood and Ardmore. "Nearly there," Frimbo said, taking his watch out again. "We're right on schedule. It will be Mile Two Million Fifty-nine."

The train slowed down, and we could see the lights of a small brick station. The porter was standing at the door of Double Bedroom K with our topcoats. "Good-by. See you again soon, Mr. Frimbo," he said, and he opened the door at the end of the car. We climbed down the steps and stood on the brick platform. The engine was rumbling a bit, and we could see that the dining car was full.

"Is Sixteen on time from Pittsburgh?" Frimbo asked the stationmaster.

"No, she's a few minutes late," he answered.

Within two minutes, the *Broadway Limited* was on its way to Chicago.

"It's seven-oh-one," said Frimbo. "One hundred and seven miles in under two hours. It's the right way to get to Paoli."

Ithaca: A Case History from Frimbo's File

I have mentioned elsewhere that I became a sports writer fifty years ago so that someone would pay me to go by train to universities in the Eastern part of the United States and report on their winter sports. I have kept up this side line ever since—I *like* football, you know. At first the problem of logistics was not a serious one. Take, for example, Cornell, at Ithaca, to which I still go two or three times a winter. Fifty years ago this was quite simple. I could pop down to Pennsylvania Station after dinner Friday night and get in a lower berth in a sleeping car on the Lehigh Valley Railroad's *Star*. The car would be set out on a side track in Ithaca in the early morning. I could sleep there until breakfast time, do my business in town, and then take the same car back to New York that night. This gave me ample time to see the game and then get about and talk to friends on campus.

The Lackawanna Railway, which begins its course in Hoboken, just across the river from New York, also ran a sleeping car to Ithaca. This was of particular interest to us rail buffs because, on the Lackawanna, Ithaca lay at the end of a branch line that could be negotiated only by a switch-back—that is, a piece of track that on a map would look like a huge "Z." The train ran down the branch line for a certain number of miles to one switch, then backed down a steep incline to another switch, then ran forward into Ithaca. Since I like to be impartial in the distribution of my wealth, I patronized in complete equality the two sleeping-car services.

First the Lackawanna sleeping car disappeared, though the train still ran down the switchback into Ithaca. Then the whole train into Ithaca disappeared. Then the Lehigh Valley sleeping car disappeared. I next resorted to other ex-pedients: in the very early hours of the morning, New York Central's *Genesee Express* to Buffalo set out a sleeping car at Syracuse for what is called the Auburn Road, a branch that dips down toward the Finger Lakes. I'd get off this sleeping car at Auburn, walk across town, have breakfast, and get on a gas-electric combined passenger-mail-and-bag-gage car run by the Lehigh Valley Railroad, which tooled down the lake through Aurora, where Wells College is, and into Ithaca. Back the same way in the evening.

When *that* service disappeared, I went back to the Lackawanna Railway, using a sleeping car that departed from Hoboken in an express train that got to Elmira, New York, at about breakfast time. I'd dust across the street to the old and extremely comfortable Mark Twain Hotel—Elmira was a Mark Twain town, of course—and a cab driver I knew there would pick me up after a late breakfast, drive me over to Ithaca, wait until the football game and the postgame press conference were over, drive me back to

Elmira, and put me back on board the Elmira-to-Hoboken sleeping car.

The Elmira-to-Hoboken sleeping car met its end a few years later. It was then necessary for me to get off another Lackawanna train at Elmira at some horrible hour, varying between two-thirty and two-fifty-five in the morning. This meant tumbling out of my roomette in a hurry, crawling on all fours to the Mark Twain Hotel, being picked up and taken to the game later in the morning, coming back and staying part of Saturday night at the Mark Twain, and arising in time to get aboard an eastbound sleeping car at two o'clock Sunday morning.

Both these services then disappeared. The next thing I could think of was to go back to the *Genesee Express,* which by now had dispensed with its Auburn Road sleeping car, and take the sleeping car that was set out in the early morning at Syracuse. This was a rather more expensive operation —fifty-five miles from Syracuse to the stadium in Ithaca. Then back in the afternoon, dinner in Syracuse, and a Saturday-night sleeper back to New York.

Next, the New York Central, with its sublime indifference to my welfare, removed the Syracuse sleeping car. I then departed at quarter past five on Friday afternoons from Grand Central Terminal in a Detroit sleeping car on the *Wolverine Limited,* which got to Syracuse—with luck —about midnight, at a new station, five miles out of town in a berry patch. I pottered over to the old Syracuse Hotel, and drove down to Ithaca and back the next day.

In a few years *this* service was withdrawn. Now I leave at four o'clock Friday afternoon on an adequate but not particularly enticing train made up solely of day coaches— the luxury of a dining car, the peace and quiet of a roomette are no longer vouchsafed me. I get to Syracuse around ten, ten-thirty at night. *But* the game in Ithaca finishes around four or four-fifteen the next afternoon, and fifty-five miles away, in Syracuse, the last train of the day to New York has already departed at three-fifty-five P.M. All right. The drive back to Syracuse. Another night in the Hotel Syracuse, where the alumni of Syracuse University are celebrating the latest defeat of their football team. Up at the unseemly hour of half past four in the morning. And off on the six-ten A.M. train to Grand Central Terminal. This is, I am told, progress. But I beg leave to doubt it.

My very last trip on the Auburn Road sleeper came about in this fashion: A good Harvard team was playing an undefeated Cornell team on a Saturday afternoon. I deemed my presence at this match to be imperative. Picking up my timetable I discovered that the Auburn Road sleeping car was no longer listed in the roster of the *Genesee Express*. In alarm I called an official at Grand Central Terminal who was a Cornell man and most likely would be attending the game. "That sleeper is still running," he said.

I replied, "That sleeping car is not in the timetable."

There was a certain amount of mumbling and mumbling and mumbling. I asked, "What's going on?"

He said, "Tell you what. Jackson and I—we're both going to the game—will meet you at Grand Central Terminal half an hour before the train departs."

I asked, "What is going on?"

He said, "Never mind. We'll explain when you get there."

At the appointed hour I arrived at Grand Central Terminal, greeted my two New York Central friends, and asked again, "What's going on? Are we all going to sit up all night

North Conway, New Hampshire, railway station

in a day coach?" "Oh, no," they said. "Come on over to the ticket counter."

I advanced to the ticket seller and said, "I'd like a roomette in the Auburn Road sleeper on Number 63 tonight."

The man looked hard at me and began reaching for his timetable. I said, "There's no use looking in the timetable; the sleeping car's not listed."

He said, "Well, sir, if that's the case, then I can't sell you a sleeping-car ticket on that train."

One of my New York Central men then pushed his nose

into my dilemma and said, "It's all right, Jack. He's with us. Give him a roomette."

So I got the roomette on the nonexistent Auburn Road sleeping car, and as we walked to the train I demanded an explanation. "Well," one of them said, "just between you and me, we're going to apply to the New York State Public Service Commission and the Interstate Commerce Commission [maybe I should say Interstate Commerce Permission —E.M.F.] to get rid of that train."

I said, "So this is the tactic."

"Well," they said, "you know. You know how things are."

Well, I knew how things are, so I called a friend of mine in Albany who was an examiner for the Public Service Commission. An examiner is a man who conducts a hearing when a railroad petitions to remove a certain service, and he questions anybody who wishes to show up to explain why the train should be withdrawn or why the train should be retained. The public-service examiner said, "Thanks very much for the tip. I'm sure this petition is going to come up."

Some months later the petition did turn up, and my friend the examiner was assigned to conduct a hearing. The lawyers for the New York Central presented their case and ended up by saying, "And, in fact, we even provide an overnight sleeping car from New York down through Auburn, and nobody uses it."

The examiner said, "Why isn't that sleeping car listed in the timetable?"

"Well," said one lawyer, "we've just left it out. After all, everybody on that line knows about it." And the examiner said, "Now, on this train you also list a sleeping car for Utica, a sleeping car for Niagara Falls, a sleeping car for

Rochester, and a sleeping car for Buffalo. But you leave out the one sleeping car on the train you want to discontinue? Isn't that a bit odd?"

My examiner friend said he didn't get a very definite answer to that.

 # Dining-Car-Steward Days

"Reminds me of the time I ran into Fats Waller in Klamath Falls, Oregon," said Ernest M. Frimbo. It was late one night and not so long ago, and we were sitting in a *boîte* near Washington Square listening to Jimmy Rowles play the piano.

"All right, we bite," we said. "Tell us the story." And we ordered him up a double brandy Alexander.

"Well," said Frimbo, "first off I'll have to tell you about my summertime career as a dining-car steward—"

"You were a steward?"

"Certainly. It was one of my devious game plans, as you will see. The story begins with a man named Gilbert Kneiss —the man who, all railway historians will concede, shortly after the Second War invented that famous train the *California Zephyr*. Kneiss, then special assistant to the president of the Western Pacific Railway, got the idea that if there was a train that was altogether homelike, delightful, comfortable, leisurely, and appetizing, a lot of people would like to spend part of their summer vacations taking it from Chicago to California. The two other railways whose participation would be needed to get this train to the Coast—that is, what is now the Burlington Northern (Chicago to Denver) and the Rio Grande Western (Denver to Salt Lake City)— fell in with the idea. And then this truly delicious train was built.

"Each *California Zephyr* had up to half a dozen dome cars: dome coaches, a dome lounge car, and an observation dome car. The concept of making reservations for dinner so that people didn't stand in the aisles with their tongues hanging out was instituted. There were all-Italian dinners with the appropriate Chianti—a novel idea—or you could live off the country: Rocky Mountain trout, California fruit, and all the rest.

"Now the story gets to me. The train was an enormous success for years, despite the general decline of railway passenger travel in this country. Mr. Kneiss, having launched this booming enterprise, started to think up more vacation trains. How about a train in which people would live for a week or two while traveling, say, from the Pacific Coast through parts of California, Oregon, and Washington through which passenger trains had never run, and even on up into Canada into the Peace River country, far north of the border in British Columbia, to what is known as the Caribou Country, Caribou being a now practically mythical forest beast from Canada? Good idea. But Mr. Kneiss had certain problems getting the *Caribou Special* started. For instance, the Western Pacific, not being a particularly large railway, didn't have many extra dining cars, or many dining-car stewards. So it wasn't long before overtures were made to me. Would I like to go on the extra board of the Western

Pacific dining-car department? This meant: if, from time to time, I was given a couple of weeks' notice, would I be willing to come out to California and take charge of one of the dining cars on a run of the *Caribou Special*?

"Would I? Well, my doctor jumped up and down and said, 'That is no way to take a rest.' But what he didn't know was that railway employees can ride on lines not open to the general public, and can ride free, on company passes. What an opportunity for a man with my ambition!"

"So you accepted?"

"Of course."

"Had you had any experience in this line of work?"

"No, but Gil Kneiss guessed that I had traveled enough to have learned the trade, and I got expert tutelage. Each *Caribou Special* carried two dining cars. I would take one and my tutor would have the other. He was a former Southern Pacific dining-car steward who, with the decline of passenger business on the West Coast, had wisely decided to try his hand as a stockbroker. Now, this may seem rather odd, but good dining-car stewards on the old crack trains—I hate that term."

"Why?"

"It's so often misused by newspaper writers. A three-car local from New York to Trenton gets derailed, and some newspaper reporter writes 'Crack Train Wrecked.' Where was I? In the best days of railway travel, when the very best people went out to California by train to browse around among the great winter resorts of Santa Barbara and Pasadena, the stewards who met with their approval received tips on the stock exchange at the end of the journey as well as tips of a monetary nature. My tutor was not the only chap I know who graduated from a dining-car stewardship to be a customer's man in a brokerage house. Well, there we were on the *Caribou Special*. He was a railway buff at heart, I was a railway buff at heart."

"What was it like?"

"It was a good long day. These trains were run rather like a cruise aboard ship. Meaning, the price of the ticket included not only a berth but all meals. Now, you and I know that when passengers on any vehicle pay for breakfast, lunch, and dinner they are going to eat breakfast, lunch, and dinner, willy-nilly. So, every chair in both dining cars was occupied between three and four times at each meal. My schedule went like this: At half past four in the morning my headwaiter would call me—there were four waiters in the car and four men in the kitchen. I would arise and make my early-morning inspection; I had to see that all the silverware had been polished. This, incidentally, is a practice that had fallen into disuse until Amtrak came along and restored polish to what silverware has survived. We opened the dining car at half past six and then there wasn't much rest until we closed down at half past ten at night. We finished breakfast, at, say, about ten. At eleven-thirty we'd start lunch, and shovel our last well-filled passenger off to his berth for an afternoon snooze at around three. At five-thirty the early birds were in for their third meal of the day. If we had a really large party aboard—say two hundred and thirty or two hundred and forty people—we'd set up four tables in the lounge car and use them for overflow meal service. Then I would have to bounce around my own dining car and slope off into the lounge car, helping the waiters and making sure that some of the pranksters—and there are always pranksters aboard—didn't try to come back and have a second breakfast. You know. They'd say, 'Oh, we left our breakfast tickets in our compartment. We'll bring them back.' An hour later, I'd see two of the kids back trying to sneak a second meal."

"How did you deal with these offenders?"

"Firmly. Give them my well-known basilisk eye, and say, 'Sonny, you've already had breakfast. Now run along.' "

"What sort of crowd did the *Caribou Special* attract?"

"Well, there were geologists who carried hammers in little cases. They seemed to think I should know every rock formation along the right of way, much of which I was seeing for the first time. These trains also attracted lady ornithologists, perhaps because we were traversing what you might call 'virgin territory.' They expected me, as the steward, to identify every bird we passed. They always looked like Eleanor Roosevelt. Can you imagine serving three meals a day to six Eleanor Roosevelts full of questions?"

"How did you answer the questions?"

"Oh, I'd say, 'Thorny-tailed Australian thrush, of course. You can tell by the bars.' You know, the old gab. Then we usually had at least one middle-aged lady of the marauding sort aboard. Someone looking for a widower with no children and a large trust fund. That was no threat to me. Frequently, people who had been under my charge the year before, or two years before, or maybe three years in a row, would tip me a dime or a quarter at the end of the fortnight, which I would simply put into the waiters' kitty. We had spendthrifts in those days, too, you know."

"Ever get any stock-market tips?"

"No, but I did have my following. Some of the passengers turned out faithfully every year. And once, when I was between trains in Union Station in Chicago, I had just heard my train for Omaha being announced and was drifting down toward the proper track, when a voice went, 'Oooh, ooh, ooh, Jack! Isn't that our steward on the *Caribou Special*?' And some sweet old lady came dashing across the concourse with her husband trailing behind. 'Mr. Frimbo, Mr. Frimbo,' she said. 'Remember us?' "

"Only too well?"

"Only too well, yes."

A pause. Jimmy Rowles launched into "Thank You So Much, Mrs. Lounsborough-Goodby."

"This was quite an experience," Frimbo resumed, "in meeting and dealing with the public from behind the counter, so to speak. It also taught me a good deal about marketing."

"Oh?"

"Well, as I say, we traveled on lines in Oregon, Washington, British Columbia that had never seen a passenger train. Along come two diners with a couple of hundred passengers eating their blooming heads off three times a day, and where do you stock up?"

"Well, where do you stock up?"

"Yes, where do we? In the towns in which we laid up overnight. We often traveled only by day so that everyone could see all the splendid scenery. We would ask one of the railway men about grocery shops in the town, and then I'd call ahead and say, 'We've been given your name; we're arriving in town; we've got a few people to feed and have to stock up; would you please stay open till seven this evening?'

"When we got to town I'd commandeer a panel truck and go down to the store and say, 'Those strawberries look very good. I'll take twenty-four boxes. And, uh, I like these peaches. I think I'll take six crates.'

"The proprietor would come up and say, 'Mister, would you mind telling me what's going on?'

"And I would say, 'I'll tell you the whole thing later. Meanwhile, I want four dozen loaves of sliced bread, and I'll take twelve pounds of butter, and, let's see, five or six sacks of potatoes.'

"By this time the proprietor was eagerly beaming."

Another pause. And then Frimbo said, "The dining-car crew men were absolutely marvelous. Life is much easier on the railways today. I don't think anyone knows what it was like many years ago, before I was a steward, when dining-car crews would work, say, all the way through from Chicago to California—a three-night job. After dinner was served, blankets would be put on the tabletops, and the dining-car and kitchen men would sleep for three nights on those tables. Now I hear talk about railway featherbedding and railway men having it so easy! Some of them do, it is true, but I cannot help thinking of my own eighteen-hour days, and of those men who worked day and night and slept on hard tabletops for three nights in a row."

One of us had a question. "Hey, I thought you were going to tell a story about Fats Waller."

"I'm coming to that. I keep getting interrupted by questions. I told you that being a steward entitled me to travel on a pass when I was off duty. Well, I once begged off on the return run of one of the *Caribou Specials* and spent a night on a freight train going through northern Oregon. I had an engine pass, which meant I could ride in the cab of an engine, and my freight set off from the town of Klamath Falls at five o'clock one evening, bound for upper California through some really wild uninhabited country. This country was so wild that several times herds of elk crossed our path and, startled or bemused by the glare of our headlight, stood stock still in the middle of the track. Twice we had to stop in order to avoid slaughtering a few elk. The moon came out about one in the morning. I rode in the cab all the way. We came to the end of the run about six in the morning, had breakfast at a twenty-four-hour-a-day beanery run by the railway, and tumbled into a railway bunkhouse. Got up later that day, and rode on my pass back on the *California Zephyr* into San Francisco. Railway engineers eat the goddamdest food. Toast and butter, German-fried potatoes, flapjacks and maple syrup, coffee and cream."

We gritted our teeth. "But what about Fats Waller?"

"Well, you see, the *Caribou Special* had set me down in Klamath Falls, and I had to wait a few hours for my freight train. I was walking along the platform when in came a north-bound train from Oakland to Portland. The Pullman on the rear end stopped right in front of me, and off stepped Fats Waller. 'Mr. Frimbo,' he said, 'what the hell are you doing here?'

" 'Mr. Waller,' I said. 'What the hell are *you* doing here?'

" 'I've got the band with me,' he said. The band was riding in the day coach; he was riding in the Pullman. 'We're playing a gig in Klamath Falls tonight.'

"I said: 'I'm taking an overnight freight train to California.'

"He said: 'Man, you're crazier than any of my musicians.' "

Frimbo on the Metroliner

We took our first Metroliner trip, from New York to Washington, D.C., in the company of Ernest M. Frimbo. We met Frimbo, by prearrangement, at Penn Station at seven in the morning, and he greeted us with his usual booming "Hello," adding "My, it's good to see you. Haven't caught sight of you since— Let's see, must have been my two-millionth mile. Well, it's up to two million eighty-two thousand three hundred and ninety-five miles now, and we'll add four hundred and fifty today. You are going to enjoy today's jaunt. The Metroliner, which is what the Penn Central calls this new high-speed train, is the first forward step taken by any form of transportation in this country in donkey's years." Frimbo was wearing a tweed suit from Bernard Weatherill in two hues of gray, a pink button-down shirt, and a stripy tie. On his head was his familiar black Homburg, and he was carrying, out of pure devilment, a maroon Qantas Airways bag. He looked fit. We said hello as soon as we were able, and he told us that it was time to get going. "The train leaves at seven-thirty, but I wanted you here a few minutes early, so you could get a good look at her," he said.

We followed Frimbo down a flight of stairs and gazed, with him, at a sleek and slightly convex six-car stainless-steel train that was humming quietly on Track 12. "Four coaches and two parlor cars," Frimbo said proudly. "Built in two-car units, and there's no locomotive. Each unit is really its own locomotive. For a faster getaway. The rounded shape is called 'tumble home' by designers. Two of the coaches have a snack bar in the middle, and the seats, as in every ordinary coach, are four abreast, with an aisle down the middle. On an airplane, they call four abreast First Class. Huh! The parlor cars on the Metroliner have one seat on each side of the aisle. That's what *I* call First Class. Each of the parlor cars also has a small kitchen at one end, and for that reason the train crews call them galley cars. The Penn Central people don't call them parlor cars, either, by the way. They call them club cars—or, to be precise, in the present instance, Metroclub cars. That's an idea they borrowed from the Canadian National Railways. The people up there decided that 'club' sounds more modern and more tony. You know—'I belong to an exclusive club.' They thought 'parlor' sounded Victorian and fusty. Of course, I myself have spent many an enjoyable hour in parlors. And many an enjoyable hour in clubs, too, for that matter."

Frimbo went aboard one of the parlor cars, and we followed him. He called out a good morning to a porter, and the porter said, "Good morning to you, Mr. Frimbo. Glad to have you aboard, sir. We'll be serving breakfast soon."

"Good," Frimbo said.

We found our seats—Numbers 24, 26, and 28. They

were salmon wing chairs, with the wings slightly raked, and they had pea-green paper antimacassars on them. We sat down, and agreed that our chairs were very comfortable. "This is the first American high-speed train to be built by someone who knows how to build railroad cars," Frimbo remarked. "They had some models run up by people who built buses, and they put in— What do you think? Plastic seats. It was awful. The Penn Central people, be it said, have gone about this in the right way."

It was now seven-thirty, and, right on the dot, and very smoothly, the Metroliner began to move out of the station. A voice said "Good morning, ladies and gentlemen" over a loudspeaker, and wished us a pleasant trip. The voice was replaced by soft music, which wobbled slightly as the train picked up speed. Frimbo caught our glance. "I know, I know," he said. "Just like the airlines. Oh, well, people probably wouldn't feel comfortable without it these days. You'll find it isn't obtrusive. This is my twenty-fifth trip on a Metroliner."

The train passed through Newark at that moment, exactly on schedule, and Frimbo started counting heads in the two parlor cars. Both were nearly full. "The Metroliners are doing a rocketing good business, and I'm very pleased," he said. "All in all, it's a damn good train. But I can't say I'm overwhelmed by its speed. That is, however, the fault of the Penn Central track. The run today will take just a minute less than three hours. When I worked in the Pentagon back in the Second World War, I used to come up to New York on the *Advance Congressional Limited*. It ran out of Washington Friday afternoons, and made one stop— at Newark, only to let off passengers. That train carried ten of the heavy old ninety-ton parlor cars and a ninety-five-ton diner, and it was scheduled to reach New York in three hours and fifteen minutes. One glorious day, we made it in three hours and ten minutes. So despite all the streamlining and yelping, the Metroliner has cut eleven minutes off the run in thirty years."

The porter now appeared with three small trays, which he placed on three small tables by the sides of our seats, and Frimbo paused to eat breakfast. Our breakfasts consisted of orange slices, corned-beef hash with grilled tomato, Danish pastry and croissants, butter, preserves, and coffee. We noticed that the porter had brought Frimbo a glass of iced tea, instead of coffee, without his having asked for it. Frimbo always starts the day with a glass of iced tea.

After breakfast, we leaned back on our pea-green antimacassars and asked Frimbo if he didn't think that transportation in the United States was improving. When he didn't reply, we looked at him and saw that he was sitting with his head propped on one arm, staring out the window at New Jersey. We repeated the question, thinking that perhaps he hadn't heard it, and he looked at us. "I heard you," he said. "That's a good question, I guess, and I was just thinking up the best answer to it. Yes and mostly no is the right answer, I think. The Metroliners are what we need, and if they have one every hour, as they keep saying they're going to, things will be moving in the right direction, but the truth of it is that transportation in this country is in one hell of a mess. I'm not talking just about the railroads this time, either. You've heard me often enough on the subject of the chicanery of railroads. It's the airlines and the bus companies, too. But I'll start with the railroads, as usual. In the first place, the railroads are hard-pressed, to give them their due. When an airline wants a new terminal, it gets the government to build it, and the men who run it are all government employees. When a bus company wants a new stop, it approaches the proprietor of a local hotel and tells him, 'We'll give you five per cent of the revenue we make on our ticket sales if we can use your hotel as a depot.' A railroad, on the other hand, is expected to build its own station, staff it, and pay real-estate taxes on it. It doesn't make much sense, does it? You and I would do very well if we were tax-exempt, like the airports. The railroads would do very well if all the signalmen were paid by the government, like the air-control staff. Of course, there are— Well, I won't call them rascals, but people in the railroad business who would just as soon forget their responsibilities to the public, cut out passenger service altogether, and go into the real-estate and hotel business. Some of the railroads are already part of these giant new conglomerates, and are doing just that. There are even some people in the Penn Central hierarchy who are nauseated by the smell of success of the Metroliners."

"But *how* do they get rid of passenger trains?" we asked. "Doesn't public necessity count for anything?"

"I'll give you a primer," said Mr. Frimbo. "You have a fast train from New York City to upstate New York at half past four in the afternoon. You push its departure time up to two o'clock, and business falls off so fast that you can ask the Interstate Commerce Commission for permission to take it off. You schedule a train to arrive in Chicago an hour and a half later than it used to, thereby missing a dozen good connections. You take off the dining cars—that's the Penn Central's favorite stunt—and make the travelers pay as much for a couple of sandwiches as they used to pay for lunch. The Pennsylvania wasn't so bad, but then after

An early Swiss progenitor of the Metroliner

the merger the New York Central men moved into the hierarchy. Now the trains are later than ever, dirtier than ever, less air-conditioned than ever, and more expensive than ever. The poor customers of the New Haven! It can cost you up to twenty per cent more to ride the coaches on what few New Haven trains are left, the parlor-car fares have gone up twenty-five per cent. For quite a while, there was talk of ending the service at the Route One Twenty-Eight station, a dozen miles this side of Boston. The argument was that in five or six years there will be a rapid-transit

line from Boston out to Route One Twenty-Eight. So the
passengers could get off there and wait five or six years.
The same sort of scheme has been on the books for Washington, where the present fine big station is to be replaced
by a rabbit hutch. Those scoundrels are such . . ."

We observed a growing empurplement of Frimbo's coun-
tenance, and we sought to divert him. Remembering that he
had persuaded us to make the final run of the *Twentieth
Century Limited* in December of 1969, we asked him when
he had made his final run on the *Century*.

"I'll be riding the *Century* again in a couple of weeks,"
he said, subsiding.

We goggled.

"Oh," Frimbo said, "the Penn Central sold it all, and
a lot of other cars besides, to the National of Mexico, and
now it runs every night—and all-Pullman, too, the way it
used to be up here—from Mexico City to Guadalajara, only
it's called *El Tapatio* now. A great train! At ten at night,
the diner is so full of happy customers that you have to be
a regular rider to get a table. It's Mexico's most popular
night club, you might say. When I see people standing up
on Penn Central trains, I ask an official I know why people
have to stand all the time. 'Shortage of equipment,' he says.
'Why don't you buy some of that stuff back from Mexico,
then?' I ask, and he pretends that he doesn't know what I
am talking about."

Frimbo shifted in his seat. "But now let's take the other
forms of public transportation in this country," he said.
"Let's talk about all those towns with one train and one bus
a day—or none at all. What happens is that the railroads
give up when the airlines move in, and then the airlines
discontinue. I can tell you a horror tale or two. I remember

flying to Grand Forks, North Dakota, one night some years
ago—there was no suitable train—and asking the stewardess
about bus service from the airport. 'Oh, there isn't any bus
service, sir,' she said. I asked about taxi service. 'Oh, there
isn't any taxi service, sir,' she said. I asked her what I was
supposed to do to get into town. 'Oh, well, sir,' she said,
'you *could* talk to the airport manager, and he *might* be able
to persuade someone to drive you.' Of course, you can always fall back on the rent-a-car, but not at that hour of
the night. And buses! I was stuck in Aberdeen, *South* Dakota, once, and the only thing for me to do was to catch the
through bus from Seattle to Chicago. It got to Aberdeen six
and a half hours late. Those are just examples that spring
to mind. Everything that can be done in this country is
being done to force people to get on the highways. And
where will they all be when we have weather like the weather
we had this past winter? Buses and airlines are fine, but in
proportion. I sometimes fly to the Coast myself. Not many
people would take the train nowadays, except on holiday.
But once you get rid of the trains, just where are you in a
bad snowstorm? Buses simply quit; the airlines are helpless.
Only the train limps through. There was hardly a day last
January and February when there wasn't something wrong
with at least one airport in New York, Baltimore, Washington, Philadelphia, or Hartford. Ninety per cent of all
intercity traffic is already in private cars. But what's the
answer? Get rid of the trains? The National Transportation
Safety Board said that last year fifty-seven thousand people were killed on the highways, and one million nine hundred and thirty thousand were injured; the amount of money
lost in highway accidents was three and a half billion dollars.
Three and a half billion dollars! And that doesn't include

job loss or hospitalization. There isn't a country in the world whose transportation is as disorganized as ours. If that three and a half billion were spent on transportation, maybe we could approach the standards of civilization."

Frimbo glanced out the window. "The crews call this stretch of track, between Wilmington and Baltimore, the race track," he said. "We are now doing a hundred and ten miles an hour."

Just then the voice on the loudspeaker announced, "We are now traveling at a speed of one hundred and ten miles per hour."

"We'll be in Washington soon," Frimbo said happily. "Then we'll have time for lunch at the Occidental Restaurant and perhaps a short visit to the Railroad Hall of the new Smithsonian Museum of History and Technology. They've got a Southern Railway old Pacific-type passenger locomotive, Number Fourteen-Oh-One, there, and she's painted the proper lovely shade of Southern Railway green. Haven't seen her in a number of years. And then we'll catch an afternoon Metroliner back to New York. It should be a *very* pleasant day indeed."

Flier

One night in the fall of 1969, Mr. Ernest M. Frimbo and we were the guests of Mr. Alan Pegler at a small dinner party in a private suite of the most comfortable hotel in Hartford, Connecticut. Mr. Pegler is a remarkable and charming Englishman. He was at that time the only person in the United Kingdom who was allowed to run steam locomotives on the tracks of British Railways. Mr. Pegler himself was the owner of the famous and beautiful steam locomotive called the *Flying Scotsman,* and that fall he brought his engine to the States, so that it could run on the tracks of our railroads. This it proceeded to do—from Boston to Houston, a distance of 2251 miles—pulling a train of nine cars, all of them also Pegler exports. These nine cars were: the only observation car in the world serving draft beer; two Pullmans used by Winston Churchill during the Second World War and named *Lydia* and *Isle of Thanet*; a brake van; a passenger coach; and four freight cars specifically designed to carry racing pigeons. The racing-pigeon traffic was for years very heavy on British rail-roads, and a number of cars were built to transport crates of the birds. These crates always had notes on them reading, for example, "Stationmaster, Barchester, Kent: Please release my birds at 4:35 A.M. on Saturday unless there is heavy fog." To help defray the costs of the whole expedition, Mr. Pegler had the pigeon cars fitted up as exhibition cars, and rented space in them to a number of important English manufacturers. He also arranged to have the train put up for a few days in every major city en route, so that as many people as possible would have a chance to get a look at it. Mr. Pegler called his train *Flying Scotsman, U.S.A.*

Frimbo and Mr. Pegler had been pals for years, and Mr. Pegler took great pleasure arranging amusements for his friend. When Frimbo went to England, Mr. Pegler always had him down to stay at his house in Nottinghamshire. The Hartford dinner party was one of Mr. Pegler's ideas for amusing Frimbo. Frimbo had arranged with Mr. Pegler to travel on the *Flying Scotsman, U.S.A.,* from Hartford to New York, and he was looking forward to the trip keenly, but Mr. Pegler was evidently worried that Frimbo would fret if he had to spend an evening in Hartford without any-thing to do, so he decided to surprise him. Frimbo was de-lighted, and the dinner was a great success. There were nine of us at table, including four quite exceptionally beautiful girls, who all had jobs on the train as guides, and a peer named Lord Napier and Ettrick. Lord Napier and Ettrick is the fourteenth Baron Napier, the fifth Baron Ettrick, and also the eleventh Baronet Napier. He knows a good deal about branch lines in southern Scotland, and one of his ancestors, named John Napier of Merchiston, who lived in the second half of the sixteenth century, invented logarithms.

Dinner was excellent, and after it Lord N. and E. moved off into a corner of the room, where, over some brandy, he and Frimbo discussed the discontinued branch lines of southern Scotland in quiet but animated tones. We took the opportunity to talk to Mr. Pegler, and as we did so we could hear in the background His Lordship saying "Yes, yes, yes, an *extraordinary* line! Yes, yes, *extraordinary!*" and "Oh, I say—no, *really?*" to Frimbo.

Mr. Pegler told us that railroading is something that bites you at an early age. His own background, we found out, was in rubber, and in his youthful days he worked for the family firm, where he is still fondly remembered for the annual *Works Special* he arranged. This was a train drawn by two steam locomotives which went to Blackpool during the festivities in that town known as the Illuminations. Later on, Mr. Pegler had devoted a good deal of his time to running the Festiniog Railway, the narrow-gauge railroad in Wales that he bought. "Last year," he said, "over three hundred thousand people came to ride on us, which is pretty good for a line that boasts nine and a half miles of track in a not particularly accessible part of Wales. We have eight steam locomotives. The *Flying Scotsman* has been my favorite steam locomotive all my life. It was the first engine in which I ever stood, as a small boy, and I bought it a few years ago, just in time to rescue it from destruction. Ever since I acquired the engine, it has been in the back of my mind to bring it over to America, and now, I am happy to say, that event has come to pass. The whole expedition has bristled with problems from the very beginning, as you may imagine. The Interstate Commerce Commission at first refused to believe that anyone but an American could build a safe steam locomotive, and one chap I talked to down there kept bringing up a boiler explosion in an English locomotive in nineteen-twelve. Seemed to be haunted by the incident. There are many stretches of America where a steam locomotive hasn't been seen for twenty-five or thirty years. I have been told that we will be the last passenger train of any sort ever to enter Dallas, which will make that city, of one point five million people, the largest city in the world—with the possible exception of some place in the interior of China—without regular train service. We are carrying two crews—one English and one American. All the cars have been painted in the original lovely livery of the Pullman Company—chocolate and cream. British Railways cars are now being painted blue and white, but for some years after the Second World War it seemed to be the policy of the post-nationalization management to change the external colors of the cars whenever a crisis of some sort erupted. Thought to be good for morale, no doubt. Two of the liveries they came up with then were affectionately known by people who liked trains as 'plum and spilt milk' and 'blood and custard.' What else can I tell you? Oh, yes —every train on the Festiniog has an observation car and a buffet car that serves gins-and-tonic, Scotches-and-soda, and other necessities of life as well as ices, cakes, and sandwiches. And, by the way, now that we have a chance to talk, isn't Ernest Frimbo a marvelous old fellow? I am terribly fond of him, you know. Shall we see if we can persuade him to accept a nightcap?"

Pegleriana

Frimbo settled himself in his favorite chair at the Lexicographers' Club. We had just arrived in New York behind Alan Pegler's steam locomotive, the *Flying Scotsman*, and Frimbo was full of Alan Pegler stories. Of course, the first one he told was mostly about himself.

"I am an official locomotive driver on Pegler's little railway in Wales, the Festiniog," he said, ordering up a Pimm's Cup No. 2, "and I may say with pride and joy that I was once in charge of a passenger train on this wild and picturesque line, which runs from the seaside up into the mountains to slate-quarry country. Hauling slate was the Festiniog's original function, in the days before synthetics, when most of England was roofed by Welsh slate. The locomotive I drove is over a hundred years old, a double-ended job, with two smoke stacks, two boilers, two sets of driving wheels, two throttles, and an open space in the middle for me and an eagle-eyed regular locomotive driver who stood there *just in case*.

"It was a rainy, misty, typically glorious Welsh summer Sunday. I wore a mackinaw, old shoes, and a Festiniog Railway cap, a good stout leather cap, which I still have. I leaned my good stout belly against the side of the locomotive, which was quite warm, grasped a throttle firmly in each hand, and hung on for dear life. Should my belly have slipped, there was nothing to keep me from dropping into the countryside. It was tricky. If the wheels started slipping going up the grade, and they sometimes did, particularly on a sharp curve—the rails were wet, remember, and therefore more than ordinarily slippery—I had to make adjustments by shutting off the steam with one throttle while keeping my other hand on the other throttle and waiting for the wheels at one end of the locomotive to stop slipping so that I could then get the wheels of both engines back into synchronization. I was inexperienced, so this situation arose several times, and to complicate my dilemma we were by now plowing through a driving rain—but the regular man was there to tell me when to give one engine more steam, when to ease off on the other."

"And did this man have anything to say about your performance?" we asked.

"Why, yes," said Frimbo, preening himself a bit. "He pointed out that we had left Portmadoc, the seaside station, four minutes late and had got to the end of the run, way up on high, one minute early, and he made a small, grudging, but congratulatory speech.

"Now about Pegler. Pegler had a country place in Nottinghamshire. If he was down in the country when I arrived from the States, he'd say, 'Come down Tuesday evening on the *Master Cutler*'—an all-Pullman train that was run in the manner of the old Cunarder *Queens*—the ideal relationship between guest and host. It ran to Sheffield, naturally, and was presided over by a most charming Mr. Dix, who represented the Pullman Company in all its glory, with quite a fetching uniform—something like what an Admiral of the Fleet would wear—with the enamel Pullman badge of office on one of his lapels. Being in charge of one of these trains was indeed quite an honor. Pegler would say, 'I suggest you have dinner on the train, because otherwise it will be too late for us to make our appointed rounds. What would you like for dinner?'

"Well, I've always had a great weakness for poached turbot, which was sometimes on the Pullman menu, but just as often not. I'd get to the station and walk down the train, and Mr. Dix would be waiting for me. 'Good evening, Mr. Frimbo. I have your seat.' 'Good evening, Mr. Dix.' 'It's not on the menu tonight, sir,' said he, whispering, 'but Mr. Pegler said you were to have the poached turbot.'

"So I felt rather at home traveling about England—that is, I felt rather at home until the afternoon when I was walking, after a late lunch, through the concourse of King's Cross station in London with two expatriate American friends of mine who lived permanently in England. I was telling them I felt as much at home in London as I felt in New York, when one of them said, with a not particularly well-bred sneer, 'Oh, you people! You've been two days in London and you think you know the whole country and everything about it.'

"As luck would have it—and this was indeed luck—we were walking by the end of the platform from which the *Master Cutler* was to depart in fifteen minutes. Now, it's the custom of the man in charge of the Pullman train to stand at the end of the platform with a chart of the cars in his command so that if any latecomers arrive without having booked a seat, he can pick one out and assign it. And so it happened that just after my friend's snide remark, Mr. Dix stepped forward, and the following conversation ensued:

"Dix: 'Good evening, Mr. Frimbo. Would you be traveling down with us to Nottinghamshire tonight?'

"Frimbo: 'Good evening, Mr. Dix. No, I'm sorry to say I will not. But Mr. Pegler and I will be going down Thursday evening with you.'

"Dix: 'Right you are, sir. Good night to you, Mr. Frimbo.'

"Frimbo: 'Good night, Mr. Dix.'

"And I walked on with my now-silent friends."

Notes and Comment

The Penn Central Railroad filed for bankruptcy in June 1970. We waited to hear from E. M. Frimbo, wanting to pass on some more of his pungent comments on that unfortunate railroad. But it wasn't until several months later that our friend gave us a ring. When he did, he said that he would have called sooner but had been busy traveling and polishing his remarks. He also said that he had two tickets for a snappy excursion train pulled by a steam engine, and that he was now prepared to "tell all" about the Penn Central, if we would meet him in Harrisburg, Pennsylvania, the following Saturday at nine in the morning.

The snappy excursion train proved to be a sumptuous affair, sponsored by an outfit called the High Iron Company, of Lebanon, New Jersey. The company was run by a jolly commodities broker named Ross E. Rowland, Jr., who is a railroad buff in his spare time. We found Frimbo seated in the lounge of an observation car that had been built for a railroad executive. The car had a private dining room, and a private tub and shower in the bathroom adjoining the master bedroom. The trip afforded many exciting moments, including the chance to debark and watch a steam engine come rushing out of a tunnel at forty-five miles an hour—an event considerably more exciting than seeing a dragon come roaring out of its cave in *Siegfried*. The train also climbed the Allegheny Mountains, west of Altoona, and managed to negotiate, under its own steam, the famous Horseshoe Curve, which the Penn Central calls "railroading's most famous geographical landmark." The curve is the trickiest part of the ascent of the Alleghenies, and it is also a magnificent feat of engineering, dating from the eighteen-fifties. The fact that our train made it up to the top astounded and confounded numerous Penn Central officials who were along for the ride and had been confidently predicting disaster. Mr. Frimbo, of course, was in high glee at the engine's triumph and the officials' frustration. "Wrong again," he said triumphantly. "A perfect, unbroken record!"

We will not describe the rest of the trip but, instead, will bring you, in toto, Mr. Frimbo's remarks, which were unusually pointed, even for him. Though this conversation—or should we call it a monologue?—took place more than four years ago, its pertinence to what is going on today seems as pointed as ever. (You must picture Mr. Frimbo sitting in an overstuffed armchair with a cool drink in one hand and a plate of toothsome canapés within easy reach.)

"My little cherubs," said Mr. Frimbo to us, "the United States of America is rapidly becoming an undeveloped country again. The Post Office is cutting down on Special Delivery, even though it charges forty-five cents a letter. I omit any reference to the Telephone Company, the electric-light companies, the bus companies, and the airlines. The railroads, as *you* know, as *I* know, as even the members of the Interstate Commerce Commission know, are disappearing. There is *no way* to get from many American towns to many other American towns these days except by automobile. The Secretary of Transportation seems to think that there is only one means of transportation: the private car. With one person in it. What mass transportation there is has become centralized on the main routes. Once you get off them, you're *dead*.

"Now, I know you want to hear about the Penn Central. And I want to talk about it. But I want you to get a picture of just how bad the Penn Central's performance has been. I am reminding you of how bad the performance of the *rest* of the industry has been, not just in looking after passengers but in delivering freight—and I am not forgetting some conspicuous exceptions—so you can see that the performance of the Penn Central has been *worse*.

"I have two points to make. Number One. It is my considered judgment that the boys at the Penn Central decided about five years ago to get out of the railroad business and into the real-estate business. I have thought about this a great deal, and it's the only explanation I can come up with that makes any sense. Here is my syllogism. The Penn Central owns great chunks of extraordinarily valuable real estate in the downtown parts of a number of major cities. This real estate would be ripe for development if only the current occupants could be evicted, or persuaded to leave, or put out of business. Most real-estate men's minds work this way —I'm not giving away any secrets. Now, the current occupants happen to be railroad stations. Ordinarily, a railroad station is very important to a community. There is, however, an occasion when a railroad station is not an important

building. That occasion arises when *there aren't any trains.*
If you happen to be in the railroad business already, and
happen to own the stations in question, the absence of trains
becomes something you can do something about. I have left
out the footnotes, in the interests of brevity, but I assure you
that many details can be furnished on request.

"Point Number Two. The railroad is a public utility.
Now, this kind of public utility is supposed to serve both
the traveling and the shipping public, in return for which
the Interstate Commerce Commission protects it from unfair competition and protects the public against monopoly.
I am sorry to have to say this, but it looks to me as though
this notion were one of those well-intentioned, and even well-
thought-out, reforms that have balled things up. And most
of the state public-utilities commissions, which also supposedly protect the public from the railroad, are doing exactly the opposite. The railroad and the other utilities are
being protected from unfair competition, all right. They are
being turned into monopolies. And all monopolists think in
the same way. The Penn Central, which, with the permission
of the Interstate Commerce Commission, has become damn
near a monopoly in this part of the country, seems to have
decided that it is its duty to provide the public with only
those services which make the largest amount of money. One
way or another, it gets subsidies for some of the less profitable services, and I agree that it should get more. But suppose the Telephone Company decided to eliminate telephone
service in the Catskills because it was not profitable. Suppose the Post Office said, 'Sorry, we're losing so much on
Rural Free Delivery we'll have to cut it out.' Would there
be a howl? Well, I'm howling now."

Falling by the Wayside

"Does anything ever go wrong?" we asked Mr. Frimbo one night when we encountered him at Raffles, that well-groomed for-members-only retreat deep in the heart of midtown Manhattan. "I mean, when you're traveling around, do you ever go completely off your trolley and end up in a ditch?"

The great lexicographer put down the bottle of Lancers with which he was anointing a dish of strawberries and gave us a long stare. "The conveyances on which I have journeyed about the world have, as you put it so inelegantly, occasionally gone off their trolley, yes. I, myself, never—I have always been too well occupied to have time for that."

"Tell us about something that went really wrong," we said.

"Well, there was the time I was returning the compliment of a guest-of-honor invitation to a banquet set up by a group of fellow wordmongers in upstate New York. It was Christmas week, and I decided that since a wholly unique and *sui generis* interurban railway across the border, in Ontario, was about to breathe its last, I would charter surreptitiously, of a Sunday, a car to tool about the more appetizing rural portions of its domain and then ask a dozen of my cronies to join up. The railway was the lamented Niagara, St. Catherines & Toronto, and part of its oddity was that though it commenced its run grandly, with all sorts of track along the streets of St. Catherines, it finally delivered its most persevering passengers in Toronto by steamship. We set off at nine that morning in our chartered car. The line we had chosen to follow had been completely covered the night before by a fresh fall of snow, so that we were literally entering upon virgin territory.

"We had been on our way a matter of three minutes when the car lurched heavily, then sank to its knees. A hasty exploration by the embarrassed interurban official who was accompanying us for the day revealed that we were hard aground; some employee, the day before, apparently needing a section of rail for some occult purpose, had removed it, unaware that before he could replace it on the Monday morning our special car would be thumpingly derailed. No damage, no injuries—simply the official's embarrassment. Presently, however, another car appeared, on the next track; we mounted our new steed, and, with two men, armed with brooms, carefully sweeping the track ahead of us to make certain that no other rails had been borrowed for the weekend, we tooled slowly into open country and then set out to make up for lost time."

"Any other incidents of that nature?" we inquired. But just then his old friend Josephine Baker, newly arrived from Paris, came onstage to sing, and we waited a full forty-five minutes for our answer.

"Yes," said Mr. Frimbo then, as though there had been no break at all in our conversation, "and the wine with which I have marinated my strawberries recalls to me a far more picturesque—oh, I might even say picaresque, a word I seldom find use for—adventure under the flag of Portugal, from which this ruby-red and refreshing beverage descends. Are you prepared to listen?"

"Indeed," we replied.

"Well, to make a long story long, I must begin with the pronunciamento that Portugal has many commendable habits aside from wine-growing, which is the basis of the mishappening I am about to relate. One of them is railways of a variety and beauty to be surpassed nowhere, and last summer, when I learned that because of a giant scheme of rehabilitation some of the most ancient and mouth-watering specimens of the steam-locomotive-builder's art were to be temporarily again plying their trade along with many less venerable examples, I decided to set off at once for Lisbon.

"As I was about to depart, word came to me from my friend David Ibbotson, an Englishman of repute among railway buffs, that he was soon to depart himself on a journey, not to Portugal but to the African Portuguese colony of Angola, where railways of equal variety and beauty also reside. The Portuguese, wherever they venture in the world, like to make everything look like home, and that includes the railways and the wines. Ibbotson disguises himself as the Dorridge Travel Service, which is properly sited for such an agency, being at Number Seven Station Approach, practically next door to the railway passenger station, in Dorridge, a thriving suburb of Birmingham. A Mr. Malcolm Crowe, Mr. Ibbotson informed me, who is a British representative of TAP, the Portuguese national airline, would be departing

from Lisbon for Angola during my stay in Portugal, his purpose the making of a documentary film for TAP—not about
the pleasures of traveling by TAP, of which, be it said,
there are a number, but about the railways of Angola. All
this, Mr. Ibbotson added, to persuade British railway buffs
to visit Angola by means of—naturally—TAP. Would I be
troubled if Mr. Crowe joined me on the passage from Lisbon
to Angola?

"I say that Ibbotson disguises himself, for the fact is
that he is as thumping a railway buff as I am, and, since he
has an excellent hold on the Portuguese tongue, a useful
companion in certain parts of the world. Crowe, too, though
an airline man, is a thoroughly knowledgeable railway buff
himself. So, further learning that Crowe, Ibbotson, and perhaps twenty like-minded Englishmen were to pass a fortnight on the railways of Angola, I snipped a fortnight from
my Portuguese itinerary and signed on for Africa."

"And the accident—your plane crashed?" we asked.

"I think not," said the great lexicographer. "As far as I
can tell, I am here not as a ghost, and in far finer trim than
you are, my friends. May I be permitted to tell my story, or
shall you assume the narrative? . . . Very well. Crowe and
I are airborne for a much greater distance than it is from
here to London, pass the night in an extremely well-
appointed hotel in Luanda, the one port in Angola where
outsize flying machines can set down, and proceed at dawn
in what may once have been a DC-3, or even a DC-Zero,
to a quite tropical port known as Lobito, and are met at
once by a Mr. Lopes, a gentleman of a school that I sometimes fear no longer keeps. Mr. Lopes, it appears, is the
P.R.O. man for the Benguela Railway, the absolute show-
piece of Angola—a railway that should be proclaimed a na-

tional monument and preserved forever exactly as it was the day we landed."

"Why do you say 'was'?" we interposed.

"I say 'was' inasmuch as a glorious custom—one of the several uniquenesses under the Portuguese flag—was coming to an end. And this is that a number of the steam locomotives of the Benguela Railway then subsisted—and some of them are still subsisting—entirely upon a diet of eucalyptus logs. Where else on earth can one happily watch the air being polluted by the soft, sweet scent of burning eucalyptus trees? It is the most life-enhancing incense I have ever inhaled."

"What other things do they do with eucalyptus in Angola?"

"Well may you inquire," said Mr. Frimbo. "They chop the logs into kindling and, on the express trains that now and then venture from Lobito into the fantastic, one-of-a-kind mountain scenery of interior Angola, they stoke the iron stoves in the wooden dining cars with it, and on top of the stoves they broil brand-new fish and lobster and other shellfish, interspersing them with secret condiments, and then they set these splendors on your dining-car table and open a bottle of that pale-green light wine, *vinho verde,* that is grown in Portugal on the slopes of the Douro Valley. The parched mountains of Angola are often dusty, and the railway is sometimes a trifle bumpy, and the narrow-gauge cars are very, *very* narrow, but the night after a dinner of this sort is a glorified dream."

"What do you do during the day in Angola?" we next inquired.

"Oh, first you go with Mr. Lopes to the Terminus Hotel, which is a small—maybe twenty bedrooms—hotel set in a quiet spot in Luanda, but almost next to the railway, and run by the railway. When you espy your now-to-be companions—Mr. Ibbotson and Company—you know that you are on location for a Somerset Maugham novel about the faraway parts of the world; Britishers in their tropicals, the silent and efficacious hotel staff shuffling about their breakfast duties, the sprinkling of the town's gentry and their ladies, the unbelievable bedrooms—these with a twenty-foot ceiling, a dressing room, an inner sleeping room, a sitting room that looks out upon a vast verandah, and the verandah looking out over the four thousand miles of South Atlantic between you and Rio de Janeiro, and palm trees conversing among themselves in the offshore breeze, and the steady lap-lap-laps of waves on the spotless beach just below. But there is work to be done—Mr. Crowe with sixty rolls of color film and his cameras and his documentary movie hardware in a tropical town where every prospect—be it architectural, floral, or railway—pleases."

We felt that now four thousand miles of South Atlantic lay between us and the story of Frimbo's mishap, but we knew from experience that the waiting game was the only one to play. "Did you go to the interior?" we asked.

"Oh, yes," he said, "though first we had to shoot the film in Lobito that Mr. Crowe wanted to shoot."

"How did that work?"

"Well, I would say, 'Maybe some footage from this spot, which will give you a different angle on the railway station and the train,' and he might say, 'Yes.' That was all. Until we got way up into the mountains, when we were visiting one of the huge eucalyptus plantations the railway maintains —seemingly square miles of them—to feed the locomotives. Below this plantation was a tiny station of the railway, at the foot of a seemingly insuperable grade, and I asked Mr. Lopes, who had volunteered to be our host and guide for the whole fortnight, if we could not travel up that grade in one of the locomotives. Senhor Lopes said that a freight train would be along in an hour, and would stop at the station to 'wood up'—I use the Mark Twain phrase for putting wood aboard the old Mississippi steamboats. The woodpile was an architectural triumph itself—half an acre of cordwood stacked thirty or forty feet high alongside the railway —and when the freight train arrived a mass of natives swarmed up this mountain of wood and began flinging logs down to comrades on the ground, who caught the logs with one hand and with the other looped them into the tender of the locomotive. For twenty minutes, the air was filled with flying hulks of wood—the most gigantic juggling act I have ever seen. Crowe was, of course, filming all of this operation. It was rather a task getting his movie apparatus into the cab of the locomotive, but we managed, and—"

"What does Mr. Frimbo wear on a journey of this sort?"

"Well, for the cities in the tropics, I take along a couple of lounge suits of lightweight gray Dupioni silk, from Italy, but, since I had had this locomotive journey in mind all day, I had come arrayed on this excursion in suitably ragamuffin clothes. Now Crowe and I were aboard the engine, in a raging heat, for eucalyptus burns like guncotton. It was an interesting scene. The cabs of these narrow-gauge locomotives are quite commodious, and with good reason, for aside from us two intruders there were an engine driver, an assistant engine driver, a stoker—whose job was to open the door of the raging furnace under the boiler and throw in eucalyptus logs as fast as he could—and two wood-passers, who stood on top of the vast pile of logs in the tender and

An Angolan Garratt locomotive

tossed them down, two at a time, to the stoker. Now Crowe had more camera angles than he could handle. Well, we started off up this grade, and it was a royal progress indeed. With my stopwatch, I calculated that we were climbing up the mountains at a steady six miles an hour, and it was an eighteen-mile ascent. The flow of scented smoke, the huge plume of glowing embers pouring from the smokestack—which the wood-passers had to keep brushing off themselves and their clothes—and the sheer, all-enveloping sound of the locomotive doing not its level best but its *uphill* best to get to the top of that mountain made a three-hour journey that I think I will never be able to beat. And when we got to the top, it was dusk, and I had an idea. 'Crowe,' I shouted, 'this blooming thing is going to take off on that wide curve around the valley ahead, and that plume of embers is going to make a photographic gem if the twilight is good enough!' It *was* good enough, and for half an hour we stood in the

deepening shadows and watched that train blasting through the oncoming night—as though a great dragon were laying waste to the countryside in pursuit of its prey."

"How far did you get into the interior?"

"As far as the officials would let us," Mr. Frimbo said. "There is this perpetual war going on in the white-ruled states of Africa, and beyond certain points a visitor simply mayn't go. Beyond that point—Silva Porto on the Benguela Railway—the trains are preceded by armed and armored engines."

"Do you ever feel sociological about situations like that?"

"Naturally," said Frimbo. "I feel that way in Russia, and then I notice the absolutely marvelous transit systems they have in their big cities—systems that move people about neatly and cleanly and at a small bit of what it costs us to move them. And when I am in Angola I think about that war, and then I think about the neatness of the Portuguese colonization, and the fact that in Angola there is a great deal of integration—a great *deal* of it, and at more than one social level. And I ponder the unreality of the situation—black nation against white nation—yet all the time I was at my journey's end in Angola the freight trains kept coming in from the hostile countries with laden freight cars from Katanga and the Congo Railway and Zaire and Zambia, and even cars of coal from the Wankie mines in Rhodesia, which is a white bastion in Africa. And I get the feeling that some magic word, some sort of mutual concession, could make the whole thing come out right and comfortable. You always *knew* I was a dreamer.

"At any rate, we were permitted to ride as far as the town of Silva Porto, several hundred miles inside Angola, and there our train turned around—literally, on a triangular piece of track. And I discovered that though I thought I was alone while the train was turning, there were three little girls and a little boy who get on the train every time it comes to Silva Porto and ride around on the triangle. They are displaced people—whites whose family had fled the upheaval in Katanga and was now domiciled in this out-of-the-way place—Belgian, or French, at a guess, for when they found that I had almost no Portuguese and I found that they had almost no English, I got their story out of them in French, our one mutual tongue."

We said, "So you didn't have that mishap you were going to tell us about."

Frimbo said, "Oh, yes indeed, but that was the following week. We had trained it back to Lobito, and flown back to Luanda, and then flown, at dawn—railroad buffs have to

become dawn-worshipers, whether they want to or not—
to an unlikely little spot called Porto Amboim, in another
of those DC-Zeros. Thence runs a *really* narrow-gauge railway upland for many miles into a set of coffee plantations,
and the railway management had laid on for us two little
gasoline-propelled open railway cars to take us up to where
its steam locomotives lurked in the tall timber; the management had also laid on for us, at the two-house hamlet where
our run ended, a surprise luncheon—two roast suckling pigs,
a dozen broiled chickens, four gigantic sort of birthday
cakes, cookies, bonbons, and a case of *vinho verde*—this for
no more than fifteen of us, including the crew and the stewardess of the DC-Zero, who said they had never been on a
journey like this ever before. Neither had any of us, but we
kept our mouths shut about that.

"The one chap who did not keep his mouth shut was the
driver of one of our open-air railway cars, whose input of
vinho verde, it turned out, was more than sufficient. In a
happy mood, we set off back to Porto Amboim and our DC-
Zero, and Crowe was filming some of the spectacular scenery when, trying to negotiate a curve at what seemed a
highly improper speed, our *vinho-verde*d driver succeeded
in derailing us as Crowe sat there carefully filming his own
incipient doom. By the time the necessary tugging and hauling and repairing had been effected, we knew we'd never get
back to the airport before night shut down operations. Those
little African airports have no floodlights, you see. So it was
dawn-worshiping again the following morning as we at last
took off on the return flight to Luanda.

"No one had been damaged in the derailment, not even
the driver, who sat down on a stone and promptly went to

sleep. Nor was Crowe's movie equipment injured. I'm going over this summer to have a look at the film he made. But I feel certain that the official version will omit that falling-off-the-rails sequence."

 *Wonderful Day*

In August 1971, the Officers and Directors of the Valley Railroad Company Requested the Honor of Our Presence Aboard the Inaugural Run at the GRAND REOPENING OF STEAM EXCURSION SERVICE on the Connecticut River Line from Essex to Deep River, Connecticut, on the *One-Hundredth Anniversary* of the First Run. The card that conveyed this invitation had a large red-pencil asterisk after the word "Directors," and a note at the bottom said, " *This refers to *me,* among others, and (speaking for my colleagues) I promise you a Wonderful Day if you turn out. But don't look for me, as I will be aboard a Trans-Siberian Railroad train, in fulfillment of a lifelong dream. I will, of course, be sorry to miss you, but I will make all arrangements; a man named Oliver Jensen (our prexy) will look after you; he's a splendid chap.—E.M.F." Since a day arranged by Frimbo is invariably a treat, we decided to turn out, and accepted the invitation.

The arrangements included a parlor-car ride from the

city to Old Saybrook, where Mr. Jensen met us with his car and drove us to his railroad's depot in Essex. Mr. Jensen was wearing a blue blazer with the insignia of the Valley Railroad on the breast pocket and a straw boater with a red-white-and-blue band, and he was smoking a corncob pipe. In the back seat of his car we noticed an engineer's striped cap and a pair of heavy work gloves. Mr. Jensen has gray hair and a lot of charm and verve, and he is also editor of *American Heritage*. On the way to the Essex depot, he explained that the Valley Railroad had the rights to 21.67 miles of track of an old New Haven branch line along the lower Connecticut River, from Old Saybrook to just below Middletown; that the V.R.R. was almost entirely a volunteer effort; that passenger service would that year be operated on weekends and holidays at least through the end of October; that the State of Connecticut was particularly interested in preserving the beauties of the area and was playing a major role in the effort; that the Lieutenant Governor himself would be present; that there were great possibilities and hopes of substantial freight service on the line, the commodities to include witch hazel, since the plant of the E. E. Dickinson Company, a firm Mr. J. described as the Standard Oil of witch hazel, was within a stone's throw of the Essex depot; that last-minute preparations were continuing feverishly, although everything was certainly well in hand; and that his, Mr. J.'s, wife, Alison, and two girls from Essex had stayed up until ten the previous night festooning the depot with bunting and decorating the engine (Number 103, built in 1925 for the Sumter & Choctaw, a logging railroad in Alabama) with sixty-four tiny American flags. The drive from Old Saybrook to Essex takes about six minutes, which demonstrates Mr. Jensen's skill at marshaling facts.

The Inaugural Run was preceded by some speechifying, and the large crowd was entertained by musical selections performed by the band of the First Company of the Governor's Footguards, Captain Dayton Palmer bandmaster and piccolo soloist. The band all wore red coats and busbies, and Captain Palmer, a man of martial aspect, with sideburns and mustachios, sported epaulets and four service medals. The Reverend Glenn Eno, pastor of the First Baptist Church of Essex, prayed, "Eternal God, our hearts are thrilled as we stand here on this momentous occasion and endeavor to bring back another moment that happened one hundred years ago," and wound up, "May Thy angel of protection be at every crossing, and we'll be careful to give You all the praise and all the glory. In Jesus' name, Amen."

Mr. Jensen said, "I'll cut this short. We're very glad you've all come out."

The first few words of the Honorable T. Clark Hull, Lieutenant Governor of Connecticut, were drowned out by the whistle of Number 103, which went off unexpectedly, so Mr. Hull unbuttoned his collar, loosened his tie, and started over. "When I was sixteen years old, at Exeter Academy, a snowy little godforsaken town—I hope no one here's from New Hampshire—I remember the Boston & Maine train came steaming in late at night or early in the morning or whenever it was, and it was always a moment of great sentiment and affection," he said, and *he* wound up, "This is going to be great for tourism, and I only wish I had the parking concession."

Then it was time for the Inaugural Run. We climbed into an open-air gondola and squeezed between the drummer from the Governor's Footguards and Liz Petrie, a lovely young reporter for the Middletown *Press*. Captain Palmer

told the band to play Number Three ("In My Merry Olds-
mobile") and said "One, two, spiel"; the band blared; and,
with a tremendous puff of smoke and cinders, many of which
soon settled in the bandsmen's busbies, the train was off.
We passed meadows, marshes, wooded hills, white clapboard
houses, cars full of waving people, an osprey, and the Connecticut River, and soon reached the town of Deep River,
where we were greeted by the Deep River Junior Ancients
Fife & Drum Corps, a group of boys and girls in lace shirts
who beat a smart tattoo. Then they and the band joined
forces in "The Battle Hymn of the Republic." Liz said that
Deep River was a factory town, unlike Essex, which was
a rich people's town, and that two weeks ago thirty-five
thousand people had assembled in Deep River to drink fifty
barrels of beer and to listen to seventy drum corps compete.

In an adjoining closed coach we found Mr. Jensen. He
was relaxing for a moment and smiling at a small boy who
had just asked him for his autograph. "I didn't expect such
a turnout," Mr. Jensen said to us. "It certainly looks as if
we were off to a good start. I hope you're enjoying yourself
as much as I am."

We said we were having a Wonderful Day.

Frimbo's Trans-Siberian Journal

The Yaroslavl Station in eastern Moscow. One hundred years old and truly a fairy-tale building, it looks as if it had been designed by Kublai Khan's court architect. Small, only two or three platforms, and, as usual, 10,000 passengers, or so it seemed to me last week, waiting to get on the daily express to Vladivostok on the Sea of Japan— seven days and nearly 5900 miles away. This is the famous *Trans-Siberian Express,* or, as the Russians call it (always have called it), the *Russia Express.* The longest passenger run in the world (by a couple of thousand miles). Also the most peculiar. And one of the most arduous—which is why I insisted that our party be accompanied the entire way by an Intourist courier.

I am shepherding a little band of five. Our purpose: to traverse this railway before its truly magnificent steam locomotives are extinct. "Is this the supreme moment for a railroad buff?"—the question was put to me in New York by one of my two Dr. Watsons. A question that presupposes that all rail buffs like the same thing. There are some buffs who like to travel only on absolutely deluxe trains. For them the *Russia Express* would not suffice. There are some who disdain anything not hauled by steam, or who like only picturesque branch lines, or whose real hobby is walking along abandoned railroad lines to see what Progress has brought. Some of us like any kind of adventure. I, myself, will go anywhere, except to some place like the Bahamas. Those islands have no railroads. What use are they?

The *Russia Express* consists entirely of sleeping cars and a dining car. There's no sitting up overnight in the day coach on long-distance passenger trains in Russia. Three kinds of lying-down accommodations: for Russians of extremely limited means, an open-berth car—four tiers of three-sided cubicles, no curtain in front. The other choices are Hard Class and Soft Class. S.C., where we are, means four-berth compartments, a lavatory at one end of the car, no hot water. I, being an early riser, get up at daybreak— half past three or four in this latitude—and nip in for shaving ahead of anyone else. Then I stand and stare out the window until breakfast, and am content.

The trip from Moscow begins on a long plain—the plain on which Russia apparently grows a vast amount of its wheat. Then, on the third morning, come the famous Ural Mountains. They are maybe 15 or 20 feet high, rather disappointing. But you are then officially in Siberia for the rest of the trip. The trip across S. is one of the most unjustly maligned trips in the world. People think of it as a land of ice and snow—with, of course, an occasional birch, behind which a convenient wolf is hiding. There *are* birch woods after the Urals—what seem like thousands of miles of birch woods. Then suddenly the country starts undulating, getting rough. You cross many wide rivers. About the fifth day, you come to real mountains. The train is climbing up a mountainside, dusting through a pass, and then descending in a vast, winding curve miles long to a valley with a big river, then taking a complete U-turn and climbing up the other side—so that for two hours, looking back, you can see the pass through which you began your descent, and watch perhaps two or three trains following, while trains that you have met an hour before you can see now crossing the river and starting up the opposite slope. Always a picturesque sight when you can look across the vast sweep of a valley and see smoking steam trains going in both directions. Freight and passenger trains are intermingled on the heavily traveled Trans-Siberian tracks; they all travel at roughly 40 m.p.h. The only way of distinguishing the *Russia Express* from any other passenger train is that the car at the beginning and the car at the rear end bear huge brass letters which stand out three or four inches, just under the eaves: POCCIR—RUSSIA, that is. And the restaurant car has a rather fine stylized birch forest on the cover of the menu.

Compartments in Russian sleeping cars are come-as-you-are, and mingling of the sexes is common. My four charges have a compartment to themselves; I am the odd man out. On three other Russian trains, I was assigned lady commissars as roommates—whether it was accident or whether it was hoped I would talk in my sleep and give away some dread secret, I do not know. Once I even accidentally got *locked* in a compartment with a lady commissar, but that is another story. On the *Russia Express* I drew two young Russian Army officers and the wife of one of them. The berths are permanent, and on a journey of this length many people don't bother to dress, spending the day in pajamas, sandals, and a dressing gown. The routine when there are ladies present, of course, is *toujours politesse*—gestures meaning "I am going to bed," "I am getting up," "Please turn your back," "Please leave the room." I had no topics of conversation with the Army officers, but my Intourist girl, realizing this was a bit of a fix for me, came in and told them I was an American who had been a railroad transport officer in the last war. Well, it turned out one of the Russians was a railway transport officer, and he kindly lent me a technical Russian magazine, of which I could not understand a word.

The Russian etiquette toward strangers goes like this: the afternoon we leave Moscow, my Intourist guide introduces me to the Army officers. All right. I go off to dinner, go to bed, and in the morning, when I come back from my very early shaving, I see two cucumbers and a tomato sitting on my pillow. Large smiles from the Army officers, and waving indicating that this is a present from them and the one wife to me. I twig to this, so at the next long stop—there is one several times every day; the engine takes on water and fuel and there is a general embarking and disembarking—I discover on the station platform a long line of women with all sorts of things to sell (this is more like Mexico or Peru or Bolivia, where people seem to make their living by selling things to eat at railway stations, than it is like Europe). I see an old lady selling huge boxes of cookies (I had noticed that my Army-officer companions didn't use the dining car—perhaps it was too expensive for them?), and I buy a box, and then when my companions are out of the compartment, I put the box on one of their pillows. When I come back after lunch—ah! Great greetings, smiles, bowings, and so forth, and so forth. The next morning, other

A dining car on the Trans-Siberian

vegetables on my pillow—and some black bread and a bit
of cheese. At the next stop I spot some likely looking vegetables and buy a sack of cucumbers (Russians are extremely
fond of cucumbers), and when my companions are out of
the way, I lay six cukes, in little oval patterns, on each
pillow. Great delight!

The first time I bought a large supply of vegetables I brought my sack into the dining car at breakfast time and poured part of them out onto the table to show my companions what I had done. Without a word to me, the restaurant-car conductor swooped down on the paper bag and the loose vegetables—it was quite a haul: tomatoes, scallions, onions, string beans, cucumbers, lettuce, and celery —and carried everything away to the kitchen. This was alarming. I had become quite friendly with the conductor and told him—through our Intourist girl—all about my own dining-car-steward days. I decided I must have violated Russian dining-car etiquette, and we sat in silence, wondering what to do. Suddenly, out popped the restaurant conductor, followed by two strapping waitresses bearing six bowls of vegetables which had been converted into salad; they set them down before us and disappeared, still without any word. We've had fresh salad every day since then.

An Intourist guide is absolutely indispensable in a Russian dining car. The reason? There is a party of five Americans on the train, sans Intourist girl, who eat at the next table. They have with them meal tickets bought in advance. They have used very few of them, even though they know the coupons are not redeemable. The menus, you see, are printed only in Russian. In Finland, which has the most unpronounceable language in the world, the train menus are printed in Finnish and Swedish—so you have a chance. In Greece the menus on the Hellenic State Railways are printed in Greek and French—which considerably eases the problem. In Russia—Russian, uncompromisingly. And nothing else. The people at the next table haven't a clue. They look at us hungrily—because with an Intourist girl everything is different. She reads the menu, and says, "This morning, let's see, we begin with caviar on toast. How does that sound?" The caviar is fresh Caspian Sea caviar, not the salted stuff we are used to in this country, and it turns out to be on the breakfast menu every second morning throughout our long journey across to the Sea of Japan.

There are also vast, indescribable soups, containing, I should say, two quarts of liquid in which what appear to be fish, meat, poultry, and perhaps a dozen vegetables are all commingled. Served boiling hot. The sideboard at one end of the car offers a vast display of cookies, bonbons, chocolates, Rumanian and Hungarian wines, Russian champagne —which is even sweeter than the champagne Germans and Mexicans like. Which is to say, probably two-thirds dissolved sugar and the rest champagne. No matter. The restaurant car is busy almost all the time—being the social center of any train on a long journey. Between meals people troop in for Russian soft fruit drinks (quite palatable) or for the inescapable and inevitable glass of tea.

Others on the train: many Russians, of course; a Japanese artist and his stunningly beautiful wife, coming home from an exhibit of his work in Paris (he is taking the train "because it is so inexpensive"—and, in fact, it is far less expensive than traveling by subway in Manhattan); Manchurians; Chinese students on their way home to Peking (they got off at an unbelievable town called Ulan Ude: wooden churches, wooden shops, wooden houses, wooden railway station, no paved streets). The Chinese spoke a bit of English and were enormously curious about us, as were we about them. Also: an enormously pretty Rumanian schoolteacher on her way to Japan, some Italians, people in Mongolian garb, Tibetan garb, and two very larky Australian girls who have abandoned a foolhardy plan of driving all the way from Helsinki to the Sea of Japan. And there are people whose race I cannot determine at all who have tried communicating with us by sign language. They are extremely eager to talk, but the sign language tells us very little. Are they perhaps Bhutanese or Nepalese?

Now, it is the last night. The two Army officers and wife got off this afternoon, and, looking forward to a night of ease—my first night alone in a week—I sat down an hour ago to write this journal, when there was a knocking on my door. I opened the door, and there stood a Russian Army officer. "Oh, sir," he said, in English, "excuse me, I hear you are a railroad transport officer in the United States Army. I am a graduate of the Railroad Transport Officers' School run by the Russian Army in Kabarovsk. I wonder if I may talk to you and ask you some questions?"

So down we sat. The questions he asked, well, they certainly did not violate any security rules. "Do you have any steam locomotives in America? What are your passenger cars like? What are your sleeping cars like? What are your stations like? . . ."

He was a very nice person, indeed, overwhelmed with excitement. There were a million other questions, all innocent. When he left he pressed on me an enamel lapel emblem with a red star and, in high relief, the face of Lenin. He put it in my lapel. This I will wear on the Russian ship which is to take us from Siberia to Yokohama, where I will prudently remove it—before I face up to the immigration officials.

P.S. FROM YOKOHAMA:

At the Russian port of Nakhodka we were required to pass through the money-changing pavilion before boarding ship. Everyone is expected to account for his money to the last fraction of a rouble. The Russians count up your cash to see whether you have exactly as much as you had declared when you entered the country, minus what you have exchanged at official exchange places (for which you should have vouchers). All this to discover whether you're spending money on the black market.

Well, I got to the money-changing pavilion, took everything from my pouch, laid it out, along with my declaration sheet, and waited to see what would happen. I had thirty-seven kinds of paper money—Russian roubles (these to be redeemed for U.S. currency), Bolivian bolivars, Cuban pesos, American dollars, Canadian dollars, New Zealand dollars, Australian dollars, Singapore dollars, Hong Kong dollars, Straits Settlements dollars, Finnish marks, West German marks, British pounds, South African rands, Italian lire, French francs, Swiss francs, Belgian francs, Moroccan francs (or dirhams), Greek drachmae, Japanese yen, Portuguese escudos, Angolan escudos, Mozambique escudos, Austrian schillings, Swedish kronor, Danish kroner, Norwegian kroner, Spanish pesetas, Argentine pesos, Thai bahts, Peruvian sols, Chilean escudos, Panamanian balbaos, Costa Rican colons, Guatemalan quetzals, and Dutch guilders. I probably had 175,000 lire (a single lira is almost worthless), some of it in 50-lire coins. As for bolivars: you give a barman in a good Bolivian hotel a 500-bolivar note as a tip.

Two soldiers started counting my money. They looked at some of the money—such as the Straits Settlements dollars—in complete bewilderment. All right. They put the Straits Settlements dollars aside and started in again. They attacked the Bolivian bolivars. Again looks of bewilderment. They put them aside. They came on American dollars,

Canadian dollars, British pounds, and got more cheerful—these they recognized. French francs they recognized. Moroccan francs brought another frown. These were put aside. Then they came upon Japanese yen. I had thought yen would not puzzle them—after all, we were taking a ship from Russia to Japan—but apparently they had never seen yen (which were all in splendid denominations, such as 1000 yen, 10,000 yen—you can easily be toting around two or three hundred thousand yen in your pocket).

Well, the recognizable money was counted—it checked against my declaration. Then the soldiers went back to the unrecognizable money and started fingering through it. They looked at each other and they looked at me; they shrugged their shoulders, stamped all the documents, and waved me on.

Frimbo's Black Homburg

We once asked Frimbo why he so often wears a black Homburg.

His answer was a story. "Once upon a time—it must have been fifteen years ago—the international network of railway-buff communications reported that three magnificent Irish railways were about to discontinue operations. One of them, the County Donegal Railways, was, I blush to say, going into the trucking business instead. So off I went, with a group of friends, including Oliver Jensen, founder of the Valley Railroad in Connecticut, to see how many beautiful steam locomotives could be rescued from the knacker. We returned with the *Lady Edith,* a beauty named —or so we were told—for the daughter of the Earl of Leitrim, founder of the Cavan & Leitrim Light Railway— but she leaves our story here.

"For three days we scoured the branch lines of the County Donegal Railways on a chartered train, staring at every deserving steam locomotive we came across, and living off the country. The manager of the railway told us that in the past forty years something like seventy-three per cent of the population of the county of Donegal had emigrated, wherefore it was *necessary* for us to live off the country. That was quite simple. We subsisted on a diet I had arranged and used for many years: local cheese, Guinness Stout, and Jacob's Digestive Biscuits—which are the finest eating goodies in the world, rubbley, not too sweet, just enough butter and sugar, nourishing and easily assimilable. Guinness is also a worthy enterprise: until just a few years ago it hauled *its* goodies around its brewery near Kingsbridge Station in Dublin by steam locomotive and then shipped some of them to outlying towns by canal on a steam barge.

"One afternoon, quite a bit after what should have been our lunch hour, we arrived at the end of a County Donegal branch line in a small fishing town named Killybegs. We alighted at the station and entered the town through the customary Irish spring drizzle. It was instantly apparent that there was neither inn nor restaurant to be had. I suggested we walk farther down the main street and find a suitable grocery. We soon came upon one, and entered this strange establishment, a long narrow shop full of characters right out of an Irish play, pipe-smoking, drawling, arguing, with the usual gruff, bluff master of the house behind the counter.

"I spotted Guinness Stout; I spotted the local cheese; I spotted the delicious Jacob's Digestive Biscuits. I was, as I often am, arrayed in my most formidable uniform—that is, a dark blue, double-breasted overcoat made of heavy horse blanketing, a speckled silk muffler, black kid gloves, and my black Homburg. I headed my hungry horde into this mixture of dried mackerel, stout, biscuits, cheese, and pipe smoke.

"The minute I entered, the chap behind the counter deserted his cronies and walked all the way down the counter. Ignoring everyone else in my group, he stopped before me, bowed, and said:

" 'Yes, milord?' "

In Memoriam

We had not a second's hesitation about deciding how we were going to spend a Memorial Day weekend when we heard that Mr. Frimbo was going off on an excursion and wanted to take us along. A Frimbo excursion means Up Bright and Early. "Never mind where; it's from here to there," he said when we met him, soon after seven Saturday morning, in the Fourteenth Street tube station on the line to Hoboken. "Where 'there' is is *my* business. Be surprised."

He was wearing a gray silk suit, a blue shirt, a striped tie, old Pennsylvania Railroad cuff links, and a wide-awake look. As we climbed the stairs at the end of our under-the-Hudson run, we could hear the sounds of a multitude overhead. The railway station in Hoboken, from which now only the Lackawanna and the Erie commuter trains run, is customarily empty on a weekend morning, and it has the air of a careworn, disused cathedral. Now it was full of people, many of them arrayed in denim engineers' caps, red or blue bandannas around their necks, and goggles pushed up on their foreheads. Over their shoulders were slung cameras and tape-recorders, and most of them bore railway insignia on their jackets and shirts. Compared to Frimbo, they were ready for a come-as-you-are party. "As you can see," he said to us, "if you provide a good train to ride, everybody will turn out. There'll be upward of eight hundred passengers aboard this excursion, even though they won't get home until late tomorrow night. This outing was planned by Ross Rowland and his friends—they're the ones who ran that trip around Horseshoe Curve—and they know what they're doing."

He led the way to Gate 3, beyond which stretched the hub of this universe—a long line of passenger cars headed by a steam locomotive. We hadn't seen a steam locomotive in Lackawanna Terminal in donkey's years. We counted a varied assortment of seventeen cars, some of which had no panes in the windows, and we stared inquiringly at Frimbo. "Taken out," he said, "so the buffs can listen to the engine."

The locomotive, Number 759, was, he told us, the last of its breed—a Berkshire type, preserved from the holocaust that had engulfed all its sisters when its first owner, the Nickel Plate Railway (technically, the New York, Chicago & St. Louis), had decided to turn them all into scrap. In its way, Number 759 looked as distinguished as Mr. Frimbo. Ross Rowland approached: "Mr. Frimbo, on schedule, as always. We're looking forward to your speech."

"Excuse me," Frimbo said to us. "I promised to dedicate this locomotive on this Memorial Day weekend to the memory of Ellis Atwood, who in his day, when the marvelous little narrow-gauge railways in Maine were expiring, got together with *his* friends and rescued as many of their engines and cars, including an absolutely miraculous period-piece wooden parlor car, as they could and hauled them down to a cranberry-bog railway he owned on Cape Cod. There they began a whole new career—carrying not cranberries but people—and they're still at it."

Grasping a microphone with a faint hint of alarm, as though it might be a cobra, Frimbo spoke feelingly about Mr. Atwood, and then he said to his audience, "When I was a young man, I commuted in and out of this station. Sometimes, when we were on our way in town for the theater, I fed my girl friend fresh oysters in the fine restaurant on the concourse. In later years, I got into Pullmans here that would take me to Buffalo, to Cleveland, even to Chicago. Today, you and I are about to board what is very likely to be the last long-distance passenger train ever to leave this grand old terminal. God bless us all."

Ross Rowland took Frimbo's arm and walked him forward. Two cars back of the engine, they paused admiringly before a venerable but well-turned-out Pullman sleeper, then climbed aboard. We followed. "What will you have?" Mr. Rowland asked Mr. Frimbo. "The young ladies in this car have instructions that our special guests are to get continuous beverage service while they're aboard."

"Iced tea, thank you," said Frimbo.

"I should have known the answer," said Mr. Rowland.

At exactly half past eight, we settled down into a plush, forest-green alcove in our conveyance just as the last long-distance passenger train pulled out of Lackawanna Terminal and into an enchantingly beautiful spring day. "Come now, Mr. Frimbo," we said. "Long-distance passenger train indeed! Where *are* we going?"

"Binghamton, New York," he said. "It's not much more than a couple of hundred miles away, and you'll be back by bedtime tomorrow."

"But—" we began.

"Everything has been arranged by Mr. Rowland," he said. "I shall be at peace for the next two days. Be likewise!"

Later, we got a whiff of the weekend's game plan. The Lackawanna and the Erie, once rivals in their journeying westward across central New York, were now as one in holy wedlock, and we were to proceed, at leisure, to Binghamton on the Erie and then come back on the Lackawanna. "Through some of the handsomest country in the whole United States," Frimbo said, "and unless trains like this come back, none of us will ever again see our glorious birthright in this proper fashion."

We were climbing now through suburban New Jersey, and—holiday or not—the station platforms were awash with spectators—so many that, Mr. Rowland informed us, we would be running quite slowly, to avoid bumping into anyone who was overly enthusiastic. "It's a bit silly to say, don't you think, that people aren't interested in trains any more," Frimbo remarked.

As Frimbo was working his way through his second iced tea, the train stopped, in a great sweep of pastureland. No station, no anything. "Photo stop," murmured a loudspeaker we hadn't noticed.

"What is going on?" we asked.

"Eight hundred people are going to get off," he said, "and then line up, mostly in someone else's way, and then the train is going to back up about a mile, and then come dashing by so that everyone can get action photographs.

This will be going on all day today and tomorrow. Out!"

Frimbo's orders are not to be countermanded, and we found ourselves jumping—and quite a jump, there being no platforms in pastureland—to the ballast beside the train. It was as Frimbo had said—a row of people, a quarter mile long, standing, kneeling, or lying down, adjusting their cameras and range finders and whatnot. It looked like the moment before Pickett's charge at Gettysburg. We asked the young man next to us what he was up to. "I'm recording the sound of the engine when it comes back," he said, in a flat voice.

"Just what for?" we asked.

"To *have* it," he said sharply.

As the train came back, a great blast of cinders fell upon us when the engine passed. "Those bandannas the buffs are wearing are not just protective coloring," Frimbo said. "They're *vital*."

"Take two!" someone shouted, as the train backed up for a second run past us.

"Now that you've discovered what it's like," Frimbo said, "stand back a little more, and you'll miss the next batch of cinders."

Nevertheless, our hands were grimy, and our faces and hair felt gritty as we climbed aboard again. "The club that owns this car has built in a remedy for that," Frimbo said, and we were shown to a lavatory that had a thick carpet, pink wallpaper, a set of mirrors, and a shower.

"Dining cars are as scarce as auks nowadays," Frimbo said later, "but Rowland has persuaded some restaurants in Calicoon, the country town we are approaching, to open up just for us at lunchtime, even if it is a holiday." There were two hundred people at the station, and four purpose-

fully antique automobiles, and on the platform two young
men were playing "Daisy, Daisy" on an electric organ and
a guitar. "A classic group of film extras," said Frimbo as
we marched across the street to a sort of Howard Johnson
lunch. The restaurant was flanked by small enterprises—
Autumn Inn, Davis Inn, Olympia Hotel, Western Hotel.
"This is a one-horse town—an *Iron* Horse town today,"
Frimbo said, "but it's still an old-fashioned summer resort.
There used to be a Friday-night train out from New York
and a Sunday-night train back. We're the last people ever
to come here by train."

The sun was hot and the humidity high; in our Pullman
after lunch, Mr. Frimbo napped until the next photo run.
This time we noticed that Ross Rowland was in the driver's
seat of the locomotive as the train backed away from us.
It came back past us like a mad thing, and then returned
to retrieve its passengers. Ross Rowland was in high spirits.
"I gave her one notch too much," he shouted down to
Frimbo, "and she just took off!"

We suggested that a restorative was now in order, and
walked forward to the lounge car that was just ahead of our
Pullman. A lot of other people, we noticed, had already had
the same idea. We sat there until a loudspeaker announced
that we were nearing Binghamton and that a fleet of taxis
and buses would move us and our luggage to the hotels we
were to pass the night in. "The rubber-tire age," Frimbo
said. "I used to walk up the street a couple of blocks to the
good old red-brick Arlington. The Lackawanna station is
still here, and its lunch counter is still in action, even if
there are no more passenger trains, because the train crews
change here, and the railway has to provide a place to feed
them. But now the hotels are on the outskirts, with their

parking lots beside them, and nobody comes downtown at night any more. This is why the hearts of cities are beginning to suffer from dry rot."

Our inn, when we finally got to it, was new and cheerful, sitting on the bank of a river, and we knew instantly, because of the bunting and the lapel pins we saw, that we were in for a Chamber of Commerce welcome. We suspected, too (and correctly), a cocktail party and banquet. The inn's quota of railway buffs reappeared, now divested of engineer's caps, goggles, neckerchiefs, and cameras. "They go back into mufti just as the party begins," said Frimbo. "Myself, I drift with the tide. We are in the hands of Ross Rowland, our good provider, and I question nothing. Press on to the cocktails and the banquet."

"Eat a hearty breakfast," said Frimbo next morning. "There won't be a real luncheon break today, and Rowland hasn't got his kitchen car. There'll be all the iced tea and rum Collinses and Danish pastry you can get down, but that will be it. The Lackawanna dining cars have all gone to Heaven."

"What were they like?" we asked him.

"Well, I need only tell you that at this very hour, in the better days, I would be making a breakfast of Lackawanna dining-car corn muffins. They were baked on the car, in a mold that shaped them exactly like ears of corn, with practically every ripe little kernel in place—so lifelike that one wanted to salt-and-butter them all over, and red-hot out of the oven." We asked no more.

We walked through the train by ourselves until we came upon a baggage car that was labeled High Iron Emporium (High Iron was the name of Ross Rowland's railway enterprise), and stared at shelves of engineer's caps, bandannas, old timetables, bar-car coasters, railway books, railway post-cards, models of engines and railway cars—and bought our-selves caps and bandannas and then a photograph of that charming old (1877) dowager of a locomotive, the *Lady Edith*. We even bought goggles.

"Well done," said Mr. Frimbo when we returned from our excursion, and "How nice!" when he saw the *Lady Edith*. "She lives in retirement down in New Jersey now. You'll recall that a few of us bought her in Ireland when she was about to be burned at the stake and gave her a good home over here."

The small, bright-eyed man who had been sitting oppo-site Mr. Frimbo got up when he saw us, smiled at us, shook hands with Frimbo, and walked away.

"Extraordinary," said Frimbo, "how being a railway buff makes the world so small. I last saw that chap three years ago, on the station platform in Grantham, a town in England a hundred miles north of London. He had come over from Gainsborough, where he taught school, to drive me to Stapleford Park, the country seat of Lord Gretton, who had invited my friend to pop over on a Sunday to visit the tiny narrow-gauge railway that runs around the grounds of Stapleford Park. My friend is a railway buff—he got all his schoolchildren interested in building a model railway, and then when the town council decided that his school had become life-expired, he bought the place and had his scholars build an exact scale model of the East Coast Main Line all the way from London to Edinburgh. And Lord Gretton is considered a patron saint of railway buffs because for years his brewery at Burton-on-Trent—he makes Bass Ale—had steam locomotives moving freight cars about the

premises. So my friend and I had a jolly ride on one of the
Stapleford Park steam engines, and felt greatly honored
when we were informed that his Lordship would allow us
to take turns driving the thing. Three years ago, and now
my friend comes walking through this car—he's over here
for a look-see at American railways, and he happened to
hear about this two-day steam-locomotive safari."

At Scranton, a lunch stop was announced, but it was only
a tea-trolley on the platform with sandwiches of processed
turkey enclosed in slices of dry white aerated bread. The
restaurant across the way was closed; the restaurant two
blocks away, in the Casey Hotel, was closed—"the grand
old Casey, with that temple-of-the-Pharaohs décor, and
that fine dining room. More dry rot!" said Frimbo. But the
station was beautiful in its forlorn old age, a remembrance
of when Scranton was capital of the anthracite coal empire
of the United States, before the First World War—and so
were the marble columns in its concourse, and the huge display, on the walls, of terra-cotta mosaics of the mythology
of the Lackawanna Railroad. "This station was built for
human beings," said Frimbo. "Something to make them
feel welcome and exalted—not give them the boxed-in, pack-
aged feeling you get in bus stations."

"Lunch" time was at an end, and we walked out onto the
platform, and toward the other end of our train. "There's a
Lackawanna business car up there," Frimbo said. "I noticed
it this morning, and I wonder who's in it." A spruce young
man was standing on the observation end of the business
car, and when he espied us he climbed down and walked
up to Frimbo. He was, he said, a vice president of the railway, and he had heard Frimbo make his speech in Hoboken
the day before, and was glad he had made it. "Of course,"

he said, "the economics of railroading today make passenger trains impossible"—and here we saw the glazed look that comes on Frimbo's face when he is listening to talk like this—"but I admit that I enjoyed traveling by train in the old days, though I haven't seen as many of them as you have, and when you remarked that this would probably be the last long-distance train to leave Hoboken I felt really sad."

"Well, yes," said Frimbo. "You see what's happening to downtown Binghamton and downtown Scranton. I hope I'm wrong about that being the last train. If I'm not, we all may have to start looking for a new country."

"So," said Frimbo after we were back in our Pullman, "there's a railway vice president with a soul. I feel better. And I'll feel even better if we make a stop on the Nicholson viaduct." The viaduct, Frimbo said, was built in the flush days of the Lackawanna—perhaps nine million dollars was spent so that express trains could get to Buffalo thirty minutes sooner. "That's the way railwaymen felt about their jobs then."

The train rolled out on the viaduct and stopped. It was so narrow that when we looked out the windows we could see nothing between us and the floor of a deep valley far below. The view was, in all honesty, magnificent from our unique, spidery perch. "The last train! No one will ever have this view again. You see that highway running down the valley? That was once the Lackawanna Railroad. When this viaduct was built, the railway sold its old line to the state for a dollar, and the state built a highway wide enough and smooth enough to accommodate the buses that helped put the railway out of the passenger business."

As the train moved out onto the Hackensack Meadows,

on the last few miles of our journey back to Hoboken, we saw the solid lines of holiday-weekend automobiles inching themselves along the highway. From the last car of the train, we saw a long loop of empty tracks stretching away into the sunset, and our arrival in Lackawanna Terminal, though a splendid one, was a lonely one.

Ernest M. Frimbo looked somber as we descended to the platform. "That does it!" he was saying. "The end of an ending. From now on, Lackawanna Terminal will be enscribed in my memory book as Point of No Return."

Turkey Hash for Breakfast

A plain white envelope arrived in the mail one Monday morning in the spring of 1972. It contained first-class railroad tickets to Philadelphia, attached to a seat check indicating that a day bedroom would be at our disposal on a train that would leave Penn Station the next morning at eight o'clock. There was nothing else in the envelope. It took no thought at all to realize what was up. Only one man would communicate with us in this fashion. We immediately canceled all our Tuesday appointments, because days with Ernest M. Frimbo are always memorable days.

We got to Penn Station the next morning at a quarter to eight. A thousand commuters, their faces registering every emotion from unhappiness to hopelessness, were scurrying toward their jobs. In their midst stood our old friend Frimbo, as fresh as a daisy. We hadn't seen him in some time, but he looked the way he always does—ready for a good time. "Good morning," he said. "I hope you're hungry. I always go to Philadelphia on the eight-o'clock, because the diner, which is not under the jurisdiction of the Penn Central, features turkey hash for breakfast. By the way, the object of our expedition today is to observe the largest auction of railroad memorabilia ever held. The Penn Central has put up for sale eighteen hundred and seventy-seven lots of assorted artifacts, and it wouldn't do to miss such an event. Come on, let's go eat."

The turkey hash was homemade. It contained chopped green peppers and came with a poached egg on top. It was accompanied by a dish of grits and a plate of hot orange muffins. The whole breakfast was delicious. Mr. Frimbo ate heartily. "That is the way to do it," he announced as he mopped up the last bite of hash with the last crumb of orange muffin. "If more people reached the office with a bellyful of turkey hash, there would be more Christian behavior." Mr. Frimbo drank iced tea with his breakfast. He said this was the proper Southern breakfast drink.

South of Trenton, we repaired to the day bedroom (it seated three) with Mr. Frimbo. He said he thought he had better give us a short briefing on the auction. "There was a public viewing of the lots last week, so I scooted down to Philly—on the eight-o'clock, of course—to check them out," he said. "The prize items are some beautiful hand-tinted street atlases of the major Eastern cities, dating from around nineteen-hundred; several albums of rare photographs of trains in the old days and of suburban homes in New Jersey and Philadelphia; some exquisite models of old Pennsy parlor cars, Pullmans, and day coaches; and a stunning painting of a happy family in a diner, entitled *Ice Water*—and I don't mind telling you I coveted that painting immediately and went back to look at it several times. I finally decided that it would be a crime to buy it for myself and remove it from public view. It's my hope that some major museum will be moved to acquire it."

The auction was held in the south concourse of Philadelphia's Thirtieth Street Station. It began at ten o'clock sharp, and the models were almost the first lots on the block. A good crowd of buffs, dealers, and collectors was in attendance. Bob Alotta, a Penn Central public-relations man, opened the auction by ringing Lot 531, described in the auction catalogue as "Brass Stationmaster's Bell, 6¾" diameter, used at Phila. Centennial Station." Bob Alotta was wearing a conductor's hat and a button that said "Philadelphia We Love You!" He is the man who thought up the auction. Another of his ideas was putting hostesses on Metroliners. The auctioneer, John Freeman, is a fifth-generation Philadelphia auctioneer, who sings the bids, in the old style, using a three-note scale based on the G below middle C. At the conclusion of the bidding on a lot, he is apt to sing the following phrase:

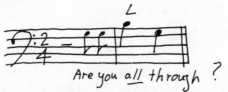

Mr. Frimbo spotted a number of acquaintances, including a dealer known to the trade as DC-7, who, Mr. Frimbo said, seemed to be bidding for a well-to-do Texas rail buff. The models sold for at least fifty dollars apiece—depression prices, according to Mr. Frimbo. A working model of a famous steam locomotive and tender that was nine feet long over-all went for twenty-three hundred dollars, and our friend nodded in approval. John H. White, Jr., the curator of the transportation collection at the Smithsonian, bought a real steam whistle once used on the real *John Bull,* one of the first locomotives ever run in the United States, for three hundred and seventy-five dollars. At one point during the bidding on the model cars, our friend leaned over and whispered, "Amtrak's probably got an agent bidding for those Pullman cars. Amtrak hasn't been willing to buy anything else from Penn Central. You will notice that every time you ride on an Amtrak train on the Penn Central lines you seem to be in a car that came from another railroad—usually a railroad that's a lot better."

We left the auction shortly before lunchtime, because Mr. Frimbo had to get back to town. We caught a train that carried a Penn Central diner, and ordered club sandwiches, at our friend's suggestion. "It's the only thing I'll eat on a Penn Central diner," he told us. "Why, just look at that menu! 'Open-Face Filet of Fish Sandwich'!" He shuddered delicately.

After lunch, we had some more talk. "I would like to get out of New York City," said Mr. Frimbo. "It's the only metropolitan region in the world without a *rapid*-transit system. I'm thinking of emigrating to England and becoming an engine driver on a small steam railroad owned by some friends of mine who have bought twelve working steam locomotives. Last summer, to bring you up to date on my travels, after I traversed Siberia by train, I sailed through two typhoons on my way across the Sea of Japan to Japan and, after ten days there, flew reluctantly to Seattle, from which town I returned to New York on the *Empire Builder* and the *Broadway Limited.* At Christmastime, I sloped off to Mexico to ride a mysterious new deluxe train that does not appear in any timetable."

Having said all this, our friend fell silent for a space.

When he spoke again, he spoke in unwontedly somber tones. Here's what he had to say: "People in this country have forgotten how to travel. They've forgotten how to do a lot of other things, too, but travel's my specialty, so I'll stick to that. Since the automobile costs more and is less convenient, all things considered, than any other form of transportation, it's bound to be a popular success these days. A girl I know conducted a serious survey recently, asking families the question 'Would you rather own a second car or send your son or daughter to college?' The overwhelming majority opted for the second car."

As we pulled into Penn Station, we noticed that, for some reason, there was a baggage car standing on the track next to ours. The door of the car was open, and it was possible to see that it was empty, except for some clean sawdust on the floor. A well-dressed woman was walking down the platform while we were getting off our train. She was heading straight for the baggage car. She entered the car just as we drew abreast of it. She looked around the car for a moment and then addressed Mr. Frimbo. "Is this the train for Florida?" she asked him.

Mr. Frimbo turned to us. "See what I mean?" he said.

Dayliner

This is the decade in which the Hudson River Day Line has spent three and a half million dollars building a new ship to replace the old sidewheeler called the *Alexander Hamilton*. Here's how the new ship stacks up against the *Hamilton*:

OLD SHIP	NEW SHIP
Name: *Alexander Hamilton*	Name: *Dayliner*
Hull: 338.6′ x 77′	Hull: 308′ x 65′
Engine: steam; 3900 hp.	Engine: 2 diesels; 3500 hp.
Passenger capacity: 3250	Passenger capacity: 3500
Top speed: 23 knots	Top speed: 16 knots
Cost: $852,000	Cost: $3,500,000

We went aboard the new ship one summer's day in 1972 to attend its christening by Mayor Lindsay. A large crowd of gentlemen in suits and ladies in hats was on hand for the occasion. It was a predominantly Irish crowd, possibly owing to the fact that the head of the Day Line, Francis J. Barry, is an Irish-American. A press representative directed the crowd to the "third floor" of the *Dayliner,* where there were seats and a podium. Occupying one of the seats was a man who was doing his best to look bent, aged, and curmudgeonly. Could it be? Indeed it was!

"What are you doing here?" we asked.

"Once they get this thing christened," said our venerable friend, "they're going to take her downriver as far as the Statue of Liberty, so that the harbor can welcome her. Now, that'll be a maiden voyage, and I've been on only one other maiden voyage in my life. I figured it was time for Number Two."

"Please tell us all," we said.

"It was the maiden voyage of the *Washington Irving,* the largest ship the Day Line ever owned and the fastest ship on the inland waters of the U.S. Fastest by far. The captain said they never really dared let her out all the way, for fear of swamping small boats."

"When was this?"

"God, I don't know how long ago that was! Sixty years, at least. It was a day just like this—bright and sunny. I was in school at the time, and I was excused for the day, provided that I stand up in front of the class on the next day and report."

"What did you say in your report?"

"My uncle was one of the naval architects who designed the ship, so, naturally, I gave him a plug. I told them what a beautiful ship it was, and described in some detail the Alhambra Writing Room, which had Moorish arches. I outlined the scene, which was one of subdued hilarity, and talked about the crowd, which was very, very bigwig. A grand repast was served in the main dining room, and I'm sure I mentioned every course. The speeches I can't remember. Fortunately, in those days there was no public-address system. Either you had a naturally commanding presence or you didn't talk."

Someone started to clap, and we looked around. There was the Mayor. The ceremonies began. Mr. Barry spoke first. Mr. Barry was wearing a blinding seersucker suit. He thanked us all for taking time out of a busy day to be there, and told us that the *Dayliner* represented three and a half million dollars of unsubsidized investment in the future of New York. He pointed out that in 1807, when Robert Fulton began regular runs up the Hudson, the fare was four dollars from New York to Poughkeepsie, one way. "Saturday, when the *Dayliner* makes her first trip to Poughkeepsie, one hundred and sixty-five years later," he went on, "the *round-trip* fare is but one dollar more!"

Frimbo applauded vigorously.

Mr. Barry then introduced Miss Summer Festival and Frank Hogan, the District Attorney. They got up and bowed. Then the Mayor spoke. He saluted the captain of the *Dayliner,* the other distinguished officers, and the crew, and the ship itself, which he called "this great vessel" and "such an exciting ship." He also had a good word for summer, referring to it as "the great summer season." The Mayor noted that tourism is now the number two industry in New York, and said he was happy to announce that the *Alexander Hamilton* had just become a permanent exhibit at the South Street Seaport and thus would not be lost to the city and its visitors. He called the *Hamilton* "a fine old sternwheeler."

"Oops!" said Frimbo, and he suggested that we tour the new vessel. We abandoned the ceremonies just as the Mayor

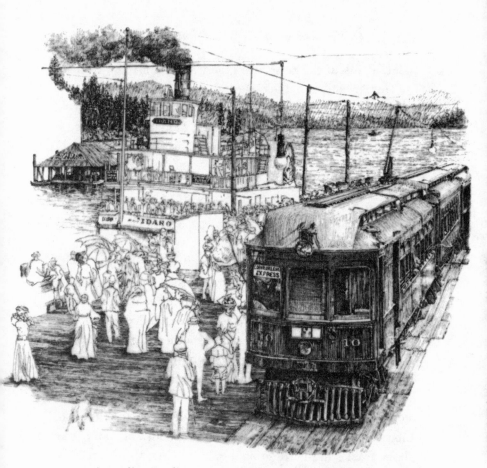

An earlier Dayliner meets the Coeur d'Alene Express

smashed a bottle of champagne on a rail, drenching Miss Summer Festival.

The *Dayliner* has four decks, a restaurant, three snack bars, and several washrooms. We inspected all these installations. "Damn it, this is bleak!" said Frimbo. "There's not enough headroom anywhere, and look at the decks! They're just steel plates coated with fire-resistant paint and anti-skid

184] *All Aboard with E. M. Frimbo*

paint. Think of the noise when there's a full load on board!"

Our friend also took exception to the *Dayliner*'s two stacks, which emerge from the aft portion of the top deck. "Diesel fumes will coat everyone not hanging over the bow, and how do you tell where the bow is on a vessel like this?" he said darkly.

Just about then, the *Dayliner* began to back out into the Hudson. After a few minutes, Frimbo brightened up. "Good heavens!" he said to us. "You're on a maiden voyage, my gossoons!"

A tug called the *Huntington* saluted the *Dayliner* with three hoarse toots. The *Dayliner* returned the salute. Other boats added their welcoming cries. A pilot boat with a tenor voice hooted at us, and a Circle Line boat called *Miss Circle Line* gave a contralto greeting. Another tug, the *Steven McAllister*, emitted three extremely hoarse but friendly cries. As we passed the Stevens Institute, in Hoboken, we could see a crowd of undergraduates on the parapet of the old Stevens castle waving at us, and, down by the Statue of Liberty, *Fire Boat Number 1* sprayed plumes of water from all its nozzles in the traditional greeting. Mr. Frimbo pointed out the oldest sign in the harbor—a large one in Jersey City, with a clock, that says "COLGATE'S SOAPS PERFUMES." It is almost fifty years old. "You know, it's really remarkable that this ship ever got built at all," Frimbo said. "Cruising inland waterways by public transport is practically at an end in this country, and the advent of the *Dayliner* at least assures that it is not altogether at an end. 'Tolerable' is the best that I can say, but I will say it: 'Tolerable.' "

25 *Letter from Japan*

My dear Contessa: The small clump of railway buffs whose destiny has for the past month been in my hands has been waved off to the railway lines in the valley below, and I am at last alone—for the nine hours before we set off this evening by ship along the Inland Sea to Kobe —to collect their bills and my thoughts. These companions of mine have, after early doubts, plunged full tilt—under my semi-direction—into the Japanese manner of life, as witness the bills I am sorting. The amenities afforded by this resort hotel, one so splendid that my name for it is Pearl of the Orient, are multifarious, and the variety of them— and the cost thereof—are set forth in presumably clear Japanese and definitely clear English. Alongside the designation "Hostess" appears the notation "2 @ 1250 = 2500 yen." A pair of my little charges, who had discovered a supper club buried in these enormous premises, last night had chartered from the management two seemly and gracile young Japanese girls, versed in such exotic imports as the

English language and the fox trot, for a stated number of hours. I myself had arranged a dinner party *chez moi,* inasmuch as my suite provides a dining room, where three young women, straight out of *Madame Butterfly,* prepared and served the dishes I had commanded, all this before the soirée in the supper club. Such is the dreary life of one who elects to journey about the world by train.

My thoughts at the moment center on the question put me by a chap at *your* dinner table the day before I left Paris for the Far East—"how can you bring yourself to visit countries whose national policies you do not approve?" I have now come upon the answer I should have had then: "If I were to live only in countries whose policies I entirely approved, I should be domiciled on the moon, and even there, of course, I should be constantly rubbing shoulders with *Russian* astronauts." More than sixty years ago, when my father, a novitiate archeologist, was beginning his exploration of the world, no one would have asked such a question. Posted to the university in Heidelberg, he took his holidays, in fourth-class railway carriages with wooden benches, wherever he and his classmates wished to go. No one suggested that they not go to England because of the British conduct of the Boer War, or that they not go to Kiev because of the Czarist hold on Russia, or to Constantinople because of the terrors of the Ottoman Empire, nor did any of his German friends suggest that he not return to the United States because of the machinations by which we acquired the site of the Panama Canal. The world must be the oyster of the lexicographer and archeologist, like my father, and of the lexicographer turned railwayman, like me. And one is ever learning.

Example: in the company of a friend in our Federal Railroad Administration and of another in our Department of Transportation, I stood alongside—a good many miles east of Moscow—a freight train from one of whose cars came a small but insistent howl. One end of this vehicle was inhabited by a crew of three or four, in minute living quarters; the remainder of it by diesel engines (the howling noise) that were blowing something into a swarm of flexible piping. Our Intourist courier said that this strange device was an air-conditioner that was feeding chilled atmosphere into a set of refrigerator cars laden with fish from the Yellow Sea en route to the capital. "Well," said my Americans, "O.K. over here, where manpower is cheap. It would never do for us." Yet one day, returned to New York, I discover in a journal devoted to the railway trade a photograph of a machine on wheels that rather resembled the one I have just described, though the legend below proclaimed that it had been built in Erie, Pennsylvania. Live and learn, my pet.

My little charges will journey with me from here to Kobe to Tokyo, where they take plane to the States. From there, I move westward, toward Paris and you.

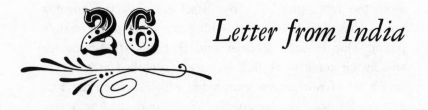

26   *Letter from India*

My dear Contessa: Much progress this past month, from Japan to India, where, inevitably, I at last found myself in a hotel that calls itself the Taj Mahal—a venerable palace on the waterfront of Bombay. A day flight from Tokyo to Bangkok, for a visit to the central railway station—an architectural fantasy run riot—and a day flight to Singapore, for a visit to another railway station of equal grandeur, an excursion upcountry into Malaysia, for a glimpse of the Malaysian State Railways, and a night or two at Raffles, in Singapore, before this further fantasy of a hotel, in every corner of which Oriental Intrigue is implicit, vanishes in the dawn of the chain hostelries that are now ringing the world; then a night flight to India. I came alone from Japan, but for three weeks now I have been joined with a group of English railwaymen and *aficionados*.

We have ranged the nation, occasionally in a sleeping car of our own provided by the munificent board of directors of Indian Railways, the title of the nationalized transport system, and we have been scorched in the overheated plains and chilled in the mountains about Darjeeling, which is as far as one may penetrate into Himalaya country, though far enough for one to catch, at dawn, the imperious Mount Everest along the northern horizon. In genuflection to the admonition "don't go near the water," I have managed well these three weeks on extremely warm tea and forthright Indian beer, but Bombay is in teetotaler territory, and what should have been the bar, waterside on the main floor, is but a tea room, and I am driven to such subterfuges as Schweppes' tonic in order to remain properly liquid.

No matter, my room is cool and quiet and air-conditioned, my bathroom's shower is the work of a sorcerer's apprentice, and I cannot stop toying with it. More than anything else, I have enjoyed the companionship of a chap whose skill at railway photography has gained him fame not simply in the British Isles but in all of western Europe. He is ostensibly a bank manager in Birmingham, back in his native England, but in real life he is a formidable railway buff, and he has been the absolute essential to this tour of India, for which Thos. Cook & Son, who have made all the arrangements, must be given extra marks. Our banker was posted to India as a Railway Transport Officer in the Second World War, and he knows all. The vocabulary of nationalization is sparse—this railway is Eastern Region, that one is Central Region, we are told—but our banker recalls the nomenclature of Empire; let a large steam locomotive chuff into view and he announces, "Bombay, Baroda & Central India," and when one more approaches, he declaims, "Assam & Bengal! Poor dear, she's a long way from home."

Names like these—I might also mention Madras &

Southern Mahratta—are both heartening and enlightening to us antiquarians. So knowing is the fellow that although he was christened a plain-spoken W. A. Camwell, we have knighted him Viceroy of India.

A week from now, we fly overnight to Rome, where I shall leave my group. There is to be an international conclave of lexicographers in the Bernini Bristol, a mere twenty minutes' stroll through some of the most superb Roman architecture—then, Termini station, whence I depart two days afterward. To you, my pet, so given to employing flying machines between Paris and Rome, may I commend the

The Taj Express, *between New Delhi and Agra*

Palatino. This express, which—granted!—involves some museum-piece cars of the Wagons-Lits operation (all, nevertheless, spotless and commodious), departs from Termini at the seemly hour of half past six in the evening. As one moves down the platform toward it, one cannot escape the fragrance of veal and zucchini being brought to the ready in the restaurant car, attached to the rear, that will accompany me as far as Genoa.

Meanwhile, having dined, I fill out a chit indicating to the border officials who I am and what my luggage contains; this, with my passport, I hand to my attendant, and then retire. No inspection at an airport, lest my luggage be found to contain a crossbow or a slingshot with which to terrify my fellow travelers; no altercation with a customs official. At Chambéry, deep in the Alps, a French restaurant car comes aboard, for a breakfast overflowing with croissants, unsalted butter, and great draughts of vigorous coffee to fortify me against the February weather I can count upon in Paris.

We arrive at Paris Lyon at nine-twenty-four. My final words: (1) be of good cheer, (2) be on time.

 *Frimbo on Cats*

Here is E. M. Frimbo's report on Intercat '73, the Second International Cat Film Festival, which convened in New York. It is not generally known that the world's greatest railroad buff is an expert on cats, but he is, and he once shared an apartment in Greenwich Village with thirteen Persians. His report:

Intercat '73 was held at the Elgin Theatre. It was organized by Pola Chapelle, a night-club singer. I was quite taken by Pola Chapelle—her attitude, her manner. She knows what cats are about. She knows what people are about. Many movies were shown, including one called *Jewish Momma Cat,* as well as the best Felix the Cat cartoon I have ever seen. Most Felix the Cat cartoons don't grab me, because Felix the Cat follows the pathetic fallacy.

I think Intercat '73 was a splendid idea, because it showed the proper attitude of people toward cats; namely, a tremendous admiration for the beasts. But, unfortunately, it also showed what urbanization can do to thinking about animals—the supposition by a number of urban people who are clearly incapable of taking care of themselves that they can take care of cats, who have been taking care of themselves for centuries without any intervention or interference by human beings. That, it seemed to me, was implicit in the whole Festival: the idea that cats are loving creatures—up to a point—that have to be looked after every minute. This was particularly evident in the *Jewish Momma Cat* picture, in which the filmmaker is obviously under the impression that his cat hasn't the vaguest idea how to give birth to children and look after them. He keeps taking her off to the hospital, when, to judge by the way he coughs on the sound track, *he* is the one who needs hospitalization. Poor man! As a matter of fact, the whole Festival proved that the only advantage man has over the cat is a movie camera. For Intercat '74 I'm going to make a movie with a cat-held camera.

As for the audience, whenever I go to something like Intercat or to see old movies—at the New School for Social Research, say—I get the impression that it's always the same cast in the seats. You get the feeling that these crowds have been assembled by assistant directors—the same freakouts, the same strange clothes, and the same earnest manner. The only thing that really changes is the placards the picketers wear. At Intercat, they were picketing for cats to become vegetarians, and vegetarian cats die of malnutrition. And one wonders, you know, how big this audience really is. You have the same two hundred and fifty people who love old movies and who love cats, and so forth and so on. Very small percentage of an urban population.

That's all for the Festival. Now to other matters. You know how hard people think it is to teach a cat anything?

Well, recent scientific research has shown that if you teach one group of cats to do tricks and then put them in with a second group of cats who don't know how to do tricks, the second group will learn quickly and easily just by watching the first group perform. Science has now confirmed my own investigations. When I was teaching one of my older Persians—Edward W. Riegelman—to do certain things, like jumping through a hoop, the old circus stunt, the others picked it up and learned to jump handily, although I hadn't taught them. This evidence calls into question many cherished theories about education, and shows that the cats should be in charge of the schools. We couldn't do worse than we are doing already, could we?

And here is some free advice for people keeping cats in the city: keep them only if the cats have access to a piece of greenery, and don't feed the cats what you eat. Cats have their own way of life, and they shouldn't eat scraps from tables. On holidays, of course, they deserve a treat. When I had my thirteen Persians, I used to feed them lobster on the Fourth of July and Decoration Day.

You look at all these city dwellers who proclaim their admiration for cats, and then you walk around town in the summer and see all the abandoned beasts on the streets. People should know that they can take their cats with them when they go away. Cats travel beautifully—unlike wines of the country. At the time I had my thirteen Persians, my mother was living in suburban Philadelphia, up in Germantown, and I used to travel back and forth weekends with the cats. The Pennsylvania Railroad porters were very snooty about cats in the parlor cars. They wanted them kept in the cages. So I transferred to the Reading Railway, which had a ferry across the Hudson and an hourly service with a parlor car to Philadelphia. I'd get off at Wayne Junction and take the local train up to my mother's house. I'd take maybe two or three or four cats down to Germantown with me in the parlor car, and the porters on the Reading were noble old boys. It wasn't long before the cats were allowed to prowl up and down the parlor car. I had a strict understanding with them that they could not jump in the lap of any customer except me. It was all right if they wanted to prance up and down and jump in an empty chair. This was the strict understanding on which they traveled. Or else they stayed home.

So one day I had three Persians—big beasts. My three very best. They were like a team of chariot horses, running up and down the carpeted parlor car at full speed. Finally, in their last sprint, they went nose, head, and tail down the aisle and landed on the top of a chair and began hissing and yowling at each other.

And a woman cried, "Porter, porter! What is all this?"

And he looked at her contemptuously and said, "Why, them's Mr. Frimbo's Persians, of course."

Now I've got one more story. You see, I was brought up in the English countryside, where animals, and particularly cats, are considered the equals of people, as they should be. Cats there accept you as their equals, too. It's a very nice relationship. We used to travel up and down constantly between the countryside and London, sometimes with the cats in tow. My father, who had a season ticket because he was commuting to the City, always traveled grandly in first class, but my mother, who was economical, often traveled third, with me. The English, you know, decided to abolish one of the three classes, so they abolished second class. That gave you the choice of going either first or third, not first or second—the real English attitude.

One afternoon we were coming back, most unusually, first class with my mother, and the ticket examiner, who knew us because we always took the same afternoon train, looked surprised at my mother's traveling first. He thought she had moved up arbitrarily from third. So he said, "Traveling first today, Ma'am?" And she said, patting the cage in which Thomas, our big cat, was sitting, "Yes. Thomas wouldn't hear of going third."

The Host
and the Guests

Ernest M. Frimbo sat in the Madison Room of the Princeton Club in New York one spring lunchtime in 1973, munching English turbot and humming an old hillbilly tune called "Flop-Eared Mule." Between bites. The first verse of that song begins, "Flop-eared mule, flop-eared mule, flop-eared, flop-eared, flop-eared mule," and the second one goes, "Real world, real world, real, real, real world, real world, real world, real, real world." It's one of his favorites. The English turbot was on hand partly because Frimbo was boycotting meat and partly because he is partial to English turbot.

Now, as it happens, we sat opposite Frimbo during that meal, and since we had not seen our friend in some time, we put a series of questions to him: "How are you? Where have you been? Are you all right? What have you been doing? Why haven't we seen you?"

He certainly looked well. He had quite a tan, and his eyes were as merry as ever.

"Things had reached the point where my doctor had said, 'I think you'd better get out of town for a good long rest,' " Frimbo told us. "I wasn't feeling good. When the town is New York, you just have to get out of it every so often. It was good advice. And the question arose: Where to go? Since I'd been everywhere.

"And a friend of mine who, hmm [here he clicked his tongue], owns a set of cars that he'd bought from the Union Pacific Railroad—namely, two sleeping cars, a dining car, and a marvelous dormitory car that houses staff—said that he was starting off on a little expedition to nowhere, because he was out of sorts, too. He thought it would be a good idea if I joined up. And he said, 'If you want to come out, I'm operating out of Texas, and we can arrange to pick you up in Houston.'

"Whereupon I said all right, I'd go out on the *Broadway Limited*. And the man said, 'I'll have someone meet you in Chicago, if you don't feel very well, and take you to lunch, and put you on the *Texas Chief* to Houston.'

"So when Mr. Frimbo gets to Houston, someone in a limousine picks him up and takes him out to a yard where this train is sitting—the two sleeping cars, the dining car, the dormitory car—and I am told there's a full staff aboard. A porter tells me, 'Your host will be along later, and his friends, some of whom I think you know, and if you wish to take a nap, I've made your room up.' And he conducts me to a magnificent compartment that will sleep three, with the air-conditioning already turned on, and a man appears and says, 'Can I get you anything from the bar?'

"Mr. Frimbo has an orange juice and takes a nap, and by the time he wakes up, the other guests have started arriving, and he's feeling a little better already, and the host comes aboard, and we're introduced to the staff; there's a secretary, and two men in the kitchen, and a man at the bar and a waiter, and a porter for each of the sleeping cars, and a general atmosphere of 'What would you like in the way of food or drink or silence or bingo?'

"The secretary had a bingo machine along, in case anybody wanted to play bingo, and a stack of magazines—you know, as the trains used to be—in case anybody wanted to read magazines. The menus were printed up, and they were always a surprise. You were presented a menu at each meal, three meals a day, ranging from oversized steaks to whatever the kitchen crew had been able to snaffle in the local market where we layed over—say, shrimps or fish or extra-good-looking strawberries, or whatever. Part stuff stored in refrigerators in the dormitory car and part living off the land—the army traveling on its stomach.

"Among the guests were a friend of mine from Birmingham, whom I had known for many, many years, and a chap from the West Coast whom I had also known, both of them ardent rail buffs. There was a doctor aboard—a doctor and his wife. I didn't know the rest of the crew. I happened to know one of the waiters; he's an old regular dining-car employee of the Southern Pacific. He greeted me by name when I arrived—to my delight.

"In the middle of the night, we started off rambling. A switch engine picked us up and tacked us onto a westbound passenger train, right behind the engine, and we started off."

"Your four cars were in front of the other cars?" we put in.

"Yes. You get better hot water that way. The closer you are to the engine, naturally, the better the hot water.

My host explained that he always asked to be put on the head end of the train. Incidentally, the host is a partner, with his brother, in a large manufacturing company on the West Coast, and when the argument comes up about can he travel on a certain train, he always says, 'Well, you know, my brother and I don't really need to ship anything in and out of our plant on your railroad.' He says, 'The truckers are coming in with these attractive offers.' The officials, he says, seem to get the message."

"And he's never been denied?"

"No, he usually manages to get—get something. Which is the way American business is conducted today. And Mr. Frimbo, being tired from the long journey to Houston and the long—overlong—stay in New York, just spent the first two or three days in, mostly in, his room, having his meals sent in if he liked, or having them in the dining car. Beautiful full-length dining car. [Here Mr. Frimbo rattled some change in his pants pocket.] And hobnobbing with the other friends—staying away from the bingo games.

"After two or three days, I began getting up and looking around. I hadn't been particularly aware of where I was going, and, all of a sudden, one morning I looked out the window and saw, among the signs along the way, kilometer posts instead of mileposts. And I asked the host what was going on, and he said, 'Well, you know, Mexican railways are much more agreeable to an expedition of this sort.' He said, 'I am planning to end this expedition in San Diego, and we've gone across the border to make it a more interesting trip.'

"I said, 'What? How is this?'

"He said, 'Oh, we had it all arranged beforehand. I knew your passport number from that journey we made out to the South Pacific a couple of years ago. Everything is in order.'

"*And,* sure enough, there was a man from the old Mexican Pullman Company in charge of the train, and a whole Mexican crew—in the kitchen, porters, everything. A delicious combination of Mexican and American cuisine appeared on our plates. You could have things as spiced as you like—*huevos rancheros,* for which everything bombastic gets thrown in, or plain, ordinary North American omelettes for breakfast. Delicious muffins and other things began appearing. [Frimbo clicked his tongue.] We went up a branch line to a town called Guanajuato, and the host said, 'Would you like to go down to the market with my secretary—it's one of the great open-air markets in Mexico—and we'll buy some fruits and vegetables?'

"So we went down to this spectacular market as big as a cathedral, and they had plantains and all kinds of incredibly wonderful fruits—juicy fruits that could be made into drinks, and so forth and so on. And we came back, each of us lugging a huge basket of goodies, put them in the dining car, and went to bed, and in the middle of the night I woke up, looked out in the light of the moon, and saw that we were on most *unlikely* trackage. The train was swaying and bumping, and so on, and the cars were swinging back and forth, and I realized we were traveling over track I had never been on before.

"Just then, I saw my host walking by in the corridor, so I asked him, 'What's up?'—this was about four o'clock in the morning—and he said, 'Oh, we're on a freight train, cutting across lots from one place to another so that we can save a couple of days. I arranged with the Mexican railroad people to put our train aboard.' He said, 'You won't have any hot water in the morning, because we're being hauled by a freight engine. But,' he said, 'we'll be making a hotel stop right after breakfast, so everybody can take a shower, or whatever.'

"So we stop off and have breakfast. And the host said, 'There's a lovely lake near here, called Pátzcuaro, and I've arranged for a motor cruiser to take us on a trip around the lake, if you don't mind walking down to the pier. It's about a mile.' So we spend the day sunning ourselves aboard the boat. He'd had a portable refrigerator full of cold drinks put aboard, and sandwiches made by the dining-car crew.

"Then we started north. Next morning, our host said, 'I think, uh, you've all had enough railroading for a while,' and we stopped off at a station, and a switch engine detached us from the passenger train we were on and took us down a siding. We got off at the siding, and he said, 'We're stopping off here for a day or two. Just take light luggage. If you need anything more, the porters will bring it to your rooms later on.'

"We walked down a lane to a literally walled hotel—a hotel with a high wall all around it, and one entrance, with an iron grille, just like the old haciendas. And we walked in there, and it turned out we had all been registered and assigned rooms in advance. Our host stood there handing out keys, and then we noticed a peculiar thing: there was nobody else in the hotel. And our host said, 'It's the off season.' He said, 'I've known the man who runs the place for years. We'll just rest here for a couple of days.'

"So *clang* goes the iron door, and there we are in our little walled city, with a swimming pool in the middle and a mariachi band for lunch and for dinner. That's why I have the tan—sitting in this walled hacienda in the sun, no one to disturb anything except the mariachi boys." Mr. Frimbo laughed, and continued laughing as he talked. "The minute the mariachi boys saw the group walking in to dinner, hustle, bustle, hustle, right behind you, set up the instruments two inches from your ear, and away they went. Six mariachi boys in fine fettle, in fine voice. It's kind of automatic, you see. Guests walk into the hotel, and the mariachi boys, who are apparently asleep somewhere, are instantly alerted for lunch and dinner.

"After we had sunned ourselves and bathed, done our drip-dry and everything for a couple of days, the host said, 'All right, we'll walk back up the lane.' We walk up the lane; pretty soon the switch engine backs down with our four cars from the railway station. We climb aboard and set out for the United States, ending up in San Diego. At which point the secretary approaches me and says, 'Most people are flying up to San Francisco, or wherever they want to go, but we assume that you, being a railway buff, will like to go on the four-o'clock *San Diegan* to Los Angeles.'

"And he hands me an envelope. It's the ticket to Los Angeles, plus a roomette on the *Super Chief* to Chicago and a roomette on the *Broadway Limited* back to New York. When I got aboard the *Super Chief*, the dining-car steward came back and knocked on my door. 'Mr. Frimbo,' he said, 'I have instructions that the dinner tonight will be on the house, with a bottle of wine. Just let me know when you wish to come in to dinner.'

"Incidentally, one of our four wonderful cars had an engine in it that would generate enough power to light all four cars and to run the air-conditioning in all four cars, in case the host wanted to have the train set out in a place where there was no way to plug in to the local supply. A couple of times, when this engine was misbehaving, I'd go outside, and there he'd be, underneath one of the cars, tinkering and making it run again. He knew exactly how to repair the thing."

Method in Your Madness

(Frimbo's Postscript to the Preceding)

When people ask me where I've been lately, and I tell them about something like that impromptu excursion into Mexico with that set of private railway cars, there is always just one more question: "How could *I* get to go on a journey like that? Should I go to my travel agency?"

And the answer is no, you should not go to your travel agency. A travel agency can fly you anywhere in the world, it can put you and your luggage in a chartered bus and move you all over Europe, it can get you in and out of two dozen hotels abroad, and see that you are fed and bedded down, without your ever having to speak to an employee for the whole three weeks. The staff of these hotels is made up entirely of what are called natives, and every country has many of these natives, speaking a large variety of languages, though almost never English. This is a safe way of traveling, for there is rarely the danger that you may have to talk to anyone who is not in your party or is not the

courier in charge of you all. The United States, too, is
largely populated by natives, many of whom speak English,
or an entertaining parody of it, and so the travel agency
does not have to worry nearly as much when it sends you
off here on a venture—package tour, I'm afraid, is the trade
term.

But then you suggest to the travel agency the most
minute alteration: you have heard that the countryside between Chicago and Minneapolis is beautiful in the summertime, and you wonder if you couldn't do it by train instead
of flying. The agency, perceiving in you the symptoms of
incipient insanity, moves in at once to quell any notion of
rebellion. "Oh, no, sir or madam," it will tell you, enun-
ciating each syllable, "there hasn't been a train through
there since the war."

But there are here and there true travelers' aides—men
whose delight is inventing unorthodox excursions to unorthodox destinations by unorthodox means of conveyance
—and these men are as methodical in their madness as the
chap who carried me off on that trip into Mexico. These
fellows plan an unusual journey, send out a prospectus to
their faithful constituency, and then are so enraptured by
the prospectus that they insist upon going along themselves.
Now and then, for instance, I push off into Latin America
with my old friend Dick Reynolds, who began life by
handling reservations on one of our most famous trains—
the old *California Zephyr*—and who now, sitting behind
the corporate name of Great Western Tours in an office at
639 Market Street, in San Francisco, sets up expeditions
south of the border to suit himself and his clients. He, too,
has his own sleeping cars and restaurant cars and lounge
cars and bar cars, he also knows any number of extremely

useful and compliant railways officials in Spanish America, and he speaks—literally—their language, which is an enormous help when things go wrong.

I have in mind especially the holiday venture during which a Mexican railway, prematurely honoring our arrival at a certain junction point, put on one of the most picturesque and imaginative wrecks in all history. At daybreak, we tooled slowly through the junction point, now converted into a disaster area, and a glance, by dawn's early light, at our schedule indicated that we were twelve or thirteen hours off base. No matter: we had our waiters, chefs, porters, enough grub to support us in style for a week without replenishment, and a wine cellar as yet scarcely tapped. But it did matter to our Mr. Reynolds: the train to whose rear we were attached was slowly but resolutely losing more time at every station, and at the far end of Mexico, on the border with Guatemala, a train he had rented solely for us argonauts—to provide us with a daylight journey through the jungle to the capital city of that country—would be waiting for us next morning, and waiting in vain, it seemed. Mr. R. always arranges to have an affable Mexican railway official or two in hand, and later in the day our cars were detached from our laggardly train, a pair of large diesel locomotives appeared, and we set off by ourselves for the border.

The part of Mexico we were to traverse that night is a bleak but amazing-looking semidesert, and most Mexicans know better than to live there, wherefore the population is sparse and the railway undernourished, but Mr. R.'s small train fled through the night—bumpety-thump—with such alacrity that we had recovered seven hours of the lost time (though not yet our breath) when we reached the border—

a small stream with a railway trestle across it. Here, on the infrequent occasions when passengers cross the border, they debark from their train and walk themselves and their luggage across, to wait who knows how many hours for the equally infrequent train to Guatemala City. But Mr. R. would have none of that. Our train turned itself around on a triangular piece of track, and then we were backing, tail first, across the trestle into Guatemala. We descended into a flotilla of customs and immigration men who had, by appointment, been waiting all day for us; our luggage descended behind us, our train moved off north into Mexico again, and there we were, on the edge of the Guatemalan jungle, in a tiny, dusty hamlet populated mainly, it appeared, by the officials swarming about us.

Mr. R., cucumber-cool, as always, gave us a smile awash with serenity, and a second later we heard the sound some of us will go to the ends of the earth to hear—the chuffing of a steam locomotive. Backing up north it came, toward the spot just emptied by the train from which we had descended, and on a narrow-gauge track that fitted neatly inside the Mexican one—the northernmost point on what had once been grandly labeled IRCA, or the International Railways of Central America. Our steam engine, hardly larger than a Shetland pony, was propelling a baggage car, a first-class coach, and—marvel of marvels—a sort of business-car-cum-sleeping-car with an observation platform on the rear. Instantly, our luggage was being popped aboard the baggage car and we were making for the observation car— a smoking lounge, three bedrooms, a kitchen, a lavatory, and an attendant arranged behind a layer of sandwiches and cold drinks. He, the sandwiches, the drinks, the whole train (all, except the locomotive, of great age and wholly

of wood) had been waiting seven hours, we discovered, and the engine was already in need of another drink for its boiler. We trundled along a mile or so to a water tank, and there the locomotive got its drink.

The railway, which had once extended through Guatemala into Costa Rica and El Salvador when it was built, had come—before it was nationalized—into the hands of a once celebrated financier known as O. Roy Chalk, who at one time had among his collection of toys not only this railway but Transcaribbean Airways and the tramcar system of Washington, D.C. The tramcars had, on his orders, all been labeled "Subsidiary of Transcaribbean Airways," and painted in a dazzling livery of his devising. It was with pleasure that we saw that our observation car was in the same livery—a trifle faded with age, as was, indeed, the O. Roy Chalk dominion, but nevertheless recognizable.

The Central American jungle is, of course, the Central

American jungle, and we have all seen it in the movies, but never quite the way we saw it then, for at times we could reach out from the open platform of our car and touch it, and as the afternoon suddenly swooned into night—sunsets in the tropics are about forty-five seconds long—we witnessed the jungle in an entirely different light. The Mexicans had put on that splendid railway wreck for us, and now the Guatemalan government had ordered three of its best volcanoes stoked up for us, and as we journeyed first along a vast jungle plain and then up into the mountains that surround Guatemala City, these volcanoes gave us a fine show —great pillars of smoke illuminated by blasts of flame and red-hot lava, and forest fires set off by that lava. The volcanoes were a bit too energetic, really, for in an hour or so a huge pall of volcanic ash began to descend upon us. The ladies in our party retreated indoors, but a few of us males, wreathing ourselves in our Burberrys and mufflers and gloves, stuck it out on the platform so that we could see the whole volcanic display. Mr. R. consulted with the Guatemalan railway official who had by now replaced his Mexican opposite numbers, and at a village a bus appeared, the ladies of our party and all our luggage were evacuated, and we survivors of the aerial bombardment proceeded through the garish night to Guatemala City, a mile or more above sea level. The full moon that appeared during our journey was altogether unnecessary. Our ladies and luggage reached our hotel a good three hours before we did—incredibly dusty and hungry—at one in the morning.

We spent a couple of days there, while the ladies got their façades restored to cleanliness and the rest of us pottered about the railway station with a guide who promised to show us every blooming steam engine still in existence in the country—a great show. On our way home, Mr. R.'s set of cars carried us to Vera Cruz—because, he said, he thought we might like to see the annual fiesta at its height, and for that he had booked a suite of rooms in a hotel along the line of march. Beforehand, so that we could see the city at leisure, he had chartered a tramcar of incalculable venerableness. Not long after we were aboard, we suddenly realized that we were rolling along not on the rails but on the pavement, and the motorman brought us to a hasty halt. Much argument between him and drivers of the tramcars, their number rapidly growing, that were collecting behind us, and the populace of the suburb turned out en masse to study the plight of the stranded foreigners and the stranded locals. Finally, someone remembered that great modern invention, the telephone, and a small truck filled with six extremely silent Mexicans arrived with tools. Twenty-five seconds later, we were on our way to the fiesta.

One more adventure on the way home: a bridge on which we had crossed without incident on our way to Guatemala had, because of someone's carelessness, collapsed, and was still being rebuilt when we started north. So the railwaymen had built what is called a shoofly—a temporary track—to get us around this problem. Our crossing was made in the middle of the night—fortunately for the more timid passengers, because the shoofly led down the steep bank of the south side of the river, crossed on the bed of the stream, so that the track was actually invisible, and ascended the steep north bank of the river. Getting us across that obstacle, one car at a time, with the two locomotives grinding and grunting on that loop-the-loop shoofly, was a spectacle indeed for those of us who stayed up to watch it. As we crossed the stream, the water came to within a foot of the floors of the cars—a chancy moment—but everything turned out all right, with Mr. R. riding on the outside of each of his cars in the blackness of the night as they came across—just to make sure.

We were three or four hours late because of all this, but again came a conference between Mr. R. and his railway officials, again we were detached from our laboring train, and again we were collected by two locomotives and shot on ahead of the rest of the train on our own. We arrived in Mexico City the next evening just in time to be attached to the much more deluxe express that would take us to the American border.

You have to look sharp to find travel agencies like Mr. R.'s. I can think of another one in this country—down in Vienna, Virginia, which is not quite a suburb of Washington. It is run by Karl Helft, another fellow traveler (if it's all right to use that expression) of mine. The agency that bears his name—Helft World Travel Ltd.—likes to explore odd parts of the globe, most especially parts that are occupied, as is Guatemala, by narrow-gauge railways that still can muster up an occasional steam locomotive. Helft has both formal and colloquial German at his tongue's tip—a most worthy asset, for the narrow-gauge railways of Europe that have survived the ravages of Progress are largely clustered in territory that has German as its primary or secondary language. A great fall of snow—an annual occurrence, naturally—sets his wanderlust adrift, and he begins telephoning friends to say that he has been talking to some railwaymen in Austria and has a collection of ironclad agreements with half a dozen narrow-gauge railways in that country that if he shows up at a certain hour in the early morning he and his friends will be put aboard a freight train for a snail's-pace journey up a long mountain valley constructed largely of snowdrifts; there will be a little hostelry and restaurant at the end of every run; there will be the local beer and sausage and fish and wine to sample at leisure; there will be an after-dinner stroll through old towns whose history and architecture are all written down in his mind, and/or an excursion on the local tram system, if there is one. The Helft brand of German is just as valid in East Germany and Poland, wherein are narrow-gauge steam railways of an age and improbability that would transfix the curator of any museum around, wherein trains to carry one along these railways can be chartered, where one lives off the countryside's local kitchen specialties and investigates the local tramlines and architecture. It is a life for the hardy railway antiquarian—long days, short nights, and no time at all to sit about and wonder what one is going to do next.

En Voiture!

Hard on the heels of a European postcard from Ernest M. Frimbo ("Europe splendid. Regards") came a letter from the great man with a Chicago postmark and an August 1973 dateline. Our old friend's letter said:

You are probably wondering why I have come back from Europe in such a great hurry when I was having a splendid time over there, dividing my spare moments between hunting for a house in England—no, not a grouse—and exploring Continental railways with two friends from the Federal Railroad Administration and the Dept. of Transportation. The reason was I had heard that two of the newest sets of French turbo trains were on their way to this country for trial runs, to be conducted by Amtrak, and I wanted to get back and see them in operation. No sooner had I got back than I had an invitation from Amtrak to make the first run—the delivery run, from Newark to Chicago.

I thought this was going to be an easy jaunt, at first, but because the turbo trains have not got certain signaling devices built into them that are required on the Newark-to-Chicago run, Penn Central put a speed restriction of 50 m.p.h. on them, which meant that the run to Chicago, instead of being one glorious single-day sprint, had to be made in two rather slower heats—the first day from Newark to Pittsburgh, the second day from P. to Chicago. Departure times were 7:00 one morning and 5:30 the next morning, which meant bed checks between 4:00 and 5:00 each morning to get us all up. The French turbo trains can run at 125 m.p.h., and, of course, in France they *do* run at 125 m.p.h. They were built for fast service on unelectrified lines, which is the reason they are turbo trains. It is hoped that they will run between Chicago and St. Louis—one run that Amtrak has in mind for them—at a top speed of 90 m.p.h. This would probably lop an hour off the schedule and mean really fast day travel for that area. The trains are a big success in France already—passenger traffic has increased 25% on the lines where the first-generation turbos have been introduced. The French plan to have 36 second-generation turbos in service in two years' time, and, in fact, the two they have just graciously sent us on lend-lease were originally part of that 36.

When the trains were unloaded, at Port Elizabeth, they seemed to be malfunctioning, and the delivery run had to be postponed until it was discovered that an American intercom device that had been put into the first train was broadcasting on the same frequency as the safety device that cut off fuel to the engines, so every time somebody had an urge to talk on the intercom the engines shut down.

The French turbo trains are not at all like the turbo trains we have in this country, in that they are comfortable, they run smoothly, they do not bump and jerk, and they never catch on fire. I talked with several American railway technicians who were on board the delivery run, and I gathered from what they had to say that there would have to be certain modifications, presumably to make these trains bump and jerk and catch on fire, before they can be approved in this country. So I was very pleased to travel on one of these turbo trains in its pristine state.

The trains have many 'disadvantages.' Aside from being quite comfortable, they have really large picture windows—*glass* ones. Over here they will have to be replaced by Lexan, because of the propensity Americans have for stoning trains. When we were switching from one track to another in North Philadelphia, the right-of-way was lined by policemen and police cars to make sure that no stoning occurred. The r-of-w was also lined practically all the way from Newark to Chicago in daylight hours by people with cameras, thus indicating that it was not true that people in this country are still uninterested in trains.

The amazing thing about the French turbo trains is that they're capable of accelerating smoothly and silently and comfortably against any opposition. For example, going west out of Altoona, Pa., there is the final climb over the eastern slope of the Alleghenies—the famous Horseshoe Curve, one of the wonders of engineering. This train just took off from Altoona and sped right up the slope like a gazelle. The fastest ride I've ever had up the Horseshoe Curve. It was lovely. Another lovely thing: These trains are what you call state-of-the-art trains. That is, they are designed to run on tracks as they are right now. The tracks between Newark and Chi in no way compare with the mainline tracks of the French National Railroads, of course, and I deliberately rode over the wheels in all the cars, at both ends, standing up and not holding on to anything, to see how they took the bad roadbed. I was not thrown around.

The train was, of course, run by two American railway engineers. (And since one of the engineers came from the Milwaukee Road, which runs trains between Milwaukee and Chicago, and the other came from the Illinois Central Gulf Railroad, which runs trains from Chicago to St. Louis, some of us are hoping that this deal is really going to go through.) But in the background, and *really* in the background, were four small, smiling, taciturn, imperturbable, reeking-with-competence, nonbilingual Frenchmen—the mechanics sent over by the builders. Since no Penn Central officials and none of the Amtrak officials on board spoke any French, the Frenchmen mostly had to demonstrate by pointing. The two engineers had been sent over to Europe for proper indoctrination in how to operate these trains, and, with the aid of an occasional point, the train proceeded on schedule —even when it got late because of public-relations stops. One moment, we were 52 minutes down on our schedule, but this train, despite being restricted to 50 m.p.h., quickly caught up on its schedule. Both evenings, we were in town on time.

The engineer's seat in the cab was beautifully sprung. I sat in it, and I've never seen anything that nice for engineers before. It's so good that when you're sitting in it and hit a lousy piece of Penn Central track you don't get that terrible *thump*. I'm thinking of suggesting that this seat be made mandatory in New York City taxicabs. Fifth Ave. certainly looks as though it were laid and maintained by Penn Central track crews.

During the journey, there was constant chatter, as there

always is when you get railway officials aboard a special run. A great deal of argument on the intercom system about refueling the train at a couple of stops. And chatter like 'Ask Crestline if they've got any 2 or 2½" nipples for the fuel feeder.' And there was a long debate about whether No. 1 diesel or No. 2 diesel fuel would be required for the refueling—a matter I thought might have been adjusted before the trip began. But that's how we operate in this country.

It appeared that the French people are not altogether sure whether we really want this train (which, naturally, I hope we do). I noticed that the ashtrays and several of the little trash bins cleverly fitted between the rows of seats were marked with the initials 'SNCF'—which stands for 'Société Nationale des Chemins de Fer Français.' The murals, of course, were all scenes of 18th-century French towns. Very handsome indeed. One participant in the run kept thinking that one of the murals looked like downtown Centralia, Ill. So it was thenceforth dubbed *Downtown Centralia, Illinois.* One of the taciturn Frenchmen had brought along a French tape for the public-address system which had everything from Chopin on a castrato saxophone to real Edith Piaf *caf-conc* Paris accordion music. The Americans were so fascinated that they insisted the tape be played and replayed.

These trains are not quite so luxurious as other French turbo trains, because Amtrak did not want what we would call a parlor car. So each train is made up of five coaches. It has an invisible and almost inaudible engine at either end, so it can be quickly reversed, if necessary, at the end of a run. In the middle, there is a kitchen and a small dining section. Naturally, nothing was served but reasonably aged sandwiches, some of which came from the Greyhound bus terminal in Pittsburgh.

The steward aboard the train was one of those old-time railroad men who always look exhausted, because they *are* exhausted, because they're called on in emergencies—an old friend of mine. Tom Middlesworth is his name. I've seen him on many break-in runs of new services. He's always sent to the front. And though he's nominally a supervisor of dining cars, he's a very handy man. The first day of the run, a chef who was supposed to show up and make the coffee didn't show up, so he had to see to it. Second morning, ditto. He got up at 3:00 that morning to make the coffee, and that's the kind of life he leads. You know, there are a bunch of old *real* railroad men, like Tom Middlesworth, who just live railroading. I've seen him waiting on table, I've seen him even in the kitchen of a dining car when the cook walked off the job. (This, incidentally, is one of the great problems in American railroading today. People assigned to jobs simply don't show up or don't phone in. You suddenly discover you're shy two porters, or you're shy a complete set of porters, or you're shy a cook and two waiters. And it's people like Middlesworth who step in and improvise. From 3:00 one morning until 10:00 the next night.)

I often wonder what would happen if the people like Middlesworth and another chap aboard the train, a great big husky guy named Boria, were allowed to run the railroads, and all the presidents and vice presidents and trustees and receivers and lawyers were let out to pasture. On the second day, I asked Boria, when they were fussing about the 2 and 2½″ nipples for the fuel feeder, what was going on, and he said, 'Oh, we'll just fuel the train the way we did yesterday.' And I said, 'Are you sure there'll be enough fuel?' And he said, 'Oh, let them fool around. There's already enough fuel in there now to get to the end of the run.'

31 Gathering

We ell, one night shortly before Thanksgiving in 1973 we set off for the Essex House in New York, where Harry Rigby, producer of *No, No, Nanette*, co-producer of *Irene*, and soon-to-be producer of *Good News*, was throwing a party for five of his leading ladies—Alice Faye, Ruby Keeler, Patsy Kelly, Jane Powell, and Debbie Reynolds. Unusual party. Black tie, sit-down supper for four hundred and twenty-three, dance band that played nonstop for almost four hours. No press agents, no disc jockeys, and no crashers.

And the first person we saw when we got there was Ernest M. Frimbo, of all people.

"What are you doing here?" we asked him.

"Well," said our old friend, "I had to get up at four-thirty this morning in Harrisburg, because I wanted to be one of the first riders on the new early-morning express that Amtrak has just put on between Harrisburg and New

York. And since I was coming to New York on this train I thought I might as well go to Harry Rigby's party."

"You know Harry Rigby, then?"

"Why, we're old friends," said Ernest M. Frimbo. "We both appeared in the same underground movie. Don't you remember Bob Downey's *Pound*? I played a penguin, and Harry Rigby was the leading penguin. I think it may be safe to say that Mr. Rigby is the only successful Broadway producer who's ever been the star of an underground movie. Isn't this a nice party? It reminds me of the dusk-to-dawn Princeton proms in the twenties."

A bearded Flemish Belgian approached Frimbo and handed him a glass of champagne. Frimbo raised the glass. "Confusion to the Walloons!" he said.

We walked around and noticed people. Julius Monk, the night-club impresario, seemed to be enjoying himself. Hazel Scott, the pianist and mother of Adam Clayton Powell III, danced to "Joy to the World." Bobby Short was there, on leave of absence from the Café Carlyle. Arnold Weissberger, the theatrical lawyer, was wearing his usual white carnation. We danced with Vadna Dibble. Vadna Dibble was a tireless attender of supper-club first nights in the old days. She's a hell of a dancer. So is Hazel Scott.

"It's kind of a relief to be here," said Julius Monk. "I've just come from a party that was kind of an imposition."

"What was it like?"

"Oh, everybody who was nobody was there."

Julius Monk left to dance with Vadna Dibble. We went to the bar and had a glass of champagne. We overheard three remarks on the way to the bar:

"I never know whether she's asking for another drink or suggesting we all go to Bermuda for a couple of weeks."

"And *that* hotel, I think, is owned by a group called Beef Wellington Associates. Could that be right?"

"He's the only man I ever met constructed entirely of foam rubber."

After a while, we decided to go home. Outside the Essex House, we found Ernest M. Frimbo waiting for a taxi. And then Hazel Scott came out holding an hors d'oeuvre on a toothpick.

"What's going on?" Ernest M. Frimbo asked Hazel Scott. "Are you waiting for the bus to Tijuana?"

"No," said Hazel Scott. "I think I'm being taken to a late restaurant where I'm not sure if there's any food. Who are you?"

"I used to work with Sonny Greer," said Frimbo.

"My God!" said Miss Scott. "That was Duke Ellington's first drummer."

"Remember those nights up at Pod's & Jerry's?" Frimbo asked her. Then he turned to us. "Pod's & Jerry's was a club in Harlem that was open from three A.M. till noon. Musicians used to go there after work to improvise."

"Let's grow old together," Hazel Scott said to Frimbo. Then her car came along.

Letter from New Orleans

Just a few months ago, Frimbo was in New Orleans. As he would, he sent us a letter:

It's old hat nowadays to think of going to New Orleans for Mardi Gras Week; you know how it is—before you've seen one, you've seen them all. But this time it was a special occasion, because a few of my friends, real honest-to-God rail buffs, decided to go to New Orleans this year in style—that is, in their own private cars.

The car I was invited to travel in, the *Pennsylvania*, has carried quantities of Presidents of the United States and was used on the funeral train that carried Senator Bob Kennedy to Washington. It was built in 1928, and built to last forever, and I think it will outlast everything, including the world, because in 1928 the men who built private cars knew what they were doing. It looks exactly as it did in the years before the Pennsy merged with the New York Central—Tuscan red with gold leaf. The present owners of the *Pennsylvania*—George Pins, a New York lawyer, who, ironically,

spends a large part of his career representing American Airlines; and his wife, Anita—have had the car done up properly inside. The car weighs ninety-one tons, and it sleeps, in
extreme comfort, only four passengers. I was awarded Bedroom A, which is the most opulent. It has a bed seven feet
long and five feet wide, a large washstand, a huge wall cabinet, a huge closet, a small chest of drawers, and a shower
bath. There are three other bedrooms in the car, none quite
as opulent as mine. Then, there is a dining room seating
eight, a properly equipped kitchen, a smoking lounge or parlor, and, at the rear, the necessary observation platform,
with the folding seats that you see in movies of forty and
fifty years ago.

There was also a quite decent wine cellar aboard, a
copious supply of perfectly polished Pennsylvania Railroad
dining-car silverware (and I mean silverware, not aluminum
substitutes), and a plentiful supply of Pennsylvania Railroad business-car crockery (a business car is a car that belongs to a railroad official), as well as the services of two old
friends of mine, Seymour Scott (of course called Scotty)
and Tony Rudd, both revered former employees of the
Pennsy dining-car department who are spending the rest of
their lives looking after Mr. and Mrs. Pins and their friends
—including me.

The *Pennsylvania* was preceded to New Orleans on the
train by another privately owned car, the *Clover Colony*,
which dates from about the same period and is one of the
last of the period-piece Pullman Company sleepers. Our
journey actually began in Washington, for the *Pennsylvania*
and the *Clover Colony* had to be sneaked down from New
York to Washington under cover of darkness, on a mail
train—this because Amtrak won't allow cars not painted

with its own flag-waving red, white, and blue on most of its trains.

When we left Washington, our two cars were on the tail end of the Southern Railway's *Southern Crescent,* which, in spite of the attitude of the Southern Railway management toward the idea of operating any passenger trains at all, is still a train on which all other American trains could well model themselves. Everything on the train is polished, everything on the train is functioning. We turned on the *Pennsylvania*'s floodlights and all stood on the observation platform as we went through the tunnel that takes trains under the city of Washington. People are not allowed outdoors when they go through that tunnel. Therefore, we were outdoors.

Dinner was the usual plainspoken but excellent business-car dinner—soup, chops, and salad, all deliciously cooked, and put away, of course, with the necessary dollops of wine. Our chef, Tony Rudd, spent nine of his forty-three years with the Pennsylvania Railroad as chef on the celebrated all-Pullman New York-to-Florida train the *Orange Blossom Special*—the most luxurious winter-season train ever devised by man. Nothing even remotely resembling a can opener was allowed on the premises. All the pies, cakes, rolls, birthday cakes were baked on board under his supervision. Cut flowers and fresh fish were taken on at every revictualing stop, and the train carried thirty-five hundred dollars' worth of wine, liquor, and champagne—these at pre-Prohibition prices—for each run. 'I don't think we'll ever see those days again,' said Tony Rudd. 'But I'm doing the best I can.'

Our journey to New Orleans—a distance of well over a thousand miles—took twenty-six hours, in comfortable, leisurely Southern fashion. Scotty stood ready throughout

the trip to open a bottle of Miller High Life beer or make a
brandy Alexander, or whatever. Wherever we stopped, railroad buffs, some of whom were officials of the Southern Railway, either came aboard or came alongside with their cameras. They stared at our car the way racegoers at Belmont
stared at Secretariat. In the early evening of the second day,
the train made its seventeen-mile trek across Lake Pontchar-
train and the marshes on a tiny wooden trestle. There's noth-

Over the Suwanee River, 1906

ing between you and the water, and in the middle you can't even see the shore. It's really like crossing the ocean on a train. We all, as one, adjourned to the rear platform and stood in the pale light of a crescent moon: most appropriate, because our train was the *Southern Crescent,* and we had brought along the name board of its ancestor, the original *Crescent Limited.* A name board was an illuminated emblem that hung on the back of famous trains in the old days.

Ours said 'Crescent Limited,' and above the lettering was an exact duplicate of the moon shining above us.

Less than ten minutes after we backed into Union Station in New Orleans, the ground crew (to use modern parlance) had hooked up a telephone, electric current, and steam to heat our water for our next five nights, while we would be living in our cars. That sounds just like living in a trailer camp, but I doubt if in many trailer camps you can come in at three-thirty in the morning from a jam session in the old French Quarter and step into a boiling-hot shower bath. And we were within convenient walking distance of everywhere instead of nineteen point five miles northwest of nowhere on Route 9A.

There were several well-got-up couples aboard who were along just for the ride and the big Mardi Gras parades. But some of us railroad buffs went on to Houston, the day before the big parades, on the *Sunset Limited,* to inspect half a dozen passenger cars that had been acquired by a group of railroad buffs and are kept in the old Houston Terminal station.

We came back the next day, having carefully timed ourselves to miss the big parades. The Southern Pacific Railroad, which runs the *Sunset Limited* for Amtrak, gave us, we thought, rather too ample assistance in this project, putting us into New Orleans at three-thirty Wednesday morning—eight and a half hours late. The railroad that accomplished this feat nets close to two million dollars a week for its stockholders.

Next morning, by which time the delightful city of New Orleans was as spotless as though nothing larger than a street tea party had occurred, we made our annual pilgrimage to the St. Charles Avenue streetcar line. The city fathers of New Orleans recently realized that doing away with anything as picturesque as their fine old trolley cars, which run along a seven-mile stretch of green between a double row of trees, would be a terrible mistake. So these cars, which are packed even when it isn't Mardi Gras, continue to trundle along the seven miles, at the exorbitant fare, including transfer, of fifteen cents.

I might add that we felt quite free about using the telephone in the *Pennsylvania* as much as we liked, because New Orleans is the only city in the United States that still charges a nickel for a phone call.

The Contessa —Again

Well, what did happen at that promised reunion with the Contessa in Paris? Was she on time at the railway station? Frimbo has entrusted us with the following account:

Yes, the Contessa was on time—for her: her customary five-minute delay. She came galloping along the platform—hatless, her fur coat wide open, her vast black mane and a porter floating behind her. My hotel room was not yet ready—not yet even empty; many air passengers were staying on because of the weather. So we decided to go to her flat, deposit my luggage, and shop until lunchtime. I bought her a flower, a book, a vial of perfume; we popped through the snow to a *brasserie* for more coffee and a brioche. "These are not very fresh," she said, and a disconcerted minion withdrew to the interior for brioches of a chaster aspect.

By cab we journeyed to the tumbledown Place des Vosges and to a restaurant whose casual frontage belied the splendor within. "Madame has not made a reservation?" our host inquired, frowning.

"François, you know that I am always much too busy for that," said the Contessa.

"Naturally," said François, hastily removing a *"Reservé"* placard from a table for four.

The cab back to the flat was in difficulties all the way; an endless supply of new snow was now arriving. "The gentleman's clothing is in a dreadful state," the maids were saying when the lift set us down at the Contessa's roof garden cum apartment. "But, Madame, forgive us; we have washed and pressed as much as we can."

In the event—weather, my drying garments—I stayed the night, while the three females of the household organized dinner and breakfast. By morning, the snow in the streets had ascended halfway to our knees. "No taxis, no planes, no trains today, my plum," said the Contessa. "I'm afraid that your obsession with travel must for now be laid to rest."

We browsed the neighborhood shops for provisions ("I have informed your hotel that it is to expect you when I tell them to expect you"), and then lunched. The afternoon must be devoted, the Contessa announced, to the revision of a manuscript she was preparing for *Paris Soir,* and it was hoped that I would not be too horribly bored by my impromptu confinement. "Perhaps a small walk," I said, as I let myself out of the flat.

"That, my sweet," said the Contessa upon my return, "was a four-hour walk."

"Yes," I replied. "Madame has, in her eagerness to deprive me of my usual way of life, overlooked the fact that the suburban trains from Austerlitz Station call at Pont St.-Michel, which even today is no more than a minute's prance from where we are now. The suburban trains, despite the inclemency of all outdoors, are doing their customary rounds today, I assure you."

"Ah," said the Contessa, "a toast: may we continue to find ways to make your world and my world companionable."

*Previously
Uncollected
Chapters*

Grand Central

Chapters 34 and 35, and Chapters 37 through 54, consist of Frimbonian material—further Frimbo trips and pieces he inspired—all of which appeared in The New Yorker *after the first edition of* All Aboard *with E. M. Frimbo came out in 1974. Whitaker and I collaborated on most of them; a couple—firsthand accounts of Frimbo's trip through the Canadian prairie and his journey on an Amtrak troop train—are Whitaker's handiwork. I speak in my own voice in Chapters 38 and 54. The original thirty-three chapters appear here just as they did twenty-two years ago, but wherever it seemed helpful I added a few introductory notes to the expanded edition's new chapters, either to update events or put them in context. For instance, the somber Grand Central story set down below eventually had a happy ending.*

In 1978, three years after our Frimbo piece appeared, the United States Supreme Court, in a landmark decision, upheld the landmarking of the station—and the constitutionality of protecting historic buildings. Thereafter, hundreds of Ameri-

can cities set up their own landmarking procedures, modeled on New York's. But it might never have happened, since New York City was initially reluctant even to appeal the lower-court decision against Grand Central. It took a ferocious citizen's campaign, founded by Kent Barwick, later New York's Landmarks Commissioner, and supported by Brendan Gill, Philip Johnson, and Jacqueline Onassis—and The New Yorker—*to shore up the city's resolve.*

And there's still more to come at Grand Central: the giant Kodak sign, which this Frimbo piece deplores, has been torn down so that morning sunlight once again floods through the east windows of the main concourse, and now the entire station is filling with scaffolding for a meticulous restoration that will at the same time find room for dozens of new shops and restaurants. A similar train-friendly transformation has already reestablished Union Station in Washington, D.C., as one of that city's liveliest destinations. Union Station's first make-over as a visitors' center, alluded to in this piece, was so wretched that visitors immediately made a wide detour around it, and the station was soon overgrown by toadstools.

Amtrak's new train station foundation will now be helping to bring new hope and new life to hundreds of stations and hundreds of cities and towns all over the country. And the icing on the cake will be the rebirth of New York's Pennsylvania Station, thanks largely to the tireless work of Senator Daniel Patrick Moynihan, who refuses to rest until the current Penn Station, that subterranean slum, has been gloriously rebuilt and given direct rail connections to both Kennedy and Newark airports, as also foreseen by the Regional Plan Association's new Third Regional Plan. *Of course, not every New York City rail victory has yet been won: for instance, despite dozens of visionary plans (and strong* New Yorker *support),*

*New Yorkers are still waiting for long-promised, new-age trol-
ley cars next to the terminal and along Forty-second Street.
Stay tuned.* —*Tony Hiss*

A few days after Irving Saypol, of the New York
State Supreme Court, decided that Grand Central Terminal
was no longer a New York City Landmark, and that the Penn
Central Railroad and its building associate, UGP Properties,
Ltd., were now free to move that station underground and
put up an office building on the site, we ducked into the newly
refurbished Grand Central Oyster Bar to think this thing out
over a few bivalves. The station is probably in no immediate
danger—who's going to start putting up another office building during the present slump? There's a new one on Sixth
Avenue not far from *The New Yorker* that has recently decided
not to open its doors; it will be cheaper to keep the building
closed than to go ahead and provide heat, light, and water
for the few tenants who have signed up. But the Grand Central
area—the station and its surrounding hotels and clubs and
shops—is the heart of Manhattan, and it needs to go on beating. We began muttering to ourself about how one of the major
accomplishments *The New Yorker* could definitely lay claim
to in its several decades of existence was that in the late forties
we managed to get the New York Central Railroad to stop
playing Muzak and commercials in Grand Central Station.
What, we groaned, could we do now?

"Well, you might ask me," said the man on the next stool
at the Oyster Bar. We looked around. By happy chance, he
was Ernest M. Frimbo, the world's leading railroad buff and

our good old friend. "I'm a man who remembers the *second* Grand Central terminal, which was being demolished when I first arrived in New York, to make way for the present, third Grand Central Terminal. The first time I walked into the concourse of *this* building—which I love very much— would have been in 1914, when I was coming down from Boston, where my family then lived, to go to school in a Friends Academy in Washington. My father, who knew some- one in the architectural firm that designed the station, was along, and he took me up to one of the offices high above the ceiling of the concourse, which were reached by a walkway through the huge, seemingly solid glass wall on the south side of the concourse. Glass on each side of the walkway. It was an eerie experience, because you looked up, and there high above you was the zodiac that adorns the ceiling of the great concourse of Grand Central—and in those days the zodiac was atwinkle with little electric-bulb stars. Nowadays, only one or two of these stars are ever shining, and they are eclipsed by the noonday sun of the huge Kodak display. And below you, on the walkway, sixty or eighty feet down, was the floor of the concourse. And just this seemingly thin glass wall on either side. It was a thrill for a little bit of a boy, and I remember I held on to my father and took every step with great care. I felt that perhaps this was a trap, and when we reached the offices I asked if there wasn't some other way of getting down out of the building. There was, of course.

"Later, as a grown-up railroad buff, I was part of a group that had the use of one of these offices, at a nominal sum, for a little meeting place, through the courtesy of one of the last good presidents of the New York Central—F.E. Williamson—when the New York Central was one of the classic railroads of the world. A little cubbyhole halfway up to Heaven where we could keep railway records, show photographs, and entertain railway officials from abroad. And then, on a Sunday morning, it was a great event to go down the street to the old Murray Hill Hotel for breakfast with all the young bloods and their young ladies.

"I'd say that in a way we're lucky to have had old Grand Central—I'm already calling it old—as long as we have had it. Because a dozen years ago or so the New York Central, no longer a classic railroad, came up with a scheme for discontinuing service from Harmon, thirty-two miles north of here, into the city, on the ground that since people were accustomed to taking buses and taxicabs in from New York City's airports, they should, uh, accept the privilege of taking a bus or taxicab in from Harmon. If *that* scheme had gone through, there wouldn't have been a Grand Central Terminal to demolish today. Just as, with the country's Bicentennial coming up, we are turning Union Station in Washington, D.C., into a visitors' center and removing the passenger trains therefrom. The passenger trains to our nation's capital will terminate nobody knows where—at a station somewhere near the visitors' center for which no plans have yet been drawn. And *that* is supposed to happen next year.

"The interesting thing is that Grand Central, if it is invited to remain with us, will be a very busy place in another couple of years. The Oyster Bar, as you can see, is already almost turning away customers, and, thanks to the bond issue passed by the voters of New York State last November, the night train to Buffalo, Cleveland, and Chicago is to be restored, and high-speed service to Albany and then west along the Mohawk Valley as far as Buffalo will be installed for the first time.

"But you want to know how to save the station? We talk

about restoring the city, making it more playful. Here's my scheme: restore Grand Central to what it was in the beginning; restore the elevated line that used to run across Forty-second Street and down to Thirty-fourth Street, then over to the East River; restore the steam ferry across the East River to Long Island City; restore the Long Island Rail Road Pullman cars from Long Island City to Montauk Point; restore the Forty-second Street trolley cars over to the old West Shore Railroad piers; and restore the steam ferry to Weehawken. It will be kind of a green belt in this perishingly overbuilt city, running all the way across from New Jersey to Long Island. It will attract millions of visitors—don't forget, there's going to be a huge new convention center right on West Forty-second—and it will be just what advanced thinking says we need, what I've always said we need: a kind of little playground, a restful spot in the middle of an overgrown city.

"By the way, everyone was delighted when we got rid of those slowpoke old trolleys back in LaGuardia's day and replaced them with new buses. Those who bothered to examine the schedules given to the drivers of the new buses replacing the slowpoke old trolleys were aghast to discover that the scheduled running time across the city for the buses—from the Hudson to the East River—was seventeen minutes longer than the scheduled time for the slowpoke trolley cars. The choice is yours."

Whitaker emerging from the side entrance of Grand Central

Louis Sullivan
in Manhattan

Frimbo (meaning Whitaker) was connected to many worlds that his New Yorker *readers only occasionally glimpsed. His interest in building better cities came from his father, Charles Harris Whitaker, editor of the* Journal of the American Institute of Architects *and the first writer in the family, whose "fiery pen," as James Marston Fitch called it, helped goad the federal government into building the country's first public housing—for First World War civilian shipbuilders. Charlie Whitaker also tried to help architects and planners he admired get through their own hard times. It was at Twelve Opossums Farm, his New Jersey country house, that Benton MacKaye, then recuperating from the death of his wife, first conceived of his continent-reshaping plan for an Appalachian Trail from Maine to Georgia. And later it was Charlie who asked Frimbo (who figures in the following piece in his Old Curmudgeon guise) to assist the frail and venerable Louis Sullivan.*

It was one of those blustery March days when it looks as though the weather's up for grabs and absolutely nothing at all can surprise you. Nice weather for pterodactyls with fifty-one-foot wingspans. We were cutting across a corner of Madison Square, thinking only of hot chocolate, when suddenly we stopped dead. The voluminous figure in front of us was our good friend the old curmudgeon, a sedentary soul if ever there was one, and he was standing quite still, staring at the Flatiron Building, while the wind tugged at his fleecy locks. What on earth? "Oh, I always come down here once a year," he said cheerfully when we accosted him. "In memory of the great Chicago architect Louis H. Sullivan. More than fifty years ago, when Sullivan was an old man, and quite broke, I worked on his book 'The Autobiography of an Idea,' which some friends of mine were publishing to try and raise some cash for the old gentleman. He came to New York on just such a cold day as this for a last look at his buildings, and my friends asked me to show him around. We went down to Bleecker Street to see an office building of his—it's now the only Sullivan building in the city—and we came up here to see the Flatiron Building, New York's first skyscraper and the handiwork of another Chicagoan, D. H. Burnham. In the old days, before a Hundred and Sixteenth and Riverside was conceived, this corner, where Broadway, Fifth, and Twenty-third collide, was known as the windiest corner in the city. Policemen chased loungers away from the front of the Flatiron Building—they stood there hoping for a glimpse of an ankle. I *think* this was the origin of the phrase 'Twenty-three skid-doo.' We also looked for other Sullivan buildings, but discovered they had all been demolished. This upset the old man so much that he began to cry in the street, so I took him to a warm place and gave him hot chocolate. You want hot chocolate, too? Well, stick with me. I'm on my way to a new restaurant."

The old curmudgeon always likes a new restaurant, and he set a diagonal course across the square. "There's nothing much to be said for Madison Square," he said, "except that baseball, which was known as the New York Game, began right here, no matter what the farmers upstate may tell you. I am pleased that the Flatiron Building has outlasted Stanford White's Madison Square Garden, which was rather too ornately decorated. The last time I was ever in *that* building was to watch a World Series—that was long before radio— on an electric scoreboard laid out like a baseball diamond. If the left fielder's light blinked, it meant he couldn't handle the ball. Then a bell rang. That meant the batter had reached first. A long wait, then another bell. He was on second. Loud cries from the audience. The suspense was terrific. Finally, a third bell! A tumult. Of course, the telegraph operator had got all this information previously and was prolonging the agony. I think a home run took ten minutes."

The restaurant the curmudgeon ducked into was Nymms, a cheerful-looking spot in the New York Merchandisers Mart, on the northeast corner of the square—a new office tower that stands on the site of what was often called the Jerome Building. "The Jerome Building deserved to go," said the curmudge. "It was later turned into the Manhattan Club, on whose premises that unpleasant cocktail the Manhattan was concocted. Ah, there's a picture of Evelyn Nesbit, the girl on the red velvet swing. In fact, it's a cutout figure of her, sitting on a swing, swinging over the bar. My father very much disapproved of her, but I think he would understand why Stanford White fell for her."

A Bordo!

Hendrik Hertzberg's Frimbo send-up, reprinted here by kind permission of Workman Publishing Company, first appeared in their 1986 New Yorker *parody book,* Snooze: The Best of Our Magazine. *The cover of* Snooze *showed Eustace Tilley,* The New Yorker*'s celebrated, top-hatted dandy, getting a pie in the face.*

In 1926 a bulky young man, new to our staff, caused a bit of a sensation by wearing a soft, ticking-striped engineer's cap to work rather than the commoner fedora or homburg. The cap was only the tip of the iceberg, as this, his first piece, shows. After almost fifty years with us, E. M. Bimbo at last stopped wearing his cap indoors and making choo-choo noises while he typed. Mr. Bimbo has always enjoyed writing about himself in the third person. Though a young man at the time of this vignette, he is already quite stuffy.

"Ah, there you are, my dear boy," said E. M. Bimbo, the world's greatest railroad bore, when we presented ourself the other day at his table in the Oyster Bar of Grand Central Station. "Do sit down. Care for a mullet? No, I expect not."

Mr. Bimbo reached into a large vat on the floor next to his table and pulled out a small, gray, wriggling, live fish. With a sharp knife, he expertly beheaded, gutted, and filleted it, then rolled it into a cylindrical shape, wrapped it in a bit of cabbage leaf, and, with a flourish, popped it into his mouth.

"A little delicacy I became acquainted with in the dining car of the Hokkaido Express," said Mr. Bimbo. "A remarkable people, the Japanese. Remarkable. First-rate trains. Extraordinary. Tip-top. Zzz."

Mr. Bimbo had momentarily dozed off, as he often does during the later stages of his luncheon, even in railroad stations. An attentive waiter glided over and gently poured a splash of ice water over the great man's head.

"Ah, that's better," Mr. Bimbo said brightly, sitting up with a start. "Well, my boy, how are you? But never mind that. I didn't ask you here to discuss your health. Nor are the Japanese on my agenda. I've got a train to catch"—and here Mr. Bimbo gestured toward the Oyster Bar's door, through which a glimpse of the waiting room, smoky, blue, and vast, could be caught—" and I have little time for idle chitchat. Purposeful activity! Discipline! That's the spirit of the age. You see, I have just returned from Italy, and it is the heartening progress of that country with respect to that spirit, and its application to the field of my special interest, which, or rather that, I have summoned you here to discuss."

Bimbo sat back and folded his hands complacently across his midsection, which, as he is extremely fat, is more than ample, and which, that day, was enclosed in a waistcoat of gray wool herringbone, the same material of which the rest of his suit was made. With his thumbs, he fiddled thoughtfully with his watch chain, which is heavy and gold, and which terminates in a timepiece that, as he once boasted to us, is accurate to within a tenth of a second per century. "As you know," he began, "I have long been interested in train schedules, of which I have an enormous, carefully catalogued collection from all over the world. I have whiled away many an afternoon paging through such schedules, reliving this or that memorable journey upon the Stockholm-to-Göteborg *jarnwag,* or the Trans-Dakota Express, or the jungle route of the *chemin de fer gabonais.* What has struck me about railway schedules, after a lifetime of study, is their almost entirely fictional nature. In my experience, the train listed in the schedule invariably arrives and departs at different times from the train that is actually upon the track. Nowhere, of course, has this been truer than in Italy, a land known more for the antiquity of its churches and the excellence of its pasta than for the promptness of its systems of transportation—that is, until recently. Are you getting all this, my boy? Or should I talk more slowly?"

"No that's fine," we said. (We write quickly, and in any case we make it a practice to use only manufactured quotations.) "What brought you to Italy?"

"Signore Mussolini was sponsoring a scientific conference, and I'd been invited. As you know, my own science is lexicograhy. Signore Mussolini's is nutritional socioengineering. He is interested in developing new uses for castor oil, particularly as an instrument of persuasion. One might even call him the George Washington Carver of castor oil, though I don't suppose he would wholly approve of the comparison."

"You didn't actually meet *Il Duce,* did you?" we asked breathlessly.

"Of course I did," Mr. Bimbo replied—rather brusquely, we thought, and we must have shown our distress, for the great polymath's face softened and he gave our hand a gentle squeeze. "There, there," he said kindly, then settled back to resume his narrative. "In fact, as it will not astonish you to learn, it was a mutual interest in railroading that brought us together. At a reception at the Palazzo Venezia, Signore Mussolini spotted the small New York Central pin I am in the habit of wearing in my lapel.

" 'You wear the badge of the Strada Ferrata Centrale del Nuovo-York, do you not?' he asked me, not with the tory sneer that some who have never met him say is habitual with him, but rather in the eager, excited tones of a small boy.

" 'Indeed I do, and so may you,' I replied in my serviceable if somewhat too French-accented Italian. And with that, I took the pin from my lapel and affixed it to his own. This is no easy task when the jacket in question is as encrusted with medals as was the one he wore. *Il Duce* is not as tall as I expected him to be, by the way. I suppose he is one of those lucky people who 'photographs well,' to use a distasteful barbarism. I remember discussing the question with Ramon Navarro in the club car of the *Pacific Queen.* We had just passed through Monterey when—"

"*Il Duce,* Mr. Bimbo," we said gently. The great man's mind, like an unbraked handcar on the down slope of the Pikes Peak narrow gauge, sometimes races ahead of where it ought to be. "You were saying . . ."

"Ah, yes. *Il Duce.* He was delighted, and naturally he

insisted on returning the favor. He had this sent to my hotel the next morning, along with a shirt to wear it with." Mr. Bimbo tapped a small silver pin in the buttonhole of his lapel—a tiny, sculpted bundle of sicks or rods with a cunning little ax-head protruding from the top. "Can't do much with the shirt, though. It's of the finest Ethiopian cotton, but the color is coal-black. I'd look like Bugsy Siegel in it."

Mr. Bimbo sighed. "In any event," he continued, "Signore Mussolini launched into an animated discussion of trains. As he spoke of the hundreds of new dining cars, sleeping cars, and cattle cars built by the state railway companies, and of the thousands of kilometres of new track he has projected as part of his scheme for the uplift of Ethiopia, his great jaw jutted forward like the smooth cowcatcher of one of the futuristic new locomotives of which he is so justly proud. He was especially keen that I visit the railway terminal he has had built in Rome. 'You are sure to agree, Signore Bimbo,' he said, 'that our new Stazione Ferroviario is a fit setting for Europe's fastest trains.' Or was it Europe's fascist trains? Ah, well, never mind. It doesn't matter."

"What happened next?" we asked.

"As *Il Duce* talked on, the other dignitaries began to mutter among themselves. After all, we were holding up the whole reception line. It was only polite to move on—as, come to think of it, we would be well advised to move on now."

Mr. Bimbo heaved himelf to his feet and maneuvered his great bulk toward the door. But he was still talking, and we trotted eagerly after him. "The last thing Signore Mussolini said to me," the great lexicographer went on, "was that I really should go to the new station the very next morning—early enough, preferably, to watch the eight-twenty to Venice pull out under full steam."

"What was it like?" we asked.

"I don't know," Mr. Bimbo replied. "You see, my cab was held up in traffic, much to my annoyance, and when I arrived the eight-twenty was only a puff of smoke and a caboose in the distance. It had left right on time. Or, as *Il Duce* would say, *in perfetto orario*."

Go Far East, Young Man

Frimbo was what train buffs call a "mileage collector," meaning someone who'll fly around the world to reach two miles of railroad track he's never been over before. Frimbo kept track of his ever-accumulating totals in what he called his "wheel reports," meticulously kept records jotted down in tiny notebooks or on the back of a press pass or flattened cigarette box—anything portable enough to make its way to the top of Sumatran mountains. Every time he passed a station, he set down a new mileage total, which, he made sure, was always accurate to the hundredth of a mile.

Lee H. Rogers, an old Frimbo friend who's become a preeminent international transportation planning consultant—he's worked in Bolivia, Ghana, and El Salvador, among many other countries, and helped plan Indonesia's modern road and rail systems—reports that the Sumatran cog railways Frimbo rode and recorded twenty years ago are still alive and still spectacular, although trains now get hauled around by less flamboyant, if far more dependable, Swiss diesels.

1,886,491.93	Villeneuve-Prairie (S.B.) [SNCF]
1,886,493.19	Villeneuve-St-Georges-Triage [SNCF]
1,886,494.45	VILLENEUVE-ST-GEORGES [SNCF]
1,886,496.34	Montgeron-Crosne [SNCF]
1,886,497.60	Yerres (S.B.) [SNCF]
1,886,498.86	Brunoy [SNCF]
1,886,502.01	Combes-la-Ville-Quincy [SNCF]
1,886,503.16	Lieusaint-Moissy [SNCF]
1,886,507.57	Cesson [SNCF]
1,886,510.09	Le Mée (S.B.) [SNCF]
1,886,511.35	MELUN [SNCF]
1,886,515.76	Bois-le-Roi [SNCF]
1,886,518.80	Fontainebleau Avon [SNCF]
1,886,523.72	Thomery [SNCF]
1,886,525.84	MORET-LES-SABLONS [SNCF]
1,886,526.47	Saint-Mammès [SNCF]
1,886,532.77	MONTEREAU [SNCF]
1,886,539.70	Villeneuve-la-Guyard [SNCF]
1,886,542.85	Champigny-sur-Yonne [SNCF]
1,886,547.26	Pont-sur-Yonne [SNCF]
1,886,554.19	SENS [SNCF]

One of Whitaker's wheel reports

September rains lashed the big plate-glass windows of the Lexicographers' Club, a club whose very existence is the best-kept secret of New York, and in the front of the bright library fire Ernest M. Frimbo, world's greatest railroad buff, fresh from two thousand miles of railroading in the Farthest East, stretched out in a comfortable chair and crossed Dacron-clad legs. Frimbo's trousers had several small holes in them. Burn marks, they looked like to us. What was this?

The Frimbo we have known for many years has invariably been impeccably dapper.

"Those, young man, are battle scars," the great man said, following the direction of our eyes. "Sumatra, you know. A gift from the ancient and honorable wood-burning locomotives of that wildly beautiful island. So many wood-burners there! And so many hills! At first, I thought it was scorpions biting my thighs. Then I realized I was aglow. 'You can't throw away those holy pants,' my companions commanded. 'They should be presented to a museum.'

"Theoretically, there are no passenger trains at all in parts of Sumatra. That is what they tell foreigners. Then you see one and ask why you can't get on it. 'Oh,' say the railway officials, 'that train is not suitable for visitors. But,' they say, 'there is a freight train that goes to the same station, and we can arrange for your party to be placed on the head end of that train.' So there we were, a band of twenty—Americans, Britons, a government official from Hong Kong; it's a group that meets once or twice a year, anywhere in the world (many of us had last met months before, when we startled the population of Florence by rolling into the main station in a cloud of steam)—in an open-platform coach directly ahead of a great big Japanese steam locomotive spewing wood smoke and char all over everything. Such are the grades that the engine must push you up. If you trailed the engine and a coupling broke, there would be little chance of saving you. These are rack-and-pinion railways—cog railways, we call them in this country. There's a center rail in the track with slots in it, and gears on the underside of the locomotives that engage these slots. The trains travel at six or seven miles an hour. It is a luxuriously willful waste of time traveling this way instead of on the decrepit Sumatran buses, but it's a wonderful way to see the jungle and the resident snakes. Over great high passes and scary bridges, twisting through wild gorges. Some of the most beautiful country in the world. The railway stations are the social centers of the dark little towns at all hours, whether a train is expected or not, and in each town we were greeted by five thousand children excited by the fact that real foreigners with cameras had been presented to them for their inspection. In one town, the local schoolteacher came aboard. 'I heard from the stationmaster,' he said, 'that you were coming again this year. School's over for the day, and we're all going home.' He and his gang of children rode out with us to the end of the line, and he kept them reasonably subdued. It was the last train of the day—maybe of the year—and while we waited for our hotel drivers to pick us up in cars and take us home to dinner, my companions thought they'd like to photograph the glorious variety of steam locomotives hanging around the railway yard under their canopies of wood smoke. Sumatra's really a paradise for anyone who has ever wanted to play with trains—West German, East German, Dutch, Japanese, Swiss, and British steam locomotives of all shapes and every dimension, from little ones the size of dogcarts to huge beasts with twelve driving wheels. But my companions found the children within six inches of their lenses. I am not a photographer, so my friends appealed to me. One little boy stuck out his tongue at me, and I staggered toward him Boris Karloff fashion, turning my fingers into claws. He shrieked with delight and ran away from me. I followed him, and so did all the children, also shrieking with delight. In two minutes, the way was clear for my friends to photograph whatever they wanted. That's life in the Indonesian highlands."

Frimbo's journey took him from New York to San

Francisco—by train, naturally. He flew from San Francisco
to Taipei for the trains of Taiwan, an island whose hundred-
and-eighty-mile-long main line has forty-six expresses a day,
and he observed in the city of Kao-hsiung the construction of
a four-hundred-and-forty-thousand-ton tanker. Then it was
off to Djakarta, in the lowlands of Indonesia. The lowlands
of Indonesia were left behind as quickly as possible. There is
oil in the lowlands, and the Indonesians there have discovered
the delights and perils of the motorcar and the rubber tire.
Automobiles, buses, and oxcarts do not blend well on the
narrow highways of the region. "Djakarta, the capital city, is
trying to develop the worst air pollution in the world," Frimbo
told us. "It has already pulled abreast of Tokyo and Los Angeles, and has shaded Mexico City. The American tourist, an
invisible ring in his nose, lands at the airport in a 747 and
feels thoroughly at home breathing this familiar atmosphere.
He lodges himself in high-rise hotels for prices greater than
you would pay at the Brown Palace, in Denver, or the Clift,
in San Francisco—hotels that know a great deal more about
the business. One Continental breakfast, obviously prepared
with a hummingbird in mind, came to four dollars and thirty-
five cents.

"So, on to Malaysia and the Eastern & Oriental Hotel, in
Penang, a city on the island that with reason calls itself the
Pearl of the Orient. The E. & O.—it's listed that way in the
Penang phone book, which is entirely in English—is the Pearl
of Penang. I like to think that at the E. & O. I sat under the
palm tree that Somerset Maugham sat under to write about
English tea planters and their difficult wives. My palm tree,
under which I usually had breakfast, lunch, *and* dinner, was
in the forecourt of the hotel, along its own private five-
hundred-foot length of seawall, and from there I could look

across the straits to the mountains on the mainland of Asia. Fighting off an occasional seagull as I dined, I watched the fishing boats arrive with prawns or lobsters, knowing that whatever they brought in would be part of my next meal. Noiseless Malay waiters padded about to ask, 'Another fresh-lime drink, sir?' I soon felt like a full-fledged wealthy colonial malefactor of the good old days. The E. & O. charges twelve dollars a day less than the Djakarta high rises, by the way.

"Across the straits lies another delight—the Malaysian State Railways, which look just about as they did when part of Malaysia was under British administration as the Federated Malay States. Sleepy, leisurely trains from a more placid part of history bumbled through the countryside while I sat in the restaurant car consuming prawn soup in a three-hundred-and-ninety-degree-heated bowl, served sometimes with seaweed, Chinese style, and beer made under license from two Holland breweries. In the morning, in the sleeping cars, bearers bring you a cup of English tea and a distinctly Malaysian ripe banana.

"Out in the jungles of Indonesia, I should have said, all the big boys—Uniroyal, Goodyear, Dunlop—have almost secret plantations, guarded by high fences and private police. One of the plantations, where we were guests, has developed the perfect solution to the energy problem. The little locomotives that snuffle through the plantation, which grows palm-oil nuts for the international soap market, burn the husks of the nuts. When day is done the hostlers in the roundhouse scoop out the ashes from the fireboxes of the locomotives and cart this highly valuable fertilizer out to where new palm-oil-nut trees are being planted. The system is self-perpetuating, and the only cost is the hand-forging of an occasional repair part for the steam engines."

Frimbo grew silent and stared into the fire. A noiseless Lexicographers' Club non-Malay waiter appeared by his side. Frimbo awoke as from a brief trance. "It's hot under this palm," he said. "Time for my four-o'clock fresh lime, please."

A Welsh Folly

Occasionally, as here, I took a Frimbonian theme and ran off with it on my own. The Prisoner has since acquired strong cult following and is now available on videotape.

I've just spent an amazing two days in the town of Penrhyndeudraeth, in North Wales, in July. I began by motoring up from Glastonbury, which was overrun with real hippies, just after throwing a Fourth of July party in London that featured a huge bowl of chili and a lot of whiskey and South African dance records. The English aren't used to juxtapositions like that. I mean, they enjoyed themselves, but they couldn't understand why. It puzzled them. They kept coming up and asking, "Did you put cannabis in the chili?" And I was off to Wales in my Budget Rent-a-Car, with my friend young Henry from New York at the wheel and hum-

ming "Men of Harlech"—it was a gorgeous day—to find
(1) the place where they made "The Prisoner," a super TV series that pitted Patrick McGoohan against the most confusing
conspiracy in history, and (2) the only narrow-gauge railroad
in the world that serves draft beer. In the series, which was
shown on CBS in 1968 and 1969, McGoohan is trapped in a
bright-colored seaside village that seems to have been assembled from every startling bit of architecture ever developed
in a warm climate. The village has towers and spires and
domes and colonnades and cottages and palm trees and a
beach and enough nooks and crannies to fill a city, and it might
be in Italy and it might be in Greece, it might be in Surinam—
well, the point is where the hell is it? Because you can't quite
place it. Patrick McGoohan can't escape from the village, because he is hounded by giant balloons, and he can never figure
out why he's there or who's running the place. He keeps asking
people in the village, "Are you No. 1?" But everyone's evasive.
"I'm No. 7." "I'm No. 2." The TV show didn't last—it went
off the air in New York City after sixteen episodes. I think it
puzzled people, and maybe it scared them a little. But I
thought it was funny because it seemed completely human in
its bizarre way, and the village continued to hop around in
my mind, owing to the question of where the hell?

Now, it was in London, at the Fourth of July party, that
Henry and I learned the truth about the village in "The Prisoner." It's up in North Wales on Cardigan Bay, on a thickly
wooded peninsula near Harlech Castle and many abandoned
slate quarries, and almost in the shadow of a great hunk of
wild Celtic mountain called the Snowdonia Massif, and it's
entirely the work of a ninety-two-year-old Welsh architect
named Sir Clough Williams-Ellis, who has been building it
for almost fifty years. We had heard about the little railway

previously, and threw it in for good measure. Neither Henry
nor I had ever been to Celtic Wales before, and I didn't know
what to expect, and certainly no one could expect Penrhyndeudraeth or the Festiniog Railway. But even aside from them
we discovered that Wales is not the same place as England.
As soon as you drive over the line from Shropshire, you get
the feeling: all bets are off. In England, the fields and the
copses and the villages are all *just so*. The county is *settled*.
The impression in England is: people arrived here several
thousand years ago, and they drew up some rules and they're
still here, and they've still got 'em, and that's that. But Wales
is unpredictable.

We see wild crags, lambs almost hidden by ferns, slate
roofs, pieces of slate stuck in the ground vertically to make
fences. And there is mist and cool air in the mountains and
warm sun down below. Just before sunset, our car is parked
in a slot marked "RESIDENTS ONLY" at Sir Clough's village,
and Henry and I have slipped behind a couple of rhododen-
dron bushes to put ties on for dinner in the main dining room.
The name of the village is Portmeirion—officially, the Hotel
Portmeirion—and a resident is anyone who has booked a room
overnight. The setting sun is glinting off the sire of a dome
and a campanile. Yellow, white, blue, and red cottages—just
like on TV—are nestled around a little beach. Low tide. It's
very still, and the only person we can see is a guy spinning
around out on the water in a blue-and-yellow rubber kayak
called *Octopus IV*. There are some city pigeons on the salt
flats, a couple of gulls are crying, the leaves of a palm tree
are just barely shimmering next to a Union Jack and a flag
of the Principality of Wales. Wowie! This place looks just like
Capri, only more so. And much cuter, too. Two very inac-

curate little cannons are trained on the bay. There's a statue of Atlas over there inscribed "TO THE SUMMER OF 1959 IN HONOUR OF ITS SPLENDOUR." Another plaque says, "1971 HIGHLY COMMENDED." Somewhere, water is splashing. Four black ducks fly overhead in formation. And there's a tree that was planted on Sir Clough's eightieth birthday. It's doing very well. And there's half of a coracle, ivy-colored. Also a half-moon in the sky. A single moo from somewhere. I feel just a litle giddy. Noël Coward songs (oh, yes, did you know that he stayed here for a week and wrote all of *Blithe Spirit* in that time?)—Noël Coward songs, I say, pulse through my mind: "In a bar on the Piccola Marina" and "Quite for no reason I'm here for the season, and high as a kite. Living in error with Maude at Cap Ferrat, which couldn't be right."

Perhaps a little dinner will calm me down. The dining room is part of a large country house—the only building on the property when Sir Clough moved in and started tinkering fifty years ago. Several older English couples are holding conversations barely above a whisper. "I did my training in oil at . . ." "We've collected old silver all our lives." "I had a horrid experience in London." The waiter brings melon, and, when he takes it away again, says, "Thank you, sir." Henry whispers, "Is that a Buddha I see before me?" "Yes." Our mood does not subside. In fact, it may be catching. A lady at the next table gets the silent giggles and cannot finish her *gâteau*.

Outside, a sign says, "TO BELVEDERE, SEA LAWN AND GROTTO."

We drive to the nearby official town of Penrhyndeudraeth for a breath. All low gray slate and all closed down. One shop

window lighted up: "ALCATRAZ UNISEX BOUTIQUE." Then
back to our Portmeirion cottage, up a winding stair.

The next day, after a spot of brekker, we have a word
with Michael Trevor Williams, hotel manager for twenty-
three years. The hotel is spotlessly and efficiently maintained.
He says that Sir Clough has been persuaded to slow down on
new construction, lest the place get out of control; that "The
Prisoner" was shot at Portmeirion one September, the film
crew arriving unexpectedly with about a hundred extras, thus
necessitating the revival of several elderly resident retired colo-
nels with brandy; that the series was never shown on Welsh
TV; that Portmeirion was never consciously intended to be
like anything, but just gay and amusing; that the hotel can
accommodate about a hundred; that among its guests have
been Richard Hughes, Bertrand Russell, a number of diplo-
mats, Alastair Sim (who comes in August), Sir Alec Guinness,
Maggie Smith, and some Americans (who expect frightful efficiency); that the hotel staff, including shopkeepers and maintenance men, numbers just over a hundred. "What else can
I tell you about this dotty place? It becomes a way of life. Oh,
will you excuse me a minute? There's the manager of the
maintenance staff, and he's very elusive. We're expecting a
visit from the fire officer tomorrow. Fire precautions are so
fierce. We spent ten thousand pounds on the main building
last year."

Mr. Williams, when he returns, says he thinks Sir Clough
will be around later in the day.

So we drive to the seaside village of Portmadoc for a ride
on the Festiniog Railway, a narrow-gauge railway with two
Fairlie double-ended locomotives, built on the premises in
1879 and 1886. The Fairlie is like a Pushmi-pullyu. Two

stacks, two boilers, and the driver stands in the middle. The Festiniog's Fairlies are as sound as bells. My friend Ernest Frimbo, the world's greatest railroad buff—who is known over here, I have discovered, as the world's greatest railroad traveler—is an honorary engineer of the line. The Festiniog was built to haul slate, and the tracks run from the seaside quite quickly into mountains. Geraniums in the station window boxes. Lace curtains on the stationmaster's windows. Bright sunshine. For sale in the station: Fetiniog pillowcases and *Sammy the Shunter,* by Eileen Gibb, about a switch engine. (" 'What's the matter Sammy?' asked Mr. Buffin, his driver. 'You're making a queer kind of noise this morning.' 'There's a nasty pain in my boiler,' whispered Sammy in a trembly voice. 'Oh dear, I do feel ill! My wheels are shaking.' ")

"I remember a narrow-gauge line at Badami, in western India," says Henry. "Very slow, and broiling in the carriages. You could walk along beside the train to get a little air. Monkeys in the trees all along the way. They didn't come in the train, though. Although—I don't know—maybe they were in first class. I was in third."

A third-class ticket on the Festiniog is £1.10. First class is £1.30. That's for a nineteen-mile-round-trip ticket from Portmadoc to Dduallt and back at a top speed of about twenty miles an hour. The Festiniog Railway has a one-foot-eleven-and-a-half-inch gauge; standard railroad tracks are four feet eight and a half inches apart. The Festiniog carries four hundred thousand passengers a year, but it is sustained in large part by volunteer labor. Gangs of schoolboys, accompanied by a master, do maintenance work on the right-of-way and other volunteers rebuild carriages, fire up the engines, sell "Sammy the Shunter" books, make bulletin boards for the stations, and in general do whatever has to be done to augment the small permanent paid staff. The Festiniog is advertised as "The Most Wonderful Railway in the Kingdom." The peak month is August, with thirteen trains a day between Portmadoc and Dduallt each way. No trains at all in January, but there are a few holiday specials at Christmastime. A first-class ticket entitles you to a seat in an observation car with large rear windows and access to the draft beer, so Henry and I decided to go first. The train had ten pony-size coaches and a puffing butterball of an engine, named *Blanche* and painted black and green with red trim and bright, shiny brass. Across a causeway and into the green countryside. We settled down in plump armchairs in the observation car and ordered pints of draft beer. Since the entire right-of-way occupies only a few feet, we had plenty of countryside to take impressions from. Swans and cows on a salt flat. A slate farmhouse with a black-and-white dog in front of its red door. Two little lambs quite unstartled and almost hidden by ferns a few feet from the rain. Harlech Castle a small gray squiggle on the horizon. A slow climb through pines, scrub oaks, and rhododendrons, past prospects and vales, to a high place where we ran along for more than a minute at eye level with a floating, soaring hawk flying over a valley a thousand feet below. Finally, at Dduallt halt, a chance to get out and stretch before a more rapid, buckety-buckety descent to Portmadoc. The engine driver delayed the return journey until the guard came running back to the train with a cup of tea.

Sir Clough Williams-Ellis, it turned out, is as remarkable as his buildings, an uncommon man even for a kingdom where the general run of subjects is uniquely unique, to say the least. Sir Clough was toasting himself before a fire when we got

Whitaker, with some Welsh friends, on the Festiniog Railway

back to Portmeirion. He is six feet two inches tall and, at ninety-two, is in excellent health. He is as bright as a button, friendly, a charmer, and something of a dandy. He had on a blue suit, a canary-yellow waistcoat, a blue-and-white polka-dot cravat, a blue silk display handkerchief, and brown suède shoes. "Well," he said, rising to his full height. "Here we are. Did you enjoy the Festiniog? Good. My uncle was chairman of the line for many years. He presented the chairmen of the Great Western Railway and the London & North Western Railway, two of the great trunk lines of Britain, with silver medals and free first-class passes on the Festiniog. They could do no more than respond with free gold passes on the G.W.R. and the L. & N.W. And my uncle, of course, then went whizzing about all over England for the rest of his life, and lived to be ninety-two."

Sir Clough, who wrote a book in 1928 warning about the

coming of megalopolis, helped develop the idea of the green belt around cities and, after the Second World War, was the first chairman of the first New Town in Britain, Stevenage. He describes himself as "rather a curiosity." "I never had any architectural training, except three months' work in the office of Sir Edwin Lutyens, the designer of New Delhi, a man whose work is now completely out of fashion, and *he* would never talk seriously about architecture. 'Very dangerous,' he would say, 'all this talk. It is bringing the ears so far forward they will act as blinkers to the eyes.' I'm a rogue architect. I was very nervous when Frank Lloyd Wright came to visit here, but he never had any formal architectural training either, and he took it like a lamb. Indeed, he conducted me around. Wonderful old prima donna, wasn't he? I first met him in 1937, when we were both on a train going to Moscow for a town-planning conference. There was a great scene at the Polish border when he refused to have his baggage examined. The authorities were about to send him home, but I walked him up and down and said, 'Oh, come off it,' and eventually he did. What I dislike about the work of some of my colleagues today is that they seem to be building for machines, and not for soft little animals such as you and me. Which may be why Portmeirion is supposed to speak for itself, but I may say it has all worked out very much as I'd first hoped and imagined. You've seen the campanile? It has an old brewery clock in its turret. It was one of the first things I built here, way back in 1928. It's quite useless, and it set a standard for everything I've tried to do here. Portmeirion is not only for my own enjoyment, it's also an outdoor museum of live architectural objects. I loathe committees unless I'm the chairman, so for many years when I was practicing architecture in London I spent most of my time on committees scribbling plans for

Portmeirion. Have you been in the dome? Or the town hall?"

"No," we said.

"Well, I'm afraid you'll have to do both. Come on."

Sir Clough strode off and began bouncing up and down a series of steep paths. Henry and I puffed in his wake, and he called remarks over his shoulder. "This urn looks a little crooked. There, that's better. It's plywood. Do you like that plaque? I happened to have a spare one, so I put it in that pediment. There's the dome. People say, 'What's it for?' I don't know. I usually tell them that, having a campanile, I was suddenly aware of an acute dome deficiency, which had to be corrected immediately. And here's the town hall."

The town hall has, underneath a cupola made from an old copper boiler, a unique seventeenth-century barrel-vaulted ceiling painted with scenes from the life of Hercules, which Sir Clough long ago rescued by dashing to a pre-demolition auction in Flintshire. "When the lot was announced," he said as we stood under the glowing ceiling, "there was dead silence. 'No bids?' asked the auctioneer. 'Yes,' I said, 'ten pounds.' 'Oh, come,' said he. Again dead silence. 'All right,' I said, 'thirteen pounds.' Now we'll see the car park. I'm very proud of that. It's the only car park I've ever seen that really *is* a park."

On the way to the car park, we passed a plaque inscribed with one of Sir Clough's mottoes: "CHERISH THE PAST, ADORN THE PRESENT, CONSTRUCT FOR THE FUTURE."

It was still a hot, hazy, bright-blue summer's day in Wales.

 *Letting Off Steam*

The Lexicographers' Club, the only Manhattan club that E. M. Frimbo, world's greatest railroad buff, calls his own, has, like other worthy midtown institutions, an exchange arrangement with a like-minded London club—in this case the Savile, where the two most popular dishes are cold steak-and-kidney pie and cold apple pie. Lunchtime conversation at the Lexicographers' is often stimulated by the presence of visiting Savileans, and last week when we dropped by the old place for a glimpse of our friend we found him just tucking into Senegalese soup, with broiled shad to follow. As we took a place at the common table beside Frimbo, the man across the table said to one of his companions, "Steam."

Frimbo's glance rose majestically from the soup to the gentleman opposite. "Steam locomotives?" he said.

"Steam cars, actually," said the gentleman. "My name's John Bunyon, and I live near Walmer, in Kent. I've just been spending the weekend driving Stanley steamers along the roads of Connecticut. Su*perb* machines! Do forty miles an hour up a hill in reverse. Go up almost anything to which they can maintain adhesion. It's a nice life. I'll be coming back in July—my hundred-and-ninety-ninth crossing—for an antique-car meet in Barre, Vermont, and I hope to drive a Doble then."

"Magnificent machine," said Frimbo. "The Doble people had a showroom on the west side of Times Square in the early twenties."

"And then the Doble company went into liquidation in April, 1931—though Doble continued to try to get steam vehicles manufactured. My great hobby," Bunyon went on, "is steam farm engines. Steam threshing machines, plowing machines, steam machines to haul farm wagons along country roads—some of them built by the nobly named firm of Ransomes, I believe. Thrilling."

"Yes," said Frimbo. "I attended a show in Nottinghamshire a few years ago of precisely that sort of machinery in steam. There was one thresher beautifully painted in a variety of colors, with a small smokestack protruding through a broad canvas awning, elegantly fringed, that stretched all the way back to where the driver sat in his cab, in front of a little pocket full of coal. Most of these farm engines were coalburners, you know. And how do you feel about steam *railway* engines?"

Bunyon said, "Well, since I live in Kent, I'm an old Southeastern Railway man myself, and I have several exquisite models of some of their earlier locomotives. Are there by any chance any steam locomotives in the States still running around your railways?"

"I'll be waving to you from one of them when you get to

Vermont," Frimbo said, "because a Bicentennial steam train
will be running there every day from July through the fall,
on what is left of the old Rutland Railroad, which is quite a
bit. In July and August, it'll be running between Bellows Falls
and Burlington; from mid-August through the foliage season,
it'll be running between Burlington and Bennington."

"Ah," said Bunyon, and he made an entry in a notebook.

Frimbo said, "Perhaps you should have come along with
me on my last trip West this spring. I stopped off for a day
in Jefferson City, that fine old riverine town on the Missouri,
for a look at another Bicentennial train, the *American Freedom Train*, which was one year old that day. It had been
hauled by various steam engines all the way from the Atlantic
seaboard to the Pacific coast, and was on its way back East.
It'll be in Harrisburg, Pennsylvania, for the Fourth of July,
and, as I was saying last year, when it began its journey, at
Wilmington, Delaware, on April 1, it's a hell of a good show.
It will be in the New York area in mid-August, but you'd
best see it en route; I saw it again last month in New Orleans,
and it should be making its way north to Birmingham, Alabama, where the magnificent steam engine that is the property
of Ross E. Rowland, Jr., the founder of the *American Freedom
Train*—the engine that started it off on its journey—will haul
it as far toward this city as the laws allow."

Mr. Bunyon made another entry in his notebook. Frimbo
and Bunyon then entered into a discussion of the efforts of
the Newcomen Society, a learned history-recording institution, to preserve the massive steam pumps that once worked
the tin mines in Cornwall. "Do you have anything of that sort
that I could see while I'm in this country?" Bunyon wanted
to know.

"Well, yes," said Frimbo. "A historical society I'm involved in has set up a museum in San Francisco to draw attention to the building that used to house the steam engines that once worked the endless cables to which the San Francisco cable cars attached themselves. The original steam engines survived the earthquake of 1906 but were replaced by electric engines in 1911."

More entries in the Bunyon notebook. "You Colonials are doing very good work," he said.

"I must accept that," Frimbo said. "And, while you're out on the Coast, go to Disneyland, in southern California, where you will see a perfectly restored narrow-gauge steam locomotive that was recovered by a friend of mine from the Godchaux sugar plantations, in Louisiana. It's still full of life, hauling passengers every day. And in Allaire State Park, near Asbury Park, in New Jersey, a narrow-gauge steam locomotive built by one of your countrymen's companies, Robert Stephenson & Company, will still be functioning this summer. And the next time you're at a steam-car rally in Connecticut, stop off at our Valley Railroad, in Essex, where, I've just heard from Oliver Jensen, its founder, we've just saved from dissolution a fine old New Haven Railroad parlor car—the kind with the green upholstered swivel seats—to provide our patrons with Bicentennial luxuries on our little steam trains."

"Narrow gauge," said Bunyon. "Down in my part of England there's that glorious little fifteen-inch-gauge Romney, Hythe & Dymchurch Railway. When you're next in London you must pop down to Walmer and let me drive you over to it."

Frimbo said, "That's the railway that ran a miniature armored train during the Second World War in case, I suppose, a nasty Nazi aircraft commander decided to take a potshot at the Dungeness lighthouse."

"Right!" said Bunyon.

At which point, bidding our two companions farewell, we wandered regretfully outdoors and back into reality.

 # Homecoming

From a letter from Shelburne, Vermont, signed by E. M. Frimbo, world's greatest railroad buff:

I'm staying at the Shelburne Inn. I used to come down here from Burlington, seven miles to the north, on a trolley car on my way to the bathing beach at Shelburne Point. The dirt highway on which the inn was situated has at last given way to macadam—Vermont compromises reluctantly with "progress." But the ell-ums alongside are even more stately, despite the ravages of the Dutch elm disease; these are, after all, Vermont elms, and Vermont was an independent republic for fourteen years in the eighteenth century, before it joined the thirteen original colonies as the fourteenth state. My way north at the beginning of every summer (since shortly after the War of Independence) commenced at Grand Central Terminal in a parlor car of the *Green Mountain Flyer*, which in eight hours took me to the Burlington depot, whence it was only a short walk to the house where my mother was born.

But Shelbourne had been the family domain (and I mean domain: six hundred and forty acres in all) until my great-grandfather sold out and went to the big city (Burlington). His domain was almost an independent country itself. The only things he bought from the outside world were iron bars and salt. He and his farmhands produced everything else they ate and wore and used. They even made the gunpowder with which my great-grandmother—according to the notches in the stock of her rifle—picked off four untoward Indians. The farm eventually became part of the vast estate of the Webb family, who by intermarriage with the Vanderbilts became high potentates in the railroad industry. I can walk from the Shelburne Inn in a few minutes to the Shelburne Museum, which is in part monument to the Central Vermont Railroad when it was under the jurisdiction of Dr. Seward Webb, as well as a monument to all the artifacts and memorabilia that will make New England a thing of joy forever. The largest artifact is the paddle-wheel steamer *Ticonderoga*, carefully beached on a grassy hillside but still looking as though she were just about to depart from her pier in downtown Burlington on her stately journey across Lake Champlain to Plattsburgh, New York, where we passengers could catch the evening Delaware & Hudson train to Montreal. We could go to Montreal on the old Rutland Railroad, crossing the northernmost reach of Lake Champlain on the only causeway ever built entirely of marble—tailings and reject slabs from the workshops of the Vermont Marble Company, down in Proctor, in southern Vermont. Or we could go to Montreal by the Central Vermont. Life really offered options in those days. All these trains disappeared, the steamship *Ticonderoga* was beached forever, and I hadn't been to Burlington or Shelburne in a dozen years. Then, a while ago, a cheerful young voice on the telephone asked me whether I would not like to return to ancestral territory in the only overland way I deem fitting. The Vermont Bicentennial Transportation Committee, in the goodness of its nostalgic heart, was preparing to foster a steam passenger train every day—except Tuesday—along the route of the old Rutland Railroad from practically the bottom of Vermont (Bellows Falls) to practically the top of Vermont (Burlington). I replied at once that if the committee would be good enough to procure for me a bedroom on the Amtrak night train to Montreal, the *Montrealer* (of course), I would be pleased to alight at Bellows Falls at three o'clock in the morning and, five hours later, join the first run of the *Vermont Bicentennial Steam Expedition*. Once aboard the *Montrealer*, I hastened to the dining car to have my first taste of two excellent dishes that the Amtrak management introduced earlier this summer for its French-speaking Canadian clientele—French-Canadian pea soup (*soupe aux petits pois à la Canadienne aux croûtons*) and quiche Lorraine. Washed down with a draught of white wine, naturally. Awaking refreshed at my accustomed hour of three, I alighted at Bellows Falls. I was approached by a policeman, who said, "I've been instructed to put you to bed for the night." In his squad car, we drove along the main street to a hotel in which not a light was shining. My escort produced a key, let me into the foyer, and said, "According to the law, I have to ask you to sign the register. Good night."

By eight o'clock, I had arrived at the new Bicentennial Parking Lot alongside the station from which the *Bicentennial Steam Expedition* would depart. A considerable crowd had already assembled, and I quickly realized, as I listened to the welcoming speeches, that this was to be not only a Bicentennial Expedition but a campaign train. I learned from the

speeches, too, that somewhere on the premises of the parking
lot the Bellows Falls Chamber of Commerce had buried a
time capsule, the contents of which were unknown to everyone
the day I was there. The *Steam Expedition* is the first regular
passenger train on the western slope of Vermont in a good
twenty years and constitutes one of the most ambitious Bicentennial projects undertaken by any state. In towns where
the old Rutland Railroad station had disappeared, the committee has put up cheerful little ones, and a half-dozen Vermont inns have undertaken to collect and deliver guests at
several of these stations. Trains will be running through Labor
Day. And why not? The track of the old Rutland Railroad—
just upgraded with a million dollars of federal money, on
behalf of the *Steam Expedition* and the freight service now
maintained over the line by the Green Mountain Railroad and
the Vermont Railway, the Rutland's heirs and assigns—runs
through some of the most beguiling landscape on this continent. As it progresses through Addison County ("Land of Milk
and Honey"), the eye and ear and nose become aware of the
proliferation of cows—black-and-white Holsteins for bulk and
brown Jerseys for creaminess—and wild flowers, from which
the county's busy bees distill some of our finest honey. None
of this honey was to be had in the little gift shop aboard the
train, but the shop offered anything up to a quart container
of Vermont Grade A maple syrup, a perfect condiment for
acres of Vermont blueberry pancakes. (Some of this acreage
is always available at the Shelburne Inn, whose management,
given proper warning, will pick you up at the Shelburne station.) The train is international, like the Amtrak dinner menu.
It is hauled by one of the last and handsomest steam engines
built for the Canadian Pacific Railway, and its cars are old

Long Island Rail Road commuter coaches—considerably upgraded.

The first run of this train got rapidly off schedule; not all
Vermont politicians are as taciturn as Calvin Coolidge, who
went to high school in Ludlow, through which this train
passes. Its progress was jolly: instead of looking like and
sounding like a mid-Manhattan political rally, what happened
in each little town, as the speeches were being made, looked
more like a ballet out of *Oklahoma!*, with the pretty wives
and daughters, when available, of the candidates weaving
through the crowds as they handed out propaganda. It was a
kind of musical chairs: the governor is running for United
States senator; the lieutenant governor is running for governor;
a state representative is running for lieutenant governor; and
the young state banking and insurance commissioner is running for secretary of state. They were all aboard; maybe I
missed a few others. One man who was definitely not aboard
was the Honorable John Liccardi, State's Attorney in Rutland,
who opened his window to greet the first test run of the Canadian Pacific loco and got a cinder in his eye. He called up
the state environmental office to complain, and was told that
the state's environmental-protection law had been waived for
this train. Vermonters know what they're doing: no-deposit,
no-return bottles are not permitted in the state; in a few
months there will be no billboards on any highways; and the
governor's food commission has just recommended that Vermonters grow more of their own food.

Which reminds me—nobody really minded the first-run
delays, and nobody went hungry. There was plenty to eat for
everyone in the grill car. There was also plenty of soot and
cinders for all—though it's much more expensive now to buy

the coal upon which steam locomotives are accustomed to subsist. The principal director of all this merriment is committee chairman and former Lieutenant Governor Jack Burgess, a well-spoken Vermonter, and a smart one, too. Burgess's principal aide-de-camp in practical matters is Bill Sprinkle, fifty-five years a railroad man, and once a navy machinist's mate. Sprinkle's major worry on the inaugural run was that something would not go wrong. Eventually, an axle under one car ran so hot that it was thought the car might have to be dropped from the train. Beaming, Sprinkle descended to the roadbed with his machinist's-mate kit and rapidly bathed and nursed the axle back to health, and we pushed on for Shelburne and Burlington.

Unlike Rockefeller's Williamsburg, the Shelburne Museum does not look like an M-G-M set for a musical about the Revolution. It looks like an old weatherworn Vermont village whose inhabitants have lovingly assembled out of their past an overwhelmingly varied assortment of things essential to or ornamental of life in old New England. They know the history of every cup and saucer, every dentist's instrument of torture, every bootmaker's nail, and they tell it with simplicity and glee. Vermont, our sister republic, is genuine Bicentennial country. It wasn't made in a day, and shows it. It really *is* two hundred years old.

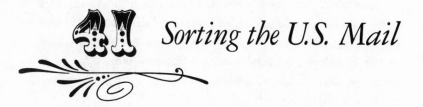 *Sorting the U.S. Mail*

The permanent shape of the United States is still undetermined—metropolitan areas, sometimes known as city-regions, have become altogether enormous and are still growing. The New York City area, for instance, is probably now about 200 miles wide, stretching from Scranton, Pennsylvania, to Montauk, at the eastern tip of Long Island. On the other hand, many deep countryside areas beyond the pull of metropolitan forces are still losing population.

Main-line American railroads, as Frimbo predicted, have been shedding trackage. On the other hand, much of their discarded branch-line mileage is in better shape than ever, because hundreds of enterprising, smallish "short lines," as they're called, have set up shop in the meantime and now operate over almost 50,000 miles of track, most of which they've upgraded themselves. In the New York area, two formerly drooping branch lines are even making sizable profits as public property, thanks in large measure to the innovative savvy of Frank T. Reilly, executive director of New Jersey's

282] *All Aboard with E. M. Frimbo*

Morris County Department of Transportation Management. It's a thriving hybrid arrangement: the county owns the tracks, in perpetuity, and a short line, the Morris & Erie, operates the freight service.

And Reilly is actually building the business: he recently helped lure a large Toys "Я" Us regional distribution center to his High Bridge Branch Railroad, and even managed to secure a million dollars in federal highway money for track work on this freight line—something never before accomplished in this country!

And 19,000 miles of abandoned trackage that even the short lines can't salvage are finding new life as "rail trails." Thanks to the can-do and unbudging insistence of thousands of citizen activists and recreationists all over the country, whose work is coordinated by the national Rails-to-Trails Conservancy headquartered in Washington, D.C., 782 former de-railed rights-of-way already welcome hikers and bikers, and another 1100 projects are in the works. It was far from the thoughts of the brilliant engineers and heroic work crews who, a hundred and more years ago, snaked railroad tracks through all of North America's rugged chains of mountains. But the very gentle grades and wide, easy curves that old steam engines had to have if they were ever to get over these jagged hills now make for thrilling, nonstressful, thumb-your-nose-at-all-the-frowning-peaks trail biking.

As to mail handling, the picture is still mixed: With the encouragement of the United States Postal Service, Amtrak is experimenting with "road-railers"—truck trailers full of (unsorted) mail bags that can be uncoupled from the back of trains in small towns and driven away. On the other hand, England still has a gleaming fleet of mail-sorting trains—and they're so efficient and productive that the Wisconsin Central, an

American railroad looking for profitable investments, has just bought control of them and will run them as a post-colonial absentee landlord.

Perhaps the third *edition of* All Aboard with E. M. Frimbo, *which presumably can be expected in 2019 or 2020, will have more definitive answers to these ongoing questions. Frimbo's "correspondent in Blue Hill, Maine," by the way, was E. B. White, whose later* New Yorker *writings were always given to Whitaker to edit.*

O̶ver a bowl of bay scallops at the Oyster Bar in his favorite railway station, Grand Central Terminal, E. M. Frimbo last week delivered himself of the following:

How to get the people out of the countryside—I guess that's the unwritten federal policy today. There are several federal agencies working on the project, but, naturally, none of them knows what the others are doing, and none of them wants to know. We need a new cabinet post—Secretary of Depopulation. Remember how easy it was, in the days when we were better organized, to get the Seminoles out of Florida and into Oklahoma? That wasn't very subtle, though, so the feds are cleverer now. They're using psychology. If life in your home town is made increasingly inconvenient, maybe you can be persuaded to move to the city, where the weight-throwing voters already live. The Interstate Commerce Commission let the railways get rid of their country passenger service, sometimes for not the best of reasons. Then the bus companies, which took over from the railways, began to whittle down

their service, sometimes to zero. Now the Civil Aeronautics
Board lets some airlines whittle down their service, too, to
zero. Suddenly, you're back in pilgrim days. If you want to
go anywhere or get anything, you do it yourself. Congress has
passed a bill, called by the trade the 4-R Act, that is so cleverly
worded that railways have started getting rid of thousands of
miles of railway lines that still carry freight to small communities. The man who owns the factory in your little town
decides to close down and move out. Your Chamber of Commerce can't find a customer for the factory, because no customer can get the freight service he wants. So the people who
worked in the factory move to jobs elsewhere. Then your
community decides to raise enough money to take over the
branch line that serves it. One way to do this is to float a
municipal-bond issue, which traditionally pays tax-exempt
interest—a device that makes the issue easier to sell. But the
feds have got news of this, and the IRS has ruled that an issue
for this particular purpose is *not* tax exempt. What the government is saying is that small towns no longer pay, so get
the hell out of them.

And now the Post Office. I just heard that they're starting
again to close rural post offices. You know the kind of small
town that had a fifth- or sixth-class post office. The postmaster
set aside a corner of his general store for post-office customers,
and his income as postmaster was mostly what he got for
selling stamps to his clients—a simple, inexpensive, *convenient* way of giving service to everyone in the township. Now
we don't care about our country cousins anymore. I've lived
in a lot of little towns. Brandon, Vermont, for instance, where
I holed up for a while, some time after—I admit—Thomas
Davenport invented the electric motor there. I was in the
household of one of the mail clerks on the local night-mail

train that ran between Burlington and Rutland. The mail came in from the south early every morning to our little post office, already sorted by the clerks on the train, and ready to be sent out instantly from the post office at breakfast time—mail that had been posted as far away as Washington, D.C., the afternoon before. I was learning to play the organ in the Congregational church, where the son of the family I was living with was the organist. When I was alone in the organ loft, I sometimes got away from the churchly manuals and started working out my own arrangement of "When It's Night Time Down in Burgundy"—until I got caught out one evening. As penance, I was required for a few weeks to go down to the railway station at half past nine at night on the days when Mr. Pollard, the father of the family, was working his way south from Burlington on the mail train to Rutland. Along with any letters of mine and of the family's, I carried a couple of tin buckets of food that Mrs. Pollard had cooked for him and a little parcel of clean laundry. Today, if I still lived in Brandon, where on earth could I post a letter at that hour of the evening and know that it would be on someone's desk in New York City before noon the next day? In my university years, I could go down to the railway station in Princeton, New Jersey, at ten-fifteen in the evening, hand letters to the mail clerk, and know that they would be delivered in Washington, D.C., the next morning.

This was the comfortable, easy pattern of communication—at three cents a throw—all over this country until the accession to the Postmaster Generalship of Arthur E. Summerfield, under Eisenhower. The Pennsylvania Railroad, which was as naïve then about the facts of life as it was years later about its horrendous merger with the New York Central, cheerfully named one of its mail cars, in big gilt letters, after the new Postmaster, even as he was setting about the dismantlement of this marvelous system of communication begun even before the Civil War. More and more mail began going out to the airports to be flown between the big cities, and that was fine for the big cities. And more mail went to the highway truckers, and that was fine for (a) the highway truckers and (b) the people who were running the Post Office patronage system; that is, local contract helps local boy make good. The mail car on the *State of Maine Express* from New York disappeared, along with the train that carried it, and my correspondent in Blue Hill, Maine, began complaining that it was taking two or three days longer for a letter to get to me from him. Well, Summerfield and his successors at last boiled the railway mail cars down to just one train—five nights a week between New York and Washington each way. It wasn't in any public timetable, and under no circumstances was it to carry passengers. But a couple of my old Pennsylvania Railroad cronies, now gone to what I hope is an extremely handsome reward, were always pleased to invite me aboard the nights they were working the train. It was an easy and early way of getting to Washington, and it cost me just the subway fare to Penn Station. I liked to get to Penn Station in plenty of time before the train departed—especially during bad weather, when, a few minutes before the train pushed off, a bunch of bags would come down the mail chute onto the platform and someone would say, "Well, where the hell do you want me to put the airmail tonight?" It was easy to spot airmail, because the mailbags that contained it were of a color not at all like the dirty gray of the standard mailbags; and the time lost while the Post Office was trucking the mail out to the nonexistent flights from Kennedy and LaGuardia and trucking it back to Penn Station was compensated for by the nimble fingerwork of the postal clerks on the train, who popped what must have been thousands of letters into this and that pigeonhole along the sides of the cars en route. So that when the train reached Baltimore or Washington, between four and five in the morning, the mail was all ready to be carted off direct to the substations in each city in time for the deliverymen to distribute it on their morning strolls. What a way to do it! Of course, it had to go. And it did: this last mail train made its final run at the end of June 1977. Philatelists arranged to post letters on it, so that they could get the mail-car cancellation on the stamps, and the letters *were* posted—twenty-five thousand of them. I'm not sure how many of them got canceled. I guess it was the first time the train had ever carried legal non–Post Office passengers: Amtrak, which wanted the train to keep running, had a bar car on the final southbound run. But I didn't feel like celebrating. Oh, I forgot one thing. The Post Office used to fine the railways for delivering the mail late. Perhaps we should start fining the Post Office now.

The Café Fanny

The Café Fanny didn't last, although George Lang is still flourishing. And the Biltmore itself is no more: its landlords smashed all its instinctive ornamentation late one night to avoid imminent landmarking, and then gave the gaunt skeleton of the old hotel unopenable windows and a new skin and proclaimed it an office tower. But the larger Grand Central District is on the rebound, with cheerful new streetlights that, courtesy of the local business improvement district, actually glow a dazzling white rather than the standard, postwar sickly orange.

One of the guests at a private party at the Café Fanny, on the ground floor of the Biltmore Hotel, the night before it opened for business was E. M. Frimbo. We turn you over to him:

I have always been fond of living in railway hotels, which are scarce in this country but rather more plentiful abroad. There is even one annexed to the station in Kuala Lumpur, the capital city of Malaysia. This is one that the British, in the days when Malaysia was part of the Federated Malay States, built with true Oriental opulence, topped by more minarets than you could count on the feet of a centipede. I was last there to attend the opening of the first Kentucky Fried Chicken in Malaysia—but I'd rather not go into that. The Biltmore has since the day the cornerstone was laid, in the early teens of this century, been a railway hotel of some renown, standing over the right-of-way of the New York & Harlem, which eventually became part of the New York Central, which eventually became part of the financial catastrophe known as the Penn Central. I have always had a proprietary interest in the Biltmore, having been for many years a shareholder in the New York & Harlem—not a bad investment, since shareholders were guaranteed a 10 percent dividend for four hundred and one years. Ah, me! The Biltmore was probably the most social railway hotel in the world when John McEntee Bowman, who was deeply involved in the annual National Horse Show, presided over it. I slept many a night there, and downed many a brandy Alexander, mostly in the rooftop supper club, where such young ladies as Jane Pickens, of the Pickens Sisters, sang—I described her in my memoirs as "pretty slim Pickens." There was also the Bowman Room, for dinner dancing, and there was the honorable custom of tea-ing and trysting under the celebrated clock in the lobby.

Hotels, like the rest of us, must swing with the times, and when Prohibition was imposed upon us—this was when I really began to dislike the concept of minority rule—the Biltmore had to start converting bars and such into shopfronts.

James Farley came to the rescue of the Biltmore and of my investment when, as Postmaser General under Franklin Delano Roosevelt, he engineered Repeal. Some of the Biltmore's shopfronts then disappeared in favor of a splendid enterprise on the corner of Madison and Forty-third called the Men's Bar. It must have been the most soft-spoken lunching place in midtown Manhattan, and it was certainly one of the most nourishing. Naturally, adjustment was in order during the Second World War, and for the specified meatless days the chef produced what I considered his greatest handiwork— eggplant steak, a vast three-inch-thick slab of this admirable vegetable gently broiled, and seasoned with a great panoply of Italian herbs. Then another swing of the times: the trains to Chicago, the trains to San Francisco and Los Angeles, even to Mexico City, that ran out of Grand Central Terminal, of which the Biltmore is an appendage, began to disappear, and the convenience of the Biltmore, a hotel beloved by all us incessant railway travelers, began to dwindle, too. Next came the ascent of women's lib and the notion that any institution blatantly labeled "Men's Bar" must be done away with. So a year or more ago there was a last supper for the assembled gentlemen, and the bar's forty-two-year career came to an end.

I head up a committee called Concerned Diners, and we were preparing a delegation to the legislature in Albany, its purpose to propose legislation setting up a state commission to designate landmark restaurants that must not be closed, when I learned that the Men's Bar was to be recommissioned in an entirely new costume, and that George Lang, a Hungarian-born restaurateur of grand repute, was to involve himself. The net result is the Café Fanny, which looks like, and is delicately scented like, the sort of age-old brasserie I am fond of frequenting when I arrive on the Donau Kurier at the Westbahnhof in Vienna. The dark woodwork, the pink-shaded brass sconces, the black-and-white checkerboard marble floor, and the hardwood floor of the slightly raised gallery that runs around three sides of the Café Fanny all represent a bit of a homecoming to me. And so does the menu, carefully captioned "Vorspeisen," "Salate," "Kaltes Buffet," and "Schnitzel Spezialitäten," *und so weiter.* "Sandwiches," murmured a young lady whom up to that moment I had thought quite—well, appetizing. "What is the Austrian word for sandwich?" she inquired, and on that double error she was sent to the showers.

It was the only untoward incident of the evening. There was music, mostly strings, and there *will be* music—violin and piano every weeknight at dinnertime. Breakfast at seven, and so on till midnight, every day of the week. There was, and there will be, pastry of devastating variety—all available, of course, *mit Schlag.* And Austrian white wines—Kremser Rosenhügler and the like—and an Austrian beer, Gösser, and all the Viennese coffees. The waiters, in their black vests and big white aprons, are another familiar touch. And why Café Fanny? Fanny Elssler was a Viennese ballerina of the mid-nineteenth century, who, the contemporary press said, took New York "by storm" in 1840, some years ahead of my arrival. George Lang told me at the party that, since all Viennese coffeehouses are named after characters, he had originally thought of naming the room the Café Augustin, after "O, du lieber Augustin," who is believed to have existed—to have been a singer-composer-poet who sang in the coffee-houses for free meals and was a friend of everyone. But the hotel people, who wanted a feminine name, and who had been doing a lot of research, came up with Fanny Elssler. She

was a familiar character to Lang, because when he was a little
boy in Hungary his parents had a porcelain figurine of her in
their dining room. I feel that the Café Fanny, like another
old favorite of mine, the Oyster Bar, is a big boost for the
renaissance of the Grand Central Terminal complex.

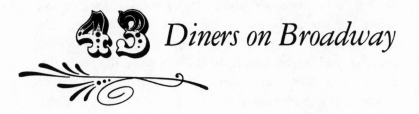 *Diners on Broadway*

E. M. Frimbo, our railway friend, recently delivered the following dissertation:

You really need a loose-leaf dictionary these days. Definitions that used to be hard and fast now dissolve into practically anything. I was brought up to think that "diner" meant a restaurant car attached to the express train on which your father was buying you breakfast on your way to your first day at school. Mine was in the English countryside, near Reading, some thirty miles west of London. Later, when I became acclimated to American ways, I discovered that "diner" also meant a dining car that at the end of its career on the rails had been bought by an enterprising restaurant man and set up, often still on its own wheels, alongside the town square. Still later I discovered that, in addition, "diner" could mean a restaurant on wheels which had been purposely built to resemble a railway dining car—at least on the exterior—and could be put wherever the owner wanted it. Most of the ve-

hicles in all three of these categories have now disappeared
from the railways and the town squares of this country. Now
when I suffer a yearning for one more meal in one of these
relics of my long, long lifetime I have to go down to Pennsylvania Station and eat aboard the club car of the *Senator,*
which departs eastbound at five-fifteen in the evening. The
Senator has no diner, but it puts me in Providence in mid-
evening, and there I simply walk down along the green that
slopes away from the station and climb aboard one of two
diners of the third variety that can be found there at night.
There's no point in leaving New York any earlier, for during
the daytime they are hidden away, gypsy fashion, in some
downtown recess. One of them has a good chef, the other does
not. I leave that up to you.

One of the parties I went to during a busy, busy week in
town was, I was told, to be held in a diner in this city, called
the Market Diner, way out West on Eleventh Avenue at Forty-
third Street. What is a Market Diner? Here I add a new entry
to my loose-leaf dictionary. A Market Diner brings evolution
about as far as it can go. From the outside, you get a vague
suggestion of diner, but once you have ascended the steps and
gone indoors you find that you are on the top level of what
can only be called a triplex. Off in the northwest corner, at
ground level, is a bar. On the top level is a restaurant large
enough to seat the population of the two Providence diners
ten times over. And in a basement there are party rooms, one
of them with a dance floor. Inside, the only resemblance to
the old town-square diners is the menu—fast food, and plenty
of it.

Or let us consider what has happened to "motel." A motel
began as an outskirts or semi-countryside sort of one-story
hotel or cluster of cabins—sometimes with a restaurant, which

almost always should have been called the Captive Audience Room. The idea was that you could park your car just outside your bedroom window and didn't need a bellhop to hustle your luggage. And it provided a scene dear to all Americans: a traveler could sit up all night and contemplate his car. Now a motel is, as often as not, in the midst of downtown, twenty stories high, and still without bellhops. You understand why I keep thinking about loose-leaf dictionaries.

But let's get to the question of why I was going to a supper party in a diner at eleven o'clock at night in what is definitely a rather rudimentary part of Manhattan. There is on Broadway a musical, *I Love My Wife,* that begins in the old-fashioned kind of town-square diner I've been talking about, and Joe Kipness and Terry Allen Kramer and Harry Rigby, who put the show together, had been thinking about where to hold a festival for the cast and the backers to celebrate an occasion almost unique in my memory: a Broadway musical's having paid off all its backers in considerably less than a year. Most seasons, of course, three-quarters of the shows produced on Broadway never pay the backers any profit at all, nor are there parties, except for the opening-night parties—and I have been to plenty of them—that end up with the reading of the newspaper notices (or should I say the obituaries?) and the declaration by the producer that he intends to fix up the show and keep it running despite the odds. You've seen it all if you saw the Fred Astaire movie of *The Band Wagon.*

Lots of cast parties are given at Gallagher's Steak House, and why not? It's in the theatre district, and it is accustomed to staying open—and cheerfully—late at night. Some happen in little East Side restaurants, some at Sardi's, and some in private houses. But there is always someone involved who would like to augment the repertory. And so it was that *I*

Love My Wife ended up in what might be called its natural habitat, a diner—a diner that was for that particular night a private nesting place, with a dance band and probably the most enormous fast-food menu in the United States. This was a menu that, like the one presented to guests at such an establishment as Lutèce, bore not a shred of price—a special Kipness-Kramer-Rigby menu born to flower but a single eve. Unaccustomed though I am to commanding a brandy Alexander even in the best of diners, I commanded one, and it arrived in perfect order. The wheatcakes that shortly followed were as thin as crêpes, and the syrup was maple-y. The full resources of the Market Diner were being put to the test by everyone else by the time I arrived. Everyone else, I might add, came early and stayed late. Sign of a good party. After all, no one is happier than a requited Broadway backer.

I settled in for a while at a table of fellow-Princetonians —yes, they get out West, too—whose principal ornament was Joshua Logan, first of the Princeton Triangle Club, next of Broadway, and now on a lecture tour. I moved on to the table of a decorator who with his American partner had recently finished redoing some rooms at the Barclay in Philadelphia. "Frimbo!" he shouted as I approached. "I've just come back from my native Japan, and I've ridden the bullet trains there. Now I'm even with you at last." I hailed Ann Miller, a tall spectacular in a shimmery, slithery dress: she looked as though she could still outfoot any competition in one of those great movie do-or-die dance routines. I hailed the pianist and leader of the dance band—Lee Evans, who had presided for quite some years over one of our best hotel dance bands and in his time had produced some of the best arrangements for some of the worst girl singers in this country. "Freedom at last!" I shouted to him as he broke into a bewitching samba. "Now,

finally, I have time to take my doctorate!" he shouted back.
Our conversation was interrupted when the waitress who had
kept my glass filled all evening suddenly bumped me, and,
turning around, I discovered that she was converting the
samba into her own version of the Hustle. Behind her, two
more waitresses were putting down their trays and beginning
to hoof, too. The wife of one of the three partners who run
the Market Diner came around the bend, frowned for a bare
moment, and then joined in the dance. Around the bend came
her husband, who quickly entered up *his* version of the Hustle.
A man whose dress and manner labeled him "co-owner" came
around the bend, yelling at his partner, "Hey! What the hell's
going on?" His confrere turned about, put his arms around
the man, and slowly moved him out of earshot, then resumed
his capers. By this time, nearly everyone else roundabout had
signed up, too. The samba ended. Lee Evans stood up and
said, "Sorry, it's two o'clock. That's all. Good night." It had
been a long time since I hadn't kept wishing a party would
end.

A 2,500,000
Milepost

Frimbo is a touch disingenuous in one part of this recollection. It's true that Amtrak's on-board merrymaking in honor of his greatest milestone came as a complete surprise to him. But, according to Arthur L. Lloyd, who recently retired as the director of public affairs for Amtrak's western division and who organized the lunch party and delivered the celebratory toast reprinted anonymously below, Frimbo and Lloyd had between them deliberately arranged the sequence of events beforehand so that Frimbo's 2,500,000 mark would be reached precisely when the Coast Starlight dramatically rounded the great horseshoe curve near San Luis Obispo. Carefully calculating Frimbo's mileage totals, as recorded in his wheel reports, they had guaranteed the inevitability of this quintessential Frimbonian moment by seeing to it that Frimbo took a thirty-six mile (no more, no less) commuter train ride the day before, from San Francisco to San Mateo and back.

Division Post [PRR]	3 618,355·40
Millham	3 618,356·30
Fair	3 618, 358·20
TRENTON	3 618, 358·50
New Jersey / Pennsylvania's	3 618,359·15
Morrisville	3 618, 359·90
Morris	2,618, 360·00
Levittown	2,618, 365·00
Edgely	3 618, 366·10
Grundy	3 618, 367·00
Bristol	3 618, 368·20
Croydon	3 618, 371·10
Eddington	3,618, 372·70
Cornwells Heights	3,618, 373·90
Andalusia	3 618, 375·10
Torresdale	3,618, 376·00
Division Post	3 618, 377·20
Holmesburg Junction	3,618, 378·60
Tacony	3 618,379·70
Wissinoming	3,618,380·70
Bridesburg	3 618, 381·50
Frankford [PRR]	3 618, 382·20

A letter just received from Ernest M. Frimbo, the eminent railway buff:

I always have a great time in San Francisco, a town that is forever full of world travelers, resident and transient. At dusk, they are apt to congregate for dinner in the Redwood Room of the Clift, my outpost when I am in that city, and the other night I came upon a dozen of them there whom I knew well. The abalone on the menu that evening was fresh out of the sea, the strawberries had all been properly marinated in kirsch, and the conversation flowed freely. One chap was just back from a mission to East Berlin (the chairman of the UIC, the confederation of European railways, is currently the doughty and uncompromising Dr. Volkmar Winkler, an East German railway official) and would be leaving on the morrow for Down Under. Another had flown in from his home in New Zealand for the annual board meeting of his corporation. A young couple, wanton dalliers in this group, were merely boarding a train to go East next day in time to intercept the QE 2 in New York and thereafter spend six weeks in Switzerland. And so it went. What was I doing, they finally wanted to know. "Oh," I told them, "a couple days from now I'll just be *bummelzuging* my way down to Los Angeles on the morning Amtrak train from Oakland. Of course, I will, as the train tops the Coast Range, a few miles north of San Luis Obispo, reach my two-and-one-half-millionth railway milepost."

"Well," said the man from New Zealand, "since none of us will be here then to see you off, let's drink a toast to that event right now."

After all these years, I know everything there is to know about the loneliness of the long-distance runner, but I felt sure that when I presented myself two days later at the station in Oakland I would find somebody aboard the *Coast Starlight* —the dining-car steward, a waiter, the barkeep—with whom I had journeyed in other days and with whom I could share a mild draught of something at the appointed milepost. Then, when I got to the station, I dicovered that boarding the train along with me were half a dozen people I recognized as friends of the world travelers with whom I had dined two nights before, all of them looking knowing and secretive. I bowed to them in my stateliest fashion, followed my attendant and my luggage into the roomette assigned me, and then ascended to the many-windowed upper level of the lounge car. The rains in California this year have done marvels for the countryside; instead of the customary dun-colored scenery, everything is Vermont green. Oakland to Los Angeles through a train window is among the great panoramas of the world, and, bemused by the unexpected greenery, I fell easily into my customary midday reverie. I was just deciding that I really must do something about celebrating my three-millionth mile in a less solitary manner—and I was figuring that I should attain this marker on the afternoon of June 10, 1984, en route from Hong Kong to the Chinese railway center of Canton— when one of my friends' friends came up top and said, "You're to report to the dining car at twelve-thirty promptly to lunch with us," and disappeared.

He was back at 12:28 to make sure. The diner was full to the brim, all forty-eight seats of it, once my escort and I had sat down at one of two tables side by side that were occupied by my friends. The fish chowder was sprinkled with the tiny shrimp that I never find anywhere but California, and the white wine of the Napa Valley was cool but exuberant. Even without benefit of Napa Valley wine, the steward, whose name badge proclaimed her to be M. Newman, and who is one of the first two women to have been put in charge of Amtrak dining cars, was looking as beamish as I was. The waiter, whose name badge proclaimed him to be T. Jones, was an old hand, so we exchanged greetings and clasped paws. After a while, I looked out the window, and said to my friends, "I'm glad not to be lunching alone on this occasion, because just five miles from now I—"

"Mr. Frimbo," said my escort, "you are a remarkably poor keeper of secrets. All is known to us." And indeed it was.

Five miles later, he rose to his feet, tapped on his wineglass with a knife, and said at the top of his voice, "Ladies and gentlemen, let us celebrate an auspicious occasion. Seated beside me is Mr. E. M. Frimbo, perhaps the world's most persistent traveler by train, who at this point, at the top of the pass over the Coast Range, far above the college town of San Luis Obispo, has reached his two-and-a-half-millionth mile. The staff will now pass among you distributing California-strawberry shortcake and champagne—on the house, of course. Dear guests, I give you Mr. Frimbo."

As I rose to take a startled bow, I could see that M. Newman, T. Jones, and another acolyte were indeed defanging bottles of champagne, to cheers and laughter.

A woman stood up at the other end of the car. "I thought that was you," she said. "Don't you remember my husband and me? You were with us in the summer of 1949 when we traveled on the Apache Railway, that marvelous logging line in Arizona. Lordy, lordy, you haven't changed a bit."

"No, Ma'am," I said. "Haven't had time."

A man came down the aisle and leaned over my shoulder. "Please stay over the weekend in Los Angeles," he said. "I've got three-quarters of a mile of narrow-gauge railway on my little ranch, and three steam locomotives to run on it." I'll be finishing off the three million miles quicker than I thought, I said to myself.

There were seconds on the strawberry shortcake, and seconds, thirds, fourths, and fifths on the champagne, so I was cheery indeed as I set off for my post on the top deck of the lounge car. Several people stood up to shake hands as I walked along the dining car. "No, no," I said. "I'm not running for governor of California—you've got Jerry Brown in office now, and he likes passenger trains."

"So do we," people kept saying. "And how can we keep the federal government from getting rid of trains like this one, and all the others?"

"Send letters to your congressmen," I said. "A lot of them can read and write."

45 Up, Up, and Away

There are no more trains to P-burg, but New Jersey Transit, which now runs trains and buses for NJ Dot, has a lot to be proud of, including the forthcoming restoration of passenger trains over an even longer and more picturesque line, the "Lackawanna Cutoff," an 80-mile run through northern New Jersey and the Pocono Mountains to Scranton, Pennsylvania. Car No. 1178 (now NJT 1) is still available for public charter, although it no longer sees daily service, and Car No. 1179 is still a restaurant in Clinton, New Jersey. Their lost sister, Car No. 1169, has been joyously rediscovered and is undergoing restoration near Morristown, New Jersey.

If you want to ride a parlor car on the way to work, MARC commuter trains from Baltimore to Washington can now accommodate you.

Bob Lewis, the impresario of this piece, is now a Floridian. He is renowned among railroaders for his vast understanding of the business, for his abundant kindness, and for carrying forward a unique railroading tradition supposedly invented

back in steam train days by a legendary engineer on the Lack-
awanna line, who achieved great fame by standing on his head
on his boiler while the engine was in motion. Lewis, a mod-
ernist, often stands on his head to celebrate great advances in
transportation technology: he's done it on three high-speed
trains—the French TGV, the German ICE train, and the
Swedish X2000, as they reached their maximum speeds—and
also while flying on the Concorde, at the very moment it
plunged through the sound barrier.

Pennsylvania Station in Newark is only fifteen
minutes away from Pennsylvania Station in New York, but
it belongs to another world, a world full of very visible trains.
You see, it's a *real* train station: there are trains whizzing in
from all directions, in an astonishing variety of colors—not
just the red-white-and-blue of Amtrak but the silver, blue-
and-white, brown, green, red, and even dark-blue-and-yellow
of the commuter trains that begin and end their careers at this
station. Hundreds of people on the dead run, and a nonstop
series of announcements, some of them almost comprehensible
on the public-address system. We had fitful opportunities to
observe all this when we alighted there at 5:20 on a fine recent
Tuesday evening and started to run, too—in the wake of the
railway buff E. M. Frimbo, as that elderly man catapulted
himself down a staircase, raced through a vast waiting room
with a forty-foot ceiling and giant chrome lanterns encircled
by the signs of the zodiac, and bounced up another staircase
to Platform 5. "Makes you think of Tokyo Central, doesn't
it?" Mr. Frimbo said as we galloped alongside him to the far

end of this platform. "But we're only in New Jersey. We're also in one of the finest architectural monuments to the concept of Art Deco—you must have noticed that as we went through the waiting room. If anything finally does happen to Radio City Music Hall, we can move the Rockettes and those *Rebecca of Sunnybrook Farm* movies over here, and the customers will never know the difference. Years from now, of course, when the New Jersey Department of Transportation, that great and benevolent institution, gets the money, we won't have to do all this sprinting, because the line we're about to travel on will be electrified, and then our next train will run right out of New York."

"E. M. Frimbo!" shouted six rather staidly attired businessmen at the end of the platform as we at last came to a stop beside them. "Glad you could join us. She'll be pulling in in a minute."

We had often wondered what sort of people E. M. Frimbo hangs out with when he's on the road, but we hadn't been sure that we were ready for one of his six-week grand tours. And then, a couple of days earlier, he had suggested that we come along on a special overnight lark with a set of his traveling companions, and we'd signed up at once. This evening, we were in the presence of Bob Lewis, the publisher of a trade publication, *Railway Age*; Tom Streeter, a railway specialist in a large Wall Street brokerage house; Arthur Yorke Allen, chairman of the firm that publishes the *Official Railway Guide*, a collection of passenger timetables that still comes out ten times a year; Porter Collins, of the Naporano Iron and Metal Company, who salvages beat-up old locomotives and nurses them back to health; and a couple of pure amateurs, who, like Frimbo himself, simply enjoy riding on trains. "I like to think of this particular group as the Friends of the N.J.

Dot Museum," Frimbo said, "which is what we call the New Jersey Department of Transportation, which has taken over the commuter trains of the now ignominiously bankrupt Penn Central, Erie-Lackawanna, Jersey Central, and Reading railways and pays for what would otherwise no longer exist."

"N.J. Dot sure is a museum," Bob Lewis said cheerfully. "It has bought cars of all vintages, from age one to age fifty-five, and that's why you see them in so many colors. That train on Track 3 has cars from the Santa Fe Railroad. The one arriving on Track 4 has cars from the Burlington, the Northern Pacific, and the Great Northern. And over there's a train with cars mostly from the Rock Island. And that streamlined car with the observation dome at one end used to go to Florida on a train called the *Silver Meteor*. Right now, on any other day, I'd be getting in that car, which belongs to my commuter club, and be off on my way home to Red Bank, on the north Jersey coast. And this dark-blue-and-yellow train coming in on our track is all Kansas City Southern, with one exception."

As though on command, the train was halted so that the one exception was only inches away from our group. "This car, gentlemen," Lewis said, "is the museum's prize antique."

Tom Streeter stepped forward and opened not a door but an elaborate brass gate and led our party not indoors but onto the ample open-air platform of the car that looked exactly like the one in which Harry S. Truman conducted his campaign for the Presidency in 1948.

"No!" we said. "There *can't* be anything like this in existence today!"

"Well, you're almost right," said Lewis. "This is the last open-platform observation car left on any scheduled passenger train in this country. And it pulls out of here at five-thirty five nights a week—Monday through Friday—on the end of a train from Phillipsburg, sixty-six miles away. I hope you've brought along a sandwich, because we won't be dining until after eight o'clock, and that will be in Easton, Pennsylvania, across the Delaware River from Phillipsburg. I organize holidays like this for Friends of the N.J. Dot now and again during the long summer evenings."

Having already been warned by Frimbo, we had fetched along a brace of sandwiches from the Fountain deli, across the street from our office, and we noticed that our new friends were equipped with bulging satchels. "Put your bags on the rear seats in the car to hold places for yourselves, and then come out again," Streeter told us.

The five-thirty for Phillipsburg was pulling out as we went back outdoors. We noticed that our solemnly accoutered companions were now armed with cameras and were waving farewell to the crowds on other platforms. "Vote for me, and I'll clean up this town!" someone right behind us shouted, and we were on our way.

The conductor came out on the platform to collect our tickets. "Eight tickets for P-burg!" he said. "What's going on out there? A convention, in that boondock?"

"We're railroad men," Porter Collins said firmly. "And we're staying outside here the whole way."

"Welcome aboard my train," the conductor said.

"I'm on home ground now," said Frimbo as the conductor went on his way. "In better times, there were thirteen trains a day out of Grand Central Terminal *alone* with cars like this. I was present at the birth of this car we're in—when it made its first run, from Jersey City to Atlantic City, as part of one of my favorite trains, the Jersey Central's *Blue Comet*. That must have been fifty years ago. There were six canvas chairs

on this platform then, and inside there was green carpeting
and two rows of wicker armchairs. As I remember it, every
car in the train was named after a comet or an astronomer.
Just ahead of this car was a restaurant car, from which, unfortunately, the porter in our car could not fetch us drinks,
because the Devil had invented Prohibition. This cheerful
conveyance was unwonted and unwanted competition to the
Pennsylvania Railroad, which had the Atlantic City business
practically to itself, with a parlor-car express named the *Nellie
Bly*—after the newspaper reporter who refused to take Jules
Verne for granted and made it around the world in seventy-
two days instead of eighty. Women's rights were, as you can
see, already in full fig in those days—in fact, the parlor-bar
car on that train was named after Jenny Lind. Prohibition
was eventually put to death, and something called Progress
eventually put the *Blue Comet* to death, but once or twice a
year thereafter, on a summery day like this, I would charter
this car and some of the *Blue Comet* day coaches from the
Jersey Central Railroad and take off with friends of mine to
such cheerily named New Jersey country seats as Egg Harbor,
Woodbine Junction, and Bivalve. The Second World War
turned me to more serious endeavors, and when peace came
I could no longer find this car. Then, one night, Bob Lewis
said to me, 'Why don't you ride down to the north Jersey coast
with me and my friends in our club car? You can have dinner
with us at home and then we'll put you on the mid-evening
train back to New York.' That club car turned out to be this
very vehicle, now No. 1178. The green carpet and the wicker
chairs had gone to their reward—such luxuries as commuter
club cars, which are subscription affairs and guarantee every
member a seat, tended to fade out during the war—but it was
still, to me, my old *Blue Comet* star. The club car lost a lot

of Wall Street patronage in 1967, when the ferryboats from downtown Manhattan to Jersey City, which was then its terminal station, stopped running, and soon after that 1178 stopped running, too. Then, a couple of years ago, Bob Lewis phoned me with the gladsome news that 1178 had had its third resurrection—this one—thanks to Dot."

It was a commuter run unlike any other we'd ever been on. Even in the suburbs of Newark, some of the stations had a neat, nineteenth-century air. A few of them were actually landscaped. And before long we broke into rolling, hill-climbing open country. Tom Streeter said, "This is old American country. The battles of the Revolutionary War were fought over this land, and you can still see the tailings of the iron mines that supplied some of our munitions for that war."

There were, we observed, no Levittowns. There were only villages, vast stretches of woodland, dairy farms, meadows full of blooming wild mustard and of cows, who never seem to learn, running away from the sound of our train. And there were small clusters of commuters getting off at every stop. For the last forty miles of the run, we had the observation car to ourselves.

"Not many passengers," we said to Frimbo.

"That's why I call N.J. Dot benevolent," he said. "It looks after its clientele not just in the big towns—Jersey is the most thickly populated state in the Union—but in the thinly peopled northern countryside as well."

We shared our roast-beef sandwiches with Frimbo, and all too soon Bob Lewis said, "Folks, I have an apology to make about this wonderful trip."

"What's that?" said Tom Streeter.

"We're almost at P-burg," Lewis said.

The train ended its run a good half mile short of the old

station in Phillipsburg, but Bob Lewis had laid on a couple of cabs to pick us up there and take us to a steak dinner at the Sheraton-Easton Inn in Easton.

"The Jersey Central once had three cars like this," Porter Collins said as we alighted. "One is now a restaurant called Union Gap, near the town of Clinton, on Route 78, on the way home. Forty years ago, we might have gone there from here on a Lehigh Valley train—but not anymore."

46 Christening Frimbo's Railroad Car

Bill Howes, the mastermind of the Chessie Steam Special celebrated in this piece, has more recently been a consultant to Ringling Brothers and Barnum & Bailey, which still sends two 55-car-long circus trains around the country every year. Each silver-colored circus train can accommodate 300 people and 155 animals and carries a "pie car," which is circus slang for a dining car.

Christening: *Marco Polo, Herbert H. Lehman, Louisa May Alcott, Davy Crockett, Thomas A. Edison, Molly Pitcher, Izaak Walton, George M. Pullman*—and now *E. M. Frimbo*, which was christened last month at a small Sunday-afternoon ceremony in Grand Ledge, Michigan, a town surrounded, as is usual in Michigan midsummers, by fine crops of Queen Anne's lace and bouncing Bet. *E. M. Frimbo* weighs a hundred and seventy-two thousand pounds, is seventy-nine feet, five and one-eighth inches long, is painted bright yellow, has a kitchen at one end and a bookstall at the other, and is now in the middle of a six-month journey that will take it through ten states, during which it will probably serve something like twenty-five hundred breakfasts of scrambled eggs and sausage, all cooked to order. The Chessie System, a railroad that embraces the Baltimore & Ohio, Chesapeake & Ohio, and Western Maryland railroads, had such a good time last year celebrating its sesquicentennial by running the third-of-a-mile-long, steam-hauled passenger train in which *E. M. Frimbo* is now inbedded over all of its lines that it decided this year to celebrate its sesquicentennial-et-unum and do the whole thing over again.

E. M. Frimbo was christened by E. M. Frimbo himself, the world's most redoubtable railroad buff, and we attended because it was the first time a railroad car had ever been named after a friend of ours. The *Chessie Steam Special* had come out to Grand Ledge from Detroit via Lansing that morning with a thousand and twenty-nine passengers, and would be returning within the hour. "I suppose," a local reporter said to Mr. Frimbo, who was busy unwrapping a bottle of Taittinger Blanc de Blancs for ceremonial use, "that this is the first time a railway car has been named after a living person."

"Well," said Frimbo, pulling a long face, "Marco Polo is gone. And so is Louisa May Alcott. And . . ."

"Enough of that!" commanded the cheerful voice of William Howes, the dapper Chessie System vice president in charge of the six-month excursion. "Let's get on with the ceremony."

But instead of cracking the bottle against the side of the car Frimbo eased out the cord and said, "Will somebody please

Whitaker, in front of "his" railroad car

give me a small glass? This champagne is too good to use all
of it to baptize even a car named E. M. Frimbo."

The car is numbered eleven, because it is the eleventh
from the giant steam locomotive, and under the numeral
is painted E. M. Frimbo's signature. "I christen thee
E. M. Frimbo," said E. M. Frimbo, moistening both numeral
and name with a dab of champers.

"Did Frimbo paint on that signature himself?" a photographer asked Howie Samelson, a full-bearded man in his late
twenties—the co-proprietor (with his wife) of the New York
railroadiana shop Broadway Limited, and the owner and operator (with a full-time staff of six) of *E. M. Frimbo*, whose
eponym was passing around glasses of Taittinger.

"No," said Samelson. "But it's an excellent forgery. We
couldn't go to Frimbo, because we wanted it to be a surprise,
so a friend of mine, after much searching, found his signature

on a postcard at an auction of railroad memorabilia. This whole train is that kind of cooperative venture. Chessie supplied today's champagne. My chef took a leave from his job with a freight-car-loading company in Chicago when he found out that the *Chessie Steam Special* would travel over tracks that Frimbo had traveled on and he had not, and I'm on board a lot of the time, too, instead of home minding the shop. Several of the cars have been lent by railway clubs, and the state of West Virginia—Lord knows why—owns one of the dormitory cars that sleep the twenty-three people permanently assigned to the train. Ross Rowland, the New York commodities broker who invented the *American Freedom Train*, owns the locomotive and the parlor car and the observation car, and he's driving the locomotive today. And when the steam locomotive was being refitted at the B. & O. shops in Baltimore, Bill Howes took off his vice-presidential three-piece suit and watch chain to work on, and mostly under, her. *E. M. Frimbo* itself is a 1948 B. & O. coach that eleven years ago was rebuilt as a food-bar car to replace a diner on some of the B. & O. Washington-Chicago trains. I bought it this spring in time to convert it into a food-bar-bookshop-souvenir car, and it'll be available to special trains all over the country in the years to come."

As Frimbo walked back with us to our large swivel armchairs in Car No. 20, Ross Rowland's fine, old-fashioned parlor car, he was waylaid by well-wishers, some of them members of the railway club at MSU—Michigan State University. "Did you know that we have our our steam locomotive?" the club's president asked Frimbo.

"Yes, I remember her well," said Frimbo. "The draftsmen at the Lima Locomotive Works, which built her in 1941, could make any old freight locomotive look as graceful as an America's Cup yacht, and they gave her the silhouette of a mighty greyhound. It's nice to know that you have both girl and boy undergraduates doing the dirty work of restoring her to order, and I'd be delighted to come out and ride in her cab when she's ready."

Sinking back in his overstuffed parlor-car chair, Frimbo said, "I never miss the chance to ride in the cab of a steam locomotive. That's why I wasn't riding with you on the way up. Ross Rowland, while he was driving the locomotive this morning, gave me a bit of private news. He and my friend George Pins, that New York lawyer who owns a clutch of Pullman cars, are conspiring to run all of them, together with this parlor car and the open-platform observation car behind us, from Penn Station in New York to Atlantic City five nights a week for first-class passengers only, starting in the middle of November. Their train will leave New York at a normal businessmen's hour in the late afternoon, but it won't start back until around half past five in the morning, an hour convenient for passengers who want to be active until the casino in that city shuts down for its siesta. They'll serve a very fine breakfast cooked on board. See you there and then."

Frimbo went on, "Today's been a good day, and totally unexpected. After all, I'm not really used to being reincarnated, and you just never know how these things are going to turn out. I might have become a candy bar, like Reggie Jackson, or a New York State Thruway, like Thomas E. Dewey. I would much rather roll through the centuries as a scrambled-egg-and-bookstall railway car."

Love among the Ruins

The New York Dock Railway, which was intermodal long before that now modish word was coined, became the New York Cross Harbor Railroad in 1983. It's still valiantly in business, and gaining renewed attention. As New York area congestion worsens year by year, it becomes ever more obvious that the little-car-floats-that-could are by far the most efficient way for bulk freight to move among New Jersey, Brooklyn, and Long Island.

The great green-and-yellow tug, the *Brooklyn III*, pride of the New York Dock Railway fleet, heading north up the East River, turned in a wide arc, and nosed cautiously into Newtown Creek, the narrow estuary that divides Brooklyn from Queens. Proceeding east, it passed two ancillary creeks, Dutch Kills and the Whale Creek Canal, and went under two bridges, the Pulaski and the J. J. Byrne Memorial, before coming to a halt alongside a huge barge on which were sitting eight railway tank cars. No railway was visible. We were standing on the upper deck of the *Brooklyn III* under a green canvas awning alongside our old friend E. M. Frimbo. "What's this all about?" we asked.

"This is how New York City grew up," Frimbo said. "There's a château ashore, which you can't see. Those tank cars were full of wine when they arrived from California, and they had to be floated across the harbor, all the way from New Jersey, so that the wine could be pumped into the château and bottled there. It's a wonderfully antique way of doing business. I happen to love it, and so does everybody on this towboat. The reason there isn't any railway here is that we built the city on an archipelago surrounded by too much water. It's had to grow up higgledy-piggledy. Maybe we should have put it somewhere else—in Albany, perhaps? And put New Haven here. After all, an archipelago is a haven. With all the interlacing of waterways hereabouts, we could have had a wonderful national park. Think of the fishing, the boating, the wildlife marshes, the oyster beds, the shad runs, the scallop beds. All that room for marinas. The cool ocean breezes. Those magnificent and smogless sunsets, which sustained an entire Hudson River school of painters. And, of course, all those darling little coves and inlets, so suitable in misty weather for smuggling. *They* kept most of us alive during Prohibition."

We could sense that Frimbo was waiting to be asked another question, so we asked one: "What's to be done about it?"

"It's already being done. Decay," Frimbo said, and we began to think about what we had just seen on our journey up Newtown Creek: boarded-up warehouses; dump trucks

discharging paving blocks and bits of macadam in any convenient open space; a derelict wooden steam cattle carrier, the
Elizabeth, submerging slowly at its moorings. The only sound
in this almost abandoned world issued from a fearsome mon-
ster of a machine, three stories high, that was devouring whole
carcasses of discarded automobiles, which shrieked and
groaned and flamed as they perished. "All illegally parked
cars, I hope," Frimbo had said. We began to remember, too,
what is to be seen from the roof of the World Trade Center:
rows of empty piers, a nearly empty harbor.

Turning the *Brooklyn III* about in a stream the size of
Newtown Creek so that she can collect and remove a car float
is an extremely deft bit of seamanship, or creekmanship. Captain Simon Holleran, who has been afloat in these parts since
the early forties, managed it without fuss. He told us, when
we talked to him later on, that at the time he began work his
company, one of a dozen railways that then floated freight
cars across the harbor, had forty-eight towboat crews. "You
could walk across the Hudson on foot, there were so many
boats on it," the captain said. Now he is one of two car-float-
towboat captains still in the trade, and his company, the New
York Dock Railway, is the only tug company carrying railway
cars across the water. New York Dock is, and always has
been, a back-yard railway. Even now that it has sopped up
its last remaining rival—another Brooklyn car-float railway,
the Brooklyn Eastern District Terminal—it measures its land
trackage in inches rather than miles: just four ports of call in
Brooklyn, each barely large enough to accommodate a few
dozen freight cars. The yardmaster at the New York Dock
toy railway yard, in what is left of Bush Terminal, in South
Brooklyn, works on the premises in a truly unique Win-
nebago—a wooden freight-train caboose wearing the house

livery of green and yellow and fitted out with telephones, an air-conditioner, a lavatory, a pantry, a refrigerator, and even a few office machines.

It is ten miles, as the New York Dock Railway plies, from the château to the old Pennsylvania Railroad yard at Greenville, in Jersey City, three miles southwest of Battery Park, where the *Brooklyn III* was to deliver the tank cars and then pick up a car float for Bush Terminal. The towboat's steady and stately nudging of the tank cars in its charge had an irresistible kind of diligence, like the work of a well-trained St. Bernard commanding a small flock of sheep. It was a leisurely journey—a lovable, picturesque, dilatory journey. "So dilatory," said Frimbo, "that when Robert Moses, head of the absolute monarchy called the Triborough Bridge and Tunnel Authority, began building pathways for trucks, and not for trains, eager shippers began to switch. And industries began packing up and moving out of town to set themselves up alongside the new highways. That's when the car floats began to disappear. Of course, if Moses or the city or the Port Authority had ever built that railway tunnel that was talked about nearly sixty years ago, from Staten Island under the Narrows to Brooklyn, maybe Trommer's and the other fine Brooklyn breweries and all the other industry that was there then would still be *in situ*. The city and the state are really beginning to worry now about keeping what industry is still around and giving it proper service. As it is, there are two ways for the cargo containers on the railway lines coming into New Jersey to reach Brooklyn without being switched to trucks. They can go a hundred and thirty-five miles up the west bank of the Hudson to Albany, cross the river, and come down the east bank another hundred and thirty-five miles to the city. Or else—and what a nutty idea this is!—the cars can be loaded on a New York Dock Railway float at Greenville and travel three enormous miles to Bush Terminal, in Brooklyn. So it turns out that one of my pet anachronisms, the New York Dock Railway, has willfully and perversely survived to become one of the quickest, least expensive, and quietest innovations of our times."

Corn on the Cob

The other day, we drifted into a characteristically strange conversation with our old friend E. M. Frimbo, the persistent railway buff. The subject was corn on the cob. All of us know about city corn: that whether we encounter it in a very good restaurant or whether we buy it enshrouded in husks and wildly plumed at an open-air Korean market or whether Gristede's sends it around already husked and stripped of its plumage, all, all of it implacably suggests that the joyous days of its youth are gone. "I know," said Frimbo. "You have to forage for it yourself. And last summer I did."

When Frimbo drops a leading remark of that sort in our lap, it is nearly always instantly followed by a long chapter of his oral autobiography. Well, then! He and friends had departed the city on another of their semiannual excursions in a railway car owned by one of them—a rolling hotel, really, with bedrooms, shower baths, a kitchen, a dining room, and a platform at the rear from which they could observe *en plain air* the passing countryside. Attaching their vehicle to first this

322

train and then that, and attended to by a ranking chef known only as Robbie and an old-school majordomo known as Harris, A. J., they had rolled through Montreal and were a hundred and fifty miles west of it when their train halted, backed up for a couple of miles, and then halted again: a demon truck driver had knocked a bridge off its pins up ahead, and a new way west must be sought out. "It was that certain hour of the afternoon, so we assembled on the observation platform and went to work on our brandies Alexander and whatnot," Frimbo said. "The air was fresh, and so was the breeze, and there was nothing but working farmland all about—not a building of any sort in view. Then our host came on deck to announce that we would be so delayed that instead of reaching Winnipeg, practically a thousand miles west, early next evening we would be arriving at three in the morning— not the finest time of day to lay in our next supply of vegetables, even on Madison Avenue in the Fifties. Beside us, in a field so vast that its limits could not be discerned, stood row upon row of ripening, tasseled corn. I rose and put together an ad-hoc victualing party, and as one man the party climbed a fence and set to work. The provender in field that size is always for cattle—no succulent Corey's Early or Golden Bantam or Country Gentleman or Black Mexican—but if you search out the ears, even of cattle corn, whose silky mane has not turned dusty brown, and if you then burrow a hard thumb through the husks and run it along the kernels, you pretty well determine which ears are, even in August, still young and tender. Stuff as succulent as that needs only a blanching in boiling water and a liberal buttering and salting. Our host was in error: we reached Winnipeg at 2:35 in the morning, not at three. But no matter; next afternoon, on one more train, en route to Edmonton, the capital of Alberta, we had a long

A young Whitaker waiting for a train

wait for an eastbound freight to get past us, and there, alongside, was another cornfield, and our ad-hoc committee was at
once reactivated."

We said that perhaps the unauthorized collecting of ears
of corn was not the real purpose of the journey.

"Well, no," said Frimbo. "You will recall that in the early
forties a very large war had begun. Soon afterward, my friends
and I got rather detached from our civilian life, and I found
myself in western Canada. There was word that the Japanese

had invaded the Aleutian Islands and were on their way to
Alaska, and there was news of Japanese submarines patrolling
the Pacific Coast, so the railways in that part of Canada were
of a sudden awash in a traffic they had not been built to cope
with. Even so, it was not easy for any one of us out there to
realize that a world war was in progress. In between the
occasional huge field of cattle corn and the occasional field of
oats or barley and the occasional hamlet, there was nothing
but prairie under that big blue sky, and in the spring, when
there was still ice on the Lesser Slave Lake, which was in our
domain, the land became an Oriental carpet as what they call
the Canada bluebell and other floral displays popped out of
the ground. And there was that silence—broken only by railway trains, made up of cars and locomotives that had been
begged, borrowed, or stolen from a dozen American railways
to help move the traffic. Then, after the Allies had beaten the
Axis back into a plowshare and Japan was folding up, the
problem arose of what to do with the German prisoners of
war who had been exported to Canada. The Japanese-
Canadian detainees were no problem; they had been put in
open camps in northern British Columbia—open because the
country round about was so stern and desolate that any of
them who ran away would starve to death in the wilderness—
and they were just released. But there were many German
prisoners of war, and the Canadian government, always mind-
ful of being short of manpower in a big country, invited these
men—who were not really men, for the prisoners I saw were
between sixteen and eighteen, and who, some of them said,
did not want to live in a ravaged Germany—to return to
Canada after repatriation and move out into the prairie country where we were and become growers of fodder corn and
wheat. I had the excellent luck to be aboard the first train—

out of Edmonton, which seems ten times bigger today—that carried a contingent of these young men into a very, very New World. Sixteen-year-old soldiers—that indicates the plight of Hitler's armies. But that first night out they were all singing —healthy-looking, well-muscled, well-fed boys. Canada was, you will recall, one of the great food-exporting nations during that war, manpower shortage or no. And when we reached the part of the land that is called the Peace River Country, after the tremendous and beautiful river that flows toward the Arctic Circle, the train stopped at what the timetable said were towns—a wooden station, three houses, a grain elevator. Two or three of the Germans were set down, and boards and nails and carpenter tools followed them, out of the train's freight cars. From there on, it was up to these young men to take care of themselves, out on the prairie of a completely foreign country, without friends, without girls—especially without girls. Two summers ago, when I was in Prince Rupert, a city on the coast of British Columbia, and saw three grim black Russian freighters and two fairly nondescript vessels flying the Chinese flag, all of them loading grain, I felt I knew what had been going on in the Peace River Country in the thirty-five years since last I visited it, and that is how the expedition in our private railway car came about. Those of us who had been there all wanted another look."

We suggested that there might have been a less complicated way.

"Sir, you don't know the country," Frimbo said. "It's not resort country, it's *working* country—corn, oats, wheat, and now oil. The roads are mostly minor, the hotels basic, the restaurants basic, too—except those run by the great grandchildren of the Chinese camp cooks who fed the men who were building the railways back in the nineteenth century. As for planes, they are few. Indeed, even the passenger trains have all been laid to rest. So, approaching an official of the Canadian National Railways who is appropriately close to the throne room, we were able to rent a locomotive to haul our train around the Peace River Country where and when we wished, and at our own pace."

We wanted to know what he had discovered.

"Oh, looking for those young Germans was like looking for the lost colony of Roanoke—those early white settlers who came over here four hundred years ago. The Peace River Country is so vast that it could swallow up a few hundred more farmers in a minute. But later, when I was telling this story at lunch on a train between Halifax and Montreal, a man spoke up. He said we had put him off the train at Watino, a couple of hundred miles northwest of Edmonton. He and two comrades had worked their farms as a communal project until he married a girl he had met at a dance hall—the daughter of a Ukrainian miner whose own father had been one of the German émigrés to southern Russia years ago. She was the first person he had met in Canada who spoke German, and that was why he married her. Now he was a salesman of something or other. We agreed, as we parted, *not* to say that it is a small world. Out in the Peace River Country last summer we had seen that much more land had been put into crops since our previous trip, yet we had also seen that man's atavistic longing for a great big open space could still be satisfied there. And we were allowed to be the first and maybe the only passenger train ever to travel on the Alberta Resources Railway, which runs through the Smoky River wilderness— and a magnificent stretch of wilderness it is. And, as so often happens when I travel with Chef Robbie and Majordomo Harris, A. J., I picked up another household hint."

Naturally, we swallowed the bait.

"The three of us were chatting after breakfast. After all, I had been traveling with Harris, in his role as Pullman and railway employee, for forty-four years. And while they were polishing the silver—and it was silver, not stainless steel or aluminum—Robbie said he had run out of silver polish. So Harris stepped to a supply cabinet and brought out a bottle of White Rock. 'Just as good as polish,' he said. 'There's a mineral in it that cleans silver like nothing else.' I watched, and it does."

Frimbo's Retreat

This trip, completed just four months before his death, was Frimbo's valedictory. He had hoped to head to India in early 1981, and to write a long-contemplated book about the early days of The New Yorker. *Instead, this expanded and annotated* All Aboard *is his lasting legacy.*

We went to a marvelous party on New Year's Eve, awash with the best of our old friends, and we half expected that E. M. Frimbo, the oldest friend of all, would be there. Someone said to us, "You seem to have forgotten that this is the time of year Frimbo goes into his annual retreat. Right now, he's on a train somewhere, shut away in his bedroom with the lights turned off." And then we remembered that we had actually witnessed the beginning of a Frimbo retreat years ago. We were spending the Christmas holidays in Pau, one of the most beautiful cities in France and certainly—with that tremendous view of the snowy Lower Pyrenees—the most beautifully sited city in France. It was pleasurably off-season in that splendid resort, and the jolliest of the few restaurants that were open for business was the railway-station buffet, at which we took most of our meals, to the accompaniment—via the buffet's jukebox—of slender female voices coping with the French lyrics of all the country-and-western American hit songs we thought we had left at home. At luncheon on New Year's Eve, Frimbo came to table carrying a handbag. "You're all the best of company," he said, "but this is the day I become, for a brief time, that cat who walks by himself." Outside stood a train so small as to be almost imperceptible, its snout pointed south, toward the Pyrenees and Spain. Frimbo's disappearance into it raised the count, he told us later, to an even dozen passengers. He was nearly alone by the time his train had wormed its way to the top of the Pyrenees and sloped off into Canfranc, the first station in Spain. He dined in solitude at the Canfranc station buffet, shut himself into his compartment in a Wagons-Lits sleeping car (he was now completely alone), and arrived early the next afternoon in Madrid. It was a railway service that then offered itself only four times a week (it now offers itself not at all), so we did not see Frimbo again for three days. "What a wonderful journey!" he said on his return. "And what a wonderful sleeping car! The walls of my compartment were mahogany inlaid with bouquets of stylized golden flowers, and the window curtains were hand-knit lace."

Last week, in a vast crowd on the concourse at Penn Station, we saw an unmistakable venerable black homburg towering above the throng, and, sure enough, E. M. Frimbo

```
1,886,434·37   Port = Villez [SNCF]
1,886,438·15   Bonnières [SNCF]
1,886,441·93   Rosny = sur = Seine [SNCF]
1,886,445·08   MANTES = GASSICOURT [SNCF]
1,886,445·71   Mantes = Station [SNCF]
1,886,450·12   ÉPONE = MÉZIÈRES [SNCF]
1,886,452·01   Aubergenville=Elizabethville [SNCF]
1,886,455·16   Les Mureaux [SNCF]
),886,458·94   Vernouillet=Verneuil [SNCF]
1,886,462·09   Villennes = sur = Seine [SNCF]
1,886,464·61   Poissy [SNCF]
1,886,467·76   Achères [SNCF]
1,886,470·28   Maisons = Laffitte [SNCF]
1,886,470·91   Sartrouville [SNCF]
1,886,472·80   Houilles = Carrières = sur = Seine  [SNCF]
1,886,475·95   LA GARENNE = BEZONS [SNCF]
1,886,480·99   PARIS (ST = LAZARE) [SNCF]
1,886,485·00   PARIS (LYON) [SNCF] [taxi]
1,886,489·41   Maisons = Alfort=Alfortville [SNCF]
1,886,490·04   Le=Vert = des Maisons (3.B.)[SNCF]
1,886,491·93   Villeneuve=Prairie (S.B.) [SNCF]
```

was under it. "Yes," he said after we had intercepted him with the inevitable question. "I got to Grand Central at five that evening, downed a handful of smelts and a glass of white wine at the Oyster Bar, boarded my train as soon as it was announced, got into bed, propped myself upright, raised the shade, and turned off all the lights. There is no finer way of going into retreat."

"And?" we said.

"I don't know when I fell asleep, but I do know that I did not hear a peep—of revelry or anything else—out of anyone or anything until a public-address system was announcing our arrival in Cleveland. My shade was still up, the sun was up even higher, but I knew that E. M. Frimbo would not bestir himself until the dining-car steward came along to inform everyone that the final moments of the breakfast hour were at hand. That was the one thing that got me out of my comfortable rolling cubicle before, in midafternoon, we attained Chicago."

We said we could understand why he had made his long-ago journey into Spain, knowing, as he did, that extinction was about to overtake that unusual approach, but we wondered where Frimbo could find in the United States a train that could take him anywhere he hadn't already been.

"You will recall that I absented myself from civilian life during two very large wars, and, in the course of my up-rooting, and in the performance of my duties, I spent a deal of time traveling on troop trains, and even helping out in the operations of them," he replied. "It seems romantic to me now—barging about for so long a time, not of my own volition but under military orders, never knowing where I would be next. But it wasn't all romance; although there were plenty of good-Joe types, who were philosophical about being inducted into the army, the draft boards sent us some fairly dubious types as well. One night when a contingent of recruits was occupying a couple of cars on a regular Baltimore & Ohio train, a draftee who had managed to conceal a gun from all of us went into the dining car and, when the steward refused to serve him any more drinks, shot the man dead. Supervision tightened up after that, I can tell you. Well, this mid-December an army friend who knows that I am what you might call a troop-train buff got me on the blower to say that a troop train—the first one I'd heart about in years—would be leaving New York on the third of January to return soldiers on Christmas leave to Fort Leonard Wood, which is really out back of beyond, a hundred and fifty miles southwest of St. Louis, at the end of a nineteen-mile branch line that had never seen a passenger train. At the fare Amtrak was asking, the train might be a sellout, but he had been promised that he could get me and a few other approved civilians aboard, even though the notices in stations along the way declared the trip was for military personnel and no one else. America is still the land of opportunity, and opportunity has to knock but once for me. So from Chicago I took a morning train to Minneapolis—I can never get tired of those many miles alongside the noble Mississippi—and a night train back to Chicago, and then a just-born train on a newly invented route to Indianapolis, where I'd collect my troop train in the morning."

A pause, and then: "That day would be the diciest part of this retreat. We were not due in Leonard Wood until after nine in the evening, less than an hour before the bus we civilians hoped to catch to get back to St. Louis in time to nab an early-morning train to Chicago. There's no accommodation at the fort for civilians, so if we missed that we'd have to wait until one in the morning for the next one, and the nearest airport would have nothing for us until after eight in the morning. I had a good look at the Indianapolis Union Station—a much celebrated architectural nonesuch—and then took a deep breath, crossed myself several times, and approached the man at the ticket window. My train was running three hours late. Never mind! The risk I was taking was worthwhile. The United States is retrograding in many respects, but the art of the troop train has really flowered. There was a car for checked luggage—checked luggage on a *troop* train! There were six day coaches, none of them more than three years old—not forty. The floors were carpeted, and

every seat was thoroughly upholstered and had its own overhead reading light. The thumping, clanging steam pipes that
warmed the cars of forty years ago had given way to a series
of little grilles behind which electricity was doing its magic.
There were two coaches with counters over which, all day
long, an Amtrak crew was dispensing food and drink of considerable variety. There was no litter in the aisles. No one
was roughhousing; no one was reading a comic. And every
one of the—by my count—465 soldiers aboard was young and
chipper and orderly. A brace of drill sergeants were patrolling
the train, but there seemed no need for them. And—novelty
of novelties—at the rear end of one coach sat in mouselike
silence a clutch (perhaps two dozen in all) of *girl* soldiers,
rather fetching in their jaunty big berets. What conversations
I picked up here and there consisted not of barroom jokes but
of talk about the problems of handling to best advantage the
complex machines of war the soldiers had to deal with. I
realized that for the first time I was in the presence of a *new*
United States Army—a wholly *voluntary* one. Out of what
I'm afraid is sheer necessity, our army is a multinational corporation, scattered almost worldwide. In one around-the-
globe trip, I came across our army in England and Germany
and Spain and Australia and Turkey, and until the recent
trouble there were clusters of it in northern Iran."

Another pause. And then: "We'd picked up just half an
hour on the long run into St. Louis. The Amtrak man who
was serving as train commander bolted into the station, and
when he emerged he said that Amtrak wanted the train dead-
headed—run empty, that is—as soon as might be possible to
St. Louis, where he'd stick it on the early train to Chicago;
and that if any of us civilians wanted to chance going back
on it instead of trying to catch that bus, we could. There was,

he added, a dormitory car at the rear of our train, where the drill sergeants and the Amtrak crew had slept, and there would be space for us there. Leonard Wood was midwinter Siberia —floodlights revealed rows of those bleak identical buildings the army is so fond of, and if there were streets between them they had vanished beneath a sea of hard-packed snow. The train was evacuated in slow march time. 'Attention!' said the loudspeakers outside. 'Men of the Fourth Brigade, you will leave the train first. Pick up your hand baggage and board the buses in front of you. Your checked baggage will be taken to the gymnasium and you will claim it there. Everyone else, stay on board.' Et cetera. I slid into an empty bed in the dormitory, and the next thing I heard was a far more welcome loudspeaker, saying, 'This train departs in five minutes for Chicago,' and I knew we were in St. Louis on time. Mission accomplished! In Chicago, I'd assemble a parcel of goodies, both protein and liquid, for the night's journey on the *Lake Shore Limited,* and not leave my bedroom aboard it until the sudden eclipse of daylight early next afternoon warned me that we were in the railway tunnel under Park Avenue, and that Grand Central Terminal was only three miles away."

A Ferryboat Comeback

Frimbo would be more than pleased by the way ferryboats have been popping up all around New York harbor in the ten years since this account first made it into print. According to Arthur Imperatore, Jr., his family's company, which is now known as NY Waterway, currently operates six commuter lines and is close to adding on at least three or four more. He's particularly excited about the prospect of giving Manhattanites their own world-class backyard beach: within the next two or three years he'll be inaugurating direct midday and weekend high-speed ferry service from the Battery in lower Manhattan to the sands of Sandy Hook, New Jersey, a glistening beach at the mouth of New York harbor that's now virtually inaccessible to New Yorkers, because the drive there is so maddeningly congested.

The *Port Imperial*, the brand-new Hudson River ferryboat that is regularly making the three-quarter-mile-long trip between West Thirty-eighth Street and a pier in Weehawken in three minutes flat, has a zippy, dashing, Coast Guard–cutter, "Miami Vice" feeling about it that immediately sets it apart from the ponderous, patient, contemplative old steamboats, like the *Elmira* and the *Binghamton*, that made the trans-Hudson run until ferry service vanished from the river almost twenty years ago—never to return, most people then thought (although the *Binghamton* has survived as a floating restaurant in Edgewater, New Jersey). At the same time, the *Port Imperial*, which is seventy-seven feet long and low-slung, white outside and blue inside, with beige benches and two decks—an open-air upper deck and an enclosed but well-windowed lower deck—has contrived to inherit three of the most prized qualities of the old steamers: it rides smoothly, operates quietly, and is a reliable boat.

Besides all that, the *Port Imperial* is relatively inexpensive, is easy to handle and maintain, and has a completely new design—a concept that popped into the head of Luther Blount, a distinguished shipbuilder in Warren, Rhode Island, when he was laid up in a hospital in 1981 after a serious operation. Blount, who was already known as the father of the modern small cruise ship and the father of the modern American stern-trawling fishing boat, now came up with the composite lightweight ferryboat, which is something like a high-speed life jacket. It has an aluminum frame, aluminum decks, and a fiber-glass skin, which keep it lightweight and fast-moving (the *Port Imperial* did about twenty-six knots on its maiden voyage), and the spaces in between are filled with polyurethane foam, which is as buoyant and virtually unsinkable as a plastic-foam cup. The foam also absorbs the noise and vibrations of the engines, just as the wooden superstructures of the old steamboats did.

The engines in this case are two General Motors engines that are similar to truck engines—a feature that helped recommend the composite lightweight ferryboat to Arthur E. Imperatore, the operator of the new Weehawken ferry service, who owns two miles of riverfront land below the Palisades in Weehawken and West New York, and plans to develop it as a city—Port Imperial—with ten million square feet of commercial space, ten thousand housing units, a major cultural center, and some kind of park by the water. He hopes to link his ferry to a new trolley line that would run along the west bank of the river and continue five miles inland to the Meadowlands Sports Complex. That would give New Yorkers direct mass-transit access to the Meadowlands, and would also mean that more New Jersey commuters could leave their cars in its parking lots, which are largely empty by day. The new ferry has already cut the commuting time of Weehawkenites drastically: it can take an hour and a half to drive from Weehawken to midtown Manhattan during the morning rush hour—and that's going through the Lincoln Tunnel, which runs almost underneath the ferry.

The maiden voyage of the *Port Imperial* took place on Wednesday, December 3, 1986, when the boat left Weehawken at 2:58 P.M., just as the sun broke through a thick bank of dark clouds; and the event was preceded by a lavish reception in a conical white tent (iced shrimp and piping-hot crabmeat au gratin) with speechmaking by almost every major political figure in New Jersey, including Governor Tom Kean, Senators Bill Bradley and Frank Lautenberg, Representative Robert Roe, and Weehawken's Mayor Stanley Iacono, who was there with his wife, Ann-Marie. Only one major personage was missing, to our way of thinking—our wonderful old friend the late Ernest M. Frimbo, the world's greatest railroad (and steamboat and ferryboat) buff, with whom, on the night before Thanksgiving in 1967, we had made the last crossing of the last of the old Hudson steam ferries, the *Elmira*, from Barclay Street to Hoboken. As the old boat slipped through the evening fog, its deep-brown sides and gold-leaf lettering gleaming faintly in the running lights of passing tugboats, while the captain held back his tears and most of the passengers devoted themselves to ripping down orange life jackets from overhead racks to take home as souvenirs, only Frimbo, his black homburg perched solidly on his head, seemed to gaze beyond the deck into a future that once again included ferryboats. How he would have beamed at the *Port Imperial* (and the shrimp and crabmeat) as it vindicated him in the belief that he had witnessed not an extinction but only a blip in the three-hundred-year story of Hudson ferry crossings. How he would have cheered the *Port Imperial*'s easy demolition of the myth that New York and New Jersey are poles apart. (Frimbo, a New Yorker, was also a Princeton man.) We could almost hear him saying, "They look at the mighty Hudson and see only a Berlin Wall or the Green Line that separates Muslim Beirut from Christian Beirut. But when New Jersey and New York are a mere three minutes apart they are by common reckoning in the same neighborhood. Because your neighborhood is defined by the distance you will go to get to a dry cleaner's or a deli or a coffee shop. For most people, that extends about three blocks—the distance they can cover, walking at a sensible pace, in three minutes."

Looking at the hundreds of people who were taking in the speeches, we realized that only a part of the crowd would make it onto the first crossing of the *Port Imperial*, which can accommodate a hundred and forty-nine. A piece of Frimbo's training sprang to mind, and we quietly slipped around to the boatside edge of the crowd, so that we would be right behind the dignitaries when it came time to embark. After all, we would never have heard the end of it from the old gent if we had told him we'd been on the second maiden voyage of the new boat. So it was that we got to the *Port Imperial* even ahead of Governor Kean, who was momentarily waylaid by a TV reporter and required the shrill cries of a New Jersey assemblyman ("Hey, Gov! C'mon, Tom!") to pry him loose. We found ourself on the afterdeck of the ferry, just a few feet above the water, standing next to Ann-Marie Iacono, the animated, dark-haired first lady of Weehawken, who was taking pictures of the *Port Imperial*—and of a New York City fireboat throwing plumes of spray into the sky to welcome the newcomer—for a scrapbook of Weehawken history she's preparing for her husband's office. "Weehawken has a lot of history to it, you know," she told us. "The man who created Ben-Gay had a thirty-two-room mansion there, Fred and Adele Astaire lived there, and Eddie Bracken moved away only recently." Behind us, a rooster tail of white water lengthened as the *Port Imperial* sped away from shore. A breeze poured into our face, and we seemed to be almost skating across the wide expanse of blue water toward the Empire State Building. Suddenly, the boat was nosing into the dock in Manhattan. It was almost too fast. Frimbo would have insisted on the *Port Imperial*'s making at least one loop in the middle of the river before heading for land.

51 The Frimbonians

The E. M. Frimbo Special, *like fifty other of Amtrak's fault-lessly turned out inaugural runs over the last twenty-two years, was presided over by Bruce Heard, who, with his usual impeccable, don't-point-the-camera-at-me suaveness, manages to remain anonymous in the telling of it. Heard, the recipient of a Frimbo-bestowed nickname ("Buster"), was probably Frimbo's all-time favorite railroader. He serves as Amtrak's Director of Special Projects and (unofficially) as its indispensable institutional memory.*

Not all of Frimbo's intimates and traveling companions ever got one of his nicknames, although I can still remember his talking mysteriously about "the Highwayman," "the Red Baron," and "Plum Blossom." How I once longed for such a Frimbo nickname! And then I was tardy once too often—and after that, no matter how much my on-time performance later improved, was always "the late T. Hiss."

Our old, old friend E. M. Frimbo, the world's premier railroad buff, has been much in the news these past weeks. At the special request of W. Graham Claytor, Jr., the president of Amtrak, the ceremonial inaugural run, on April 4, 1991, of the railroad's new Hudson River service down the West Side of Manhattan into Pennsylvania Station was officially styled the *E. M. Frimbo Special*, and each of three hundred guests aboard the train was handed an Amtrak press release detailing the great man's legendary career. On the sixth, the last day of Amtrak service into Grand Central Terminal—which for seventy-four years had been the final destination for all passenger trains traveling south from Niagara Falls or Buffalo or Montreal or Albany—press cameras flashed as sixteen train lovers boarded the *Black Diamond*, a seventy-five-year-old open-platform observation car, for a trip to Albany and back: a sentimental journey dedicated to Frimbo's memory and featuring a carefully researched sit-down luncheon based on Frimbo's favorite old death-takes-a-holiday, the-hell-with-cholesterol dining-car recipes: lobster Newburg (garnished with hand-cut watermelon pickles), creamed-spinach soufflé, saffron rice, toasted corn bread, and strawberries in heavy cream.

The debonair and farseeing Frimbo during his lifetime had a railroad car named in his honor, but, of course, few railroad passengers, however celebrated in their day, are singled out for even greater honors ten years after leaving this world. As we climbed aboard the *E. M. Frimbo Special*, which smelled faintly both of fresh paint and of champagne (a bottle of Glenora Brut, which is made in New York State, had just been sloshed across its prow), and again as, two days later, we stood swinging in the April sunset out on the observation platform of the *Black Diamond*, we had our hand wrung and our back whacked by a succession of Frimbo well-wishers, and we began to understand why the old man's name commands respect among a new generation of railroaders. Back in the dark days before Amtrak, when those who admired trains lived in dread of each new timetable, because so often it would mean only absences, disfigurements, and heartache, as famous old trains were canceled or else had their running times extended so that they just missed the connections they had once made so handily, the railroads had few public champions, and Frimbo's tirelessly stouthearted defense of trains rang out across the land almost the way Churchill's voice rallied England after Dunkirk. The United States, if it let its railways slip away, Frimbo warned, would become the largest underdeveloped country in the world.

The real news today, we found out to our pleasure, is not just that, against all odds, train travel has survived in this country. It's that there is now a world of Frimbonians out there—among them some seemingly unlikely converts—trying to create a national high-speed-railroad system that will take dread and frustration out of transportation and replace them with such all but forgotten qualities as enjoyment, ease, convenience, and a sense of community. Even some members of the Bush Administration seem to be getting the message. Gil Carmichael, a former Volkswagen dealer and highway advocate from Mississippi, who is now serving as the head of the Federal Railroad (he was one of the honored guests aboard the *E. M. Frimbo Special*), goes around the country giving speeches about the need for what he calls "ethical transportation," meaning a transportation system that doesn't kill people, doesn't waste fuel, doesn't pollute the air, and doesn't cost more than the country can afford. "Railroads," he told us as the inaugural special streaked past a dozen swans bobbing gently on the Hudson, "are the one mode that fits almost automatically within these parameters."

As the train slid into Manhattan over its new trackage, we caught up with Senator Alfonse D'Amato, another born-again-Frimbonian, who had a seat in the head car of the *E. M. Frimbo Special*. (D'Amato has been a key player in the new Hudson River service: at almost the last minute, he came up with eleven million dollars in federal money that enabled the new Manhattan right-of-way to be double-tracked and thus avoid a considerable amount of snarled traffic.) For a moment, it seemed as though we were back in conversation with our old friend Frimbo, because all that the senator wanted to talk about was how trains link people together. "In 1944, when my grandfather moved from Brooklyn out to Island Park, he bought a house only two hundred and fifty yards from the town's Long Island Rail Road station, and because everybody walked by our house to go down to the station we knew everybody in town," he said. "The sense of neighborhood extended all the way into the city, too, because the same crowd gathered every workday to play pinochle on the train. We were a nice community because of the train—better informed, even, because the train ride also gave people time enough to read the papers. The new Hudson River service, which brings Long Islanders and upstaters into the station for the first time, won't be a boon just for travelers. It will extend a New York State sense of commonality, so that people from Albany and folks from Island Park won't be cut off from each other's psyche and knowledge."

On Saturday, at the invitation of Richard A. Horstmann, one of the owners of the *Black Diamond*, we went on board the car for a private, twilight run up the Hudson. As dusk fell, we wandered out onto the observation platform. The blue peaks of the Hudson Highlands hovered just over our head, and almost at our feet small waves smacked against the riverbank and a newly awakened chorus of spring peepers sang out into the gathering night. Then Horstmann turned on the car's running lights, so that the track fading away behind us took on a golden glow, and we stood there listening to the clickety-clack of the wheels. This time, the cadences of the motion itself seemed to take on Frimbo's voice. "Be of good cheer," we heard the rails say. And Frimbo's own battle cry: "Get on a train!"

Down the Track

Most of the predictions in this chapter are still on track, if slightly behind schedule. Wayne E. Davis remains one of American railroading's great modern heroes, and it's now expected that Amtrak's trains from Boston to Portland, Maine, will enter service in the fall of 1996. Electrification of the Northeast Corridor tracks between New Haven, Connecticut, and Boston will be completed later this decade, and new Amtrak high-speed trains will be running over the line in 1999.

Two spectacular train rides this summer that weren't published in any 1991 timetable—one that was a luxurious slither through steep Pennsylvania mountains, and one that was entirely stationary—have given us a look at how American passenger trains, which almost disappeared twenty years ago, may evolve over the next two decades. Unnoticed by the tens of thousands of shoppers and train riders who surge through Washington's gleamingly restored Union Station every day, the *Marco Polo*, which was once Franklin D. Roosevelt's private railroad car and is now the property of the Norfolk Southern Railroad, sits unassertively in a dim half-light at one end of Track 7. Inside, however, it is astir and aglow: an executive chef bustles among simmering pots in the kitchen; stewards hover attentively, unobtrusively; there's an Oriental rug on the floor of the observation lounge and a crisp white tablecloth and fresh flowers on the dining-room table. It's never alluded to by anyone on board—a reticence that perhaps strengthens the illusion—but the general effect is that F.D.R. might rejoin the assembled company at any moment.

F.D.R.'s buoyant presence is particularly inspiring to some of the members of Amtrak's brain trust, who have their headquarters upstairs in Union Station and have often had much to fear besides fear itself. Back in 1971, when Amtrak (officially, it's the National Railroad Passenger Corporation) began operations, many people thought that it would be lucky to last a couple of years. As recently as ten years ago, Amtrak made only forty cents for every dollar it spent, but this year it expects to make at least eighty cents, and it has now set itself the aim of covering its operating costs completely by the end of the decade. These days, even the Bush Administration, which at first talked, as the Reagan Administration had, about scuttling Amtrak, is showing respect and proposing funding (although not huge sums). Last month, when we accepted an invitation to join three Amtrak executives for lunch on the *Marco Polo*, we were impressed by the matter-of-factness with which they talked about setting, and achieving, big new goals. At first, as we all sipped iced tea and nibbled on hors d'oeuvres, talk centered on two names. One was that of Senator Daniel Patrick Moynihan, the author of the new Surface Transportation Act, which will for the first time provide states with what's already being called "flexibility money"; that is to say, it will allow them to divert federal money they get for highways into commuter-rail or light-rail or other mass-transit projects. Moynihan's watchword, ringing through the debate in Congress, has been "We have poured enough concrete!"

The second name, new to us, was that of Wayne E. Davis, a retired bank vice president from Portland, Maine, who in the last two years has mounted a remarkable citizens' campaign to restore passenger trains to his state. Maine, whose highways are increasingly congested, is one of three states in the lower forty-eight that Amtrak doesn't yet reach, and service to Maine from Boston was withdrawn way back in 1965, six years before Amtrak came on the scene. Davis started his campaign quietly: only twenty-one State of Mainers showed up at his first meeting, in 1989, to listen to him talk about how in a given time period two railroad tracks could carry as many people as a fifteen-lane highway. But a lot more have started listening since, and by early this year ninety thousand had signed a petition saying that they wanted their trains back. Only a few weeks ago, the Maine legislature, which had just spent months in an agonizing budget battle, passed a bill authorizing the state to find at least forty million dollars for passenger trains. Now it seems possible that trains will be heading Down East again by 1993.

Over lunch, our Amtrak hosts—Elyse G. Wander, the vice president for corporate planning and development; David J. Carol, a senior director for government affairs; and Sue S. Martin, a senior director for public affairs—began to look even further ahead. According to hasty notes we scribbled between courses, here are some just-beyond-the-horizon developments.

"Amtrak will become the airports' best friend," we wrote down—a summary of several things we learned. Today's Metroliners, which have a top speed of 125 miles an hour, and scoot between midtown New York and downtown Washington in as little as two and a half hours, already dominate that travel market, carrying more passengers daily than either the Trump (later USAir) Shuttle or the Pan Am (soon to become Delta) Shuttle. Amtrak, which plans to raise speeds between New York and Washington to 150 miles an hour, shaving fifteen minutes off the present running time, is also in the process of electrifying its main-line tracks between New York and Boston. The old New Haven Railroad, which had big plans after the First World War, was never able to extend electrification any farther north than New Haven, so the best time possible between New York and Boston these days is three hours and fifty-five minutes, but by 1996 the extended electrification will help make a three-hour run possible. Thirty percent of the passengers who enter Boston's Logan Airport are headed for New York, so a high-speed train between the two cities could make it possible for Boston *not* to build a second airport, and thereby save five billion dollars. And out West there's a rail corridor with the same potential: Portland, Oregon, to Seattle to Vancouver. At a state transportation hearing in Seattle this spring, officials from the Port of Seattle, which operates the Seattle-Tacoma Airport, now clogged with travelers for both Portland and Vancouver, surprised almost everyone in the room by pleading for more trains.

Another note merely says "the Amtrak look"—a reference to plans intended to make the railroad a more substantial, more everyday, and more recognizable part of people's lives all around the country. One way of doing this will be by introducing a transcontinental train from Los Angeles to Miami, Florida, and such a train will be a first: because American railroads were built either east or west of the Mississippi, we have never, even in the palmy days of crack expresses, offered ourselves any through trains. Amtrak also wants to see twice-a-day service on all its long-distance routes, so that, say, the only eastbound train out of Erie, Pennsylvania, doesn't leave at 3 A.M. And the railroad hopes at long last to design its own rolling stock, with crisp, angular lines and an unmistakable look, thus casting off its ragtag appearance. Right now, Amtrak is operating sleeping cars that were elderly when it inherited them, in 1971, from a variety of defunct passenger lines, and even the rounded, cigar-tube design of the Metroliners was introduced, back in 1969, by the Penn Central Railroad.

"Newfound champions" is what our last note says, and the only way to explain that one is to mention our day-long tour on what we've already started to think of as the Retroliner. Our second train ride, from New York to Pittsburgh, was a preview run of Amtrak's latest innovation, the Keystone Classic Club. It's a smoothly gliding observation car in which overstuffed armchairs are scattered about and which is allowed to carry only twelve people (ten passengers and two attendants) at any one time, along with a superabundance of food and drink, served practically nonstop. The route, which climbs around the Horseshoe Curve—an eighteen-fifties engineering marvel that catapults trains up over the Allegheny Mountains—and which descends along the gorge that in 1889 carried the raging waters of the Johnstown Flood, is now part of an experiment backed by the National Park Service to enhance awareness of America's industrial heritage. And the idea of the Keystone Classic Club was suggested to Amtrak by one of its directors, Paul M. Weyrich, who is both a dedicated enthusiast of passenger trains and the founder of the staunchly conservative Heritage Foundation. (Weyrich tells interviewers he suspects that President Reagan put him on the Amtrak board on the assumption that he detested trains.) A close associate of his, William S. Lind, who is the director of the Free Congress Foundation's Center for Cultural Conservatism, and is also the associate publisher of the *New Electric Railway Journal*, was one of the passengers on the Keystone Club Car the day of our journey, and he told us that now is the time for Amtrak to start wooing affluent travelers who are under the delusion that a train is only a Greyhound bus on rails.

"I see a strong urge toward retro-culture," Lind said as the train circled Horseshoe Curve. "That doesn't mean wanting to repeat the past; it means retracing our footsteps to the point where we took a wrong turn and lost our way. Americans need to know where our strength comes from." With a whoosh, the Keystone Club Car swept into the Gallitzin Tunnel, at the crest of the Alleghenies. Two armies—the Confederates and the Nazis—have tried and failed to blow up this tunnel, and it has now been in service for more than a hundred and thirty years.

Rogers E. M. Whitaker, 1900–1981

Rogers E. M. Whitaker, who died on Monday, May 11, 1981, at the age of eighty-one, was best known to *New Yorker* readers for his many appearances in The Talk of the Town under the thin disguise of E. M. Frimbo, world's greatest railroad buff. Less visible until now has been the fact that in his fifty-five years at the magazine Whitaker's presence and intelligence permeated almost every part of *The New Yorker*, contributing to, among other things, the way each of its pages looks and reads. The semifictional Frimbo, dapper and impeccable in his black homburg, the tails of his old tan mackintosh swirling in the steam hissing from a mighty locomotive, sometimes seemed larger than life. The real man was not always as endearing, but he had more sides to him and he attained greater stature.

Rogers Whitaker was born in Arlington, Massachusetts, on January 15, 1900. His father, Charles Harris Whitaker, was a vivid man, a lecturer on architecture, who crossed the Atlantic fifty times on steamships, and who, as editor of the

Journal of the American Institute of Architects, was an important figure in American architectural publishing. When Whitaker was nine, his father told him he was old enough to travel by himself on trains. At the end of Whitaker's sophomore year at Princeton, his father declined to pay any more tuition fees and gave him forty dollars and letters of introduction to three New York publishers. The young Whitaker's reaction was to plunge into publishing, dedicate himself to his work, learn whatever he could. "Work, for the night is coming" was one of his watchwords. From then on, he cherished his ability to pay his own way, and always dressed like someone with a large private income. The Metropolitan Museum of Art has taken an interest in his wardrobe; one of his handmade Bernard Weatherill tweed sports coats, with buttons on the sleeves that really button, has gone over to its Costume Institute.

When Whitaker got to New York, in 1920, he immediately adored it. He felt, as so many did then, that he had permanently acquired the freedom of the city—to go anywhere, at any time of the day—and that intelligence, wit, and a certain blend of tolerance and nerve would see him through any situation. He lived in a theatrical boardinghouse, down the hall from Mae West, and, later, in a Greenwich Village apartment with fifteen Persian cats. He sold advertising for a trade magazine, and he worked at the *Times* checking bridal announcements for hoaxes placed by rejected suitors. In 1925, he bought the first issue of *The New Yorker* and decided he had found the place where he wanted to work. A year later, he landed a job there as head of the makeup department, and he spent six years laying out each issue and refining the format. During this time, he also helped found our fact-checking department, teaching checkers that a fact is only as pure as the disinterestedness of its source. Then, as chief proofreader and head of the copy desk, he worked to develop the editorial query as an instrument for polishing a writer's intentions. Eventually, he was made an editor and worked directly with writers. Harold Ross bragged about Whitaker's eye for the bad, the flat, and the inapposite in a piece of writing, and attributed much of the magazine's early success to Whitaker and his colleague Hobart Weekes—two men who together could tussle with the prose of a loosely trained newspaperman and turn it into language.

Whitaker was a big man—six feet two and built like an ex–football player. He had pink cheeks, a large head, large features—except for narrow, hooded eyes—and a large stomach. He got handsomer with age. He spoke in a sort of gruff drawl. Some of the thirty or more writers Whitaker worked with over the years were scared of him, but many of them felt blessed. "He always got my point, and he was always interested in what I was trying to say," one of those writers has said. "He showed enormous courtesy to my writing."

Another writer recalls: "He had such superb confidence in the language that it never crossed his mind it might be impossible to say whatever it was I was trying to say. So when I floundered he just fixed the sentences. 'There's always a way,' he would say, and he would find it."

"He had something of the great, crusty authority of Dr. Johnson," still another writer has said. "Our phone calls were a genuine education. His attention to grammatical detail ultimately had a kind of moral force, because to his way of thinking each issue of the magazine had to be as nearly perfect as possible. It might be the only copy of the magazine some reader would see."

In 1934, Whitaker, while continuing to serve *The New*

Yorker in other capacities, began forty-six years of covering college football for the magazine—signing his columns "J.W.L.," because an early managing editor liked the look of these letters. Whitaker bought a huge pair of binoculars and wore a vest of real tiger skin under a big raccoon coat to Princeton games. He preferred to write about colleges that didn't give athletic scholarships, because he enjoyed watching games played without hope of reward or fear of punishment. Harvard's head coach, Joe Restic, said shortly before his death, "Whenever I talked to him, I felt like I was talking to another coach—one who appreciated that when football is played by young people who love competition it serves them well the rest of their years."

In the early thirties, Whitaker had taken on another chore for the magazine, which lasted forty years—going to supper clubs and cabarets and writing short reviews of them for the Goings On About Town section. (From 1943 to 1963, over the initials R.E.M.W. or R.W., he also wrote about these clubs and cabarets in the column Tables for Two.) Whitaker found that he liked nothing better than dining in the Persian Room, taking in the midnight show at the Copacabana or the late show at the Blue Angel, and then trundling off to an after-hours spot in Harlem or the Village before diving into a big breakfast of turkey hash and orange muffins, ducking into a hotel barbershop for a quick shave and a shine, and reporting to his desk promptly at 10 A.M. He quickly made friends with the musicians and comics he wrote about, and he was often invited to climb on a train with Duke Ellington when the Ellington band went on tour. He helped a number of performers—Harry Belafonte, Debbie Reynolds, Orson Bean, Jonathan Winters—get their first Broadway-musical parts. He gave Cy Coleman, the composer of *Little Me, Sweet Char-*

ity, and *Barnum*, his first rave when Coleman was a very young jazz pianist. "Growing up," Coleman has said, "I always wanted to be a concert pianist, and Whitaker's praise really got me started on a career I wasn't yet quite sure I wanted. It sent me spiraling in a strange way." (Coleman later wrote *On the Twentieth Century* with Whitaker in mind.) Whitaker also gave Lenny Bruce his only good notice when Bruce first opened at the Blue Angel. In the night-life world, for reasons that are lost to history, he was known as Popsie. "Popsie Whitaker reigned supreme," Bobby Short has said. "He was one of the few who *knew*, one of the few wise men I've met, and it was gratifying to know we were getting across to someone as intrinsically stylish as he was. The little blurbs he wrote were actually brilliant reviews that exerted a terribly important influence, because in two or three words he had it out flat exactly what you were up to. If you were bright, you picked it up and went on from there."

During all these years, Whitaker never stopped taking train trips whenever a moment opened up—an evening ride to Philadelphia, a weekend ride to Chicago and St. Louis, a week of rides in Switzerland or India or Japan or New Zealand. His totals were staggering—2,748,636.81 miles by train formally accounted for (and he confided near the end of his life that he was at least several years behind in his arithmetic), seventy-eight trips across the Atlantic, twelve across the Pacific—but in his view he was always only doing something sensible and practical. "If I rode around in a Buick all weekend," he used to point out, "no one would say a word."

And Whitaker put his knowledge of trains to good use. During the Second World War, the United States Army commissioned him in the rank of major in the Traffic Control Division of the Transportation Corps, so that he could help plan the routing of troop trains. (Trains accounted for more than 97 percent of the troop movements in this country during the war.) In 1970, he was a key witness at an Interstate Commerce Commission "train-off" hearing that denied the Penn Central Railroad permission to discontinue all thirty-four of its long-distance passenger trains west of Buffalo and Harrisburg. In the mid-seventies, he worked as a secret consultant to Paul Reistrup, then the president of Amtrak: Whitaker would ride on troublesome trains and report privately on their problems. "Service is better today because of the work Frimbo did," Reistrup has said. "It was really beneficial to riders—particularly in scheduling and marketing. He would tell me it was no wonder our morning train to Princeton had no business, because there was no evening train back from Princeton. Our schedulers had never round-tripped it. I spotted him one day when he was on an unannounced trip out West—he booked tickets under forty-eight different aliases, so no one would know what he was up to—and I thought he was sort of nodding off. Only to be expected, at his age, I said to myself. Then he looked up and saw me, and I noticed that he had his pocket watch—set, as always, to New York time—in his hand. 'Just judging our speed by timing the catenary poles,' he said. He never earned his living on railroads—unless you count the couple of weeks in the summers of 1957, 1958, and 1959, when he volunteered his services as a dining-car steward on the Western Pacific's *Caribou Country Special*—but whenever I talked to him I thought I was talking to a real railroad man, and specifically, to an employee of the New York Central passenger department. Each railroad had its own personality in the old days, and the Central had real class. It wasn't uppity, like the Pennsylvania."

At the end of 1975, Whitaker retired as an editor and, at

the age of seventy-five, settled down as a full-time reporter.
He wrote Talk of the Town pieces and pieces for the *Times,
Travel & Leisure*, and *The Official Railway Guide*. In addition, he wrote a book, *Decade of the Trains: The 1940's*; he
was consultant editor to *Fodor's Railways of the World*; and
he wrote the foreword, the song blurbs, and the singer's biography for *The First Blossom Dearie Songbook*. Not long
before his seventy-seventh birthday, he test-drove a moped in
Central Park for another piece. A musical comedy about
him—*Frimbo*—played in Grand Central Terminal in the fall

*The logo and a performance photo-
graph from* Frimbo, *a musical
comedy, 1982*

of 1980, and in October of that year the National Association of Railroad Passengers presented him and Frimbo with a joint certificate of appreciation for "their vital contributions" to passenger service.

At the end, there was yet another transformation—one that surprised those who had never seen sweetness in Whitaker. His greatest strength for many years—his pride in making his own way in the world—had also kept him at a distance from some whose company he might otherwise have enjoyed. He was stubborn, and he could often be harsh and wounding. But when he was hospitalized with cancer in early 1981 and started to lose a great deal of weight he somehow at the same time shed the large burdens of hurt and suspiciousness he had carried ever since he was yanked out of Princeton. He endured a great deal of pain in the hospital without complaint, and the Whitaker of the final days was a tiny, bright-eyed man—alert, valiant, courteous, and endlessly kind.

Whitaker's battered homburg and his manual typewriter

Frimbo's Peak

This chapter, first published in 1983 and by far the longest in the book, introduces the "outdoor Frimbo," as I think of him, Rogers' extraordinary younger brother, Francis, who now lives and works at the Rocky Mountain School in Carbondale, Colorado, which has built him his own forge. Francis Whitaker, at eighty-nine, now regularly goes on jaunts around the world as elaborate and as Frimbonian as any ever undertaken by his elder brother. He recently sent me a note from the Queen Adelaide Restaurant, *the dining car on board the* Indian Pacific, *the most famous train in Australia, which runs from Sydney to Perth:*

"There are a few times," he wrote, "when a door opens suddenly on a new phase of the world. It happened thirty years ago, when I first went snorkeling with Portia. And it happened again this month when I first saw Australian Aboriginal art —a whole new world for me, but thousands of years old, and all color, dots and lines, and abstract designs. A great experience coming so late in life."

Francis Whitaker, who has been a blacksmith for sixty-one years, invited me out to Colorado a while back to help him fasten a brass plaque he had made in honor of his brother Rogers to a railroad tie ten thousand and fifteen feet above sea level. Here is my friend John Haber's photograph of the 14″ × 6″ plaque:

My first thought when I saw this plaque was that Rogers Whitaker, who for many years was my friend, colleague, and officemate at *The New Yorker* (where he had been nicknamed Frimbo), and whose rail trips I had occasionally chronicled in The Talk of the Town, had been even more extraordinary than the inscription indicated, because I knew that his Frimbo mileage—which can be divided out to more than fifty thousand miles a year for more than fifty years—was all done on nights, holidays, vacations, and weekends away from his work editing manuscripts, reviewing night-club acts, and writing a football column for the magazine. It was after I had spent a few days with Francis Whitaker that I began to discover how many different stories, each one as remarkable or as commonplace as Rogers' own story, come together in the plaque

Rahway [PRR]   2 618, 319.20
Union   2 618, 319.40
Coloniz   2 618, 321.30
Iselin   2 618, 322.40
Metro Park   2 618, 322.60
Menlo Park   2 618, 323.80
Metuchen   2 618, 325.60
Lincoln   2 618, 325.80
Kilmer   2 618, 328.60
Edison   2 618, 328.70
Park   2 618, 330.20
New Brunswick   2 618, 333.10
County   2 618, 334.60
Jersey Avmo Main   2 618, 334.80
Adams   2 618, 337.30
Dems   2 618, 340.30
Monmouth Junction   2 618, 342.80
Midway   2 618, 343.00
Pkzimsbow   2 618, 347.20
Nassau   2 618, 348.70
Princeton Junction   2 618 348.80
Laurence   2 618, 353.00
Division Post [PRR]   2 618, 355.40

that honors him. Since then, back in New York, I have also
been thinking about how much has had to survive and remain
available during the last half century for even a small plaque
with Frimbo's name on it to be exactly where it now is.

Frimbo's plaque is in Cumbres Pass, a narrow gap in the
San Juan Mountains, a range of jagged peaks, nine to fourteen
thousand feet high, in the southern Rockies. The range is
about a hundred and fifty miles long and runs gradually down-
hill to the southeast into New Mexico. It is empty country

and poor country, for the most part, and very beautiful. The mountains are thirty-five-million-year-old volcanoes, scraped by glaciers that disappeared twelve thousand years ago. Cumbres Pass, a couple of miles north of the New Mexico border, is a small meadow with a few tall, straight Engelmann spruce trees that is crossed by three paths: State Highway 17, a two-lane road that was paved about twenty years ago; the ghost of an old dirt road used by miners and homesteaders in the 1870's; and a single narrow-gauge railroad track, now over a hundred years old and only about twice the width of a cow path.

There are four seasons in the high mountains, Coloradans say—winter, spring, fall, and winter. Early in the last week of September, the aspen groves on the slopes below Cumbres turn a pale gold. A couple of weeks later, the trees drop their leaves. During the double winter, from late October until about the last week in May, Cumbres—except for the state highway, which is regularly plowed—is entirely covered with the dry, light, blowing, drifting snow that falls at altitudes of eight thousand feet and higher. There are generally eight or nine feet of snow on Cumbres all winter. One winter, a total of forty-one feet fell; the largest single snowstorm on record left three and a half feet in less than twenty-four hours. In the Cumbres spring, when the winds are gentle, Black Angus and red-and-white Hereford cattle crop lush green grass; towering thunderheads form a white line of mock mountains along the peaks in the clear blue afternoon sky; and, near Frimbo's plaque, purple, blue, bright-red, yellow, and white wild flowers—asters, lupine, fireweed, miniature sunflowers, and Indian paintbrush, which is usually fiery red but paled here by the subalpine altitude—bloom among gray-black cinders

cast aside by panting little fifty-eight-year-old steam locomotives that clamber up and down the railroad track over the
pass.

Driving through Cumbres Pass—the first and less spectacular of two passes on an hour-long trip over an empty road
between the small town of Chama, New Mexico, and the
equally small town of Antonito, Colorado—is an experience
that barely gets into short-term memory. At Cumbres, there's
a sensation that a slight rise in the road has just become a
slight dip in the road, and there's a road sign that says
"Cumbre Pass, Elev. 10022 feet" (the highway climbs seven
feet higher up the pass than the railroad), but there aren't any
vistas or panoramas. Cumbres is hemmed in by hills, so you
don't think about braking to a stop and rolling down the
window, and if it occurred to you to look over your shoulder
you'd be gone before you had even turned around. There are
a hundred and thirty-six named passes in Colorado, and a car
can get over half of them without a strain, at least in the
summer.

An arrival at Cumbres at a speed of ten miles an hour
behind one of the *I-think-I-can, I-think-I-can* steam engines
of the Cumbres & Toltec Scenic Railroad is, however, an
achievement. It's not something you can do all the time—the
trains run only from the first week in June through the second
week of October. When they do run, there's one train a day
for Cumbres; it leaves Chama at ten in the morning. Standard-
gauge railroad track is four feet eight and a half inches
wide—an arbitrary but substantial figure that some say is
based on the distance between the ruts worn by chariots and
wagons in the stones of the old Roman roads of Britain. The
rails on the Cumbres & Toltec Scenic track are only three feet
apart, and the ground has been cleared for only a few feet on

ROUND-TRIP EXCURSION TICKET

New Mexico Express

CUMBRES & TOLTEC SCENIC RAILROAD

P.O. BOX 789, CHAMA, NEW MEXICO, 87520

Date ___ MONDAY AUG - 9 1982

CAR: _Q_ SEAT: _27_

DEPARTS: CHAMA, N.M., 10:00 A.M.

N⁰ 11736 — 82

either side of the track. A ride over track of this width is fascinating: it has as much immediacy as a bicycle ride, but you seem to be gliding just above the ground in a dream. Cumbres is an hour away from Chama by train, and it's generally ten degrees colder. The whole trip, twisting through mountain valleys, past stands of pine, cottonwood, and aspen, along ledges cut into the bulging sides of mountains, is up a grade so steep that the engine repeatedly throws off roiling columns of gray-black coal smoke sixty feet high, like a bottle releasing a different genie every second. The engine is often as much as sixteen feet higher than the final car on the train it pulls. When the train gets to Cumbres, the first level place it has encountered in an hour, it has to stop, so that the engine can absorb several thousand gallons of water. And when it gets there it has reached what just happens to be the highest point in the country traversed by passenger trains. So there it is—Cumbres. Frimbo's peak.

Cumbres was certainly never planned to be the highest point railroad passengers could reach, and the experience of Cumbres was not thought by most travelers to have anything to do with their purpose in traveling. Cumbres was just one more thing to put behind you. The sixty-four-mile track between Antonito and Chama was installed in the early 1880's and was only a small segment of a much longer line, now mostly gone, that linked Denver with the towns of Durango and Silverton, way west in the San Juans, where in the 1870's gold and silver had been discovered. There was a small station at Cumbres—there still is. There was even a post office there until 1937, which was really just for railroad workers—the grade up from Chama was so steep that sometimes as many as three extra engines had to be added on in Chama and cut out at Cumbres. But the miners' race to the mining camps was not the only race across Cumbres: the railroad itself, the Denver & Rio Grande, was racing to reach Durango before its rival, the Santa Fe Railroad, could run tracks there. Thus, for a long time, Cumbres wasn't the highest point for passengers, because there were several thousand miles of narrow-gauge track all over the Colorado Rockies, reaching many parts higher than Cumbres (narrow-gauge track was cheaper to build than standard-gauge, and could make sharper turns through the mountains). Then for a time, after all the narrow-gauge track that reached points higher than Cumbres had passed out of use, Cumbres was only *potentially* the highest point for passengers, because only freight trains ran over the line. In 1951, Alfred E. Perlman, the general manager of the Denver & Rio Grande Western, who wished to close down the line to Durango altogether, had discontinued passenger service on it—service that had included, daily, an open-platform observation car and a buffet-parlor car, beloved of Frimbo, where you could get a steak dinner for a dollar and fifteen cents—because without the daily passenger trains snow would accumulate more often at Cumbres and it would cost

Railroad siding along Cumbres-Toltec track in Chama, New Mexico

more to clear it away, and this increase in cost would make it easier for the railroad to apply to the Interstate Commerce Commission for permission to abandon the whole Durango line as a losing venture. (Perlman, who later became the president of the New York Central Railroad, used similar tricks —except when foiled by Frimbo and some of his friends—to close Eastern branch lines.) But after the passenger trains had been withdrawn the Durango line started making money

again. In the 1950's, there was a huge dicovery of oil and gas
at the far end of the line, near Farmington, New Mexico, and
the pipes needed to bring them out of the ground had to be
brought in on railroad flatcars.

Cumbres finally became the highest point for passengers
only thirteen years ago, when the track from Antonito to
Chama, no longer needed to supply the oil and gas fields, was
saved by preservationists from Colorado and New Mexico,
who persuaded the two states to set up the only two-state-
owned railroad in the country: the Cumbres & Toltec Scenic,
a tourist railroad that would inherit much of the Denver &
Rio Grande Western narrow-gauge freight equipment, thus
preserving the most spectacular part of a working narrow-
gauge mountain railroad. No one knows how long Cumbres
will go on being the highest point, because the Cumbres &
Toltec Scenic is expensive to operate and, although registered
as a National Historic Landmark, hard to publicize in the
middle of mostly uninhabited country, and a great many people have never heard of it. Kyle Railways, Inc., the private
operating company for the line, is hoping to put things on a
stable basis by tapping the vast market of Texans who could
drive to the railroad's two terminuses on their vacations.
(There are eleven Texans for every New Mexican or for every
two Coloradans.) But there it is, for now—Cumbres. And you
can get there on a train—part of the time, at least. Even if
you have to drive to get to the train.

I had Frimbo's plaque on my lap when I heard most of
this information about the high pass. It was the morning of
the day that the plaque was going to be put in place, and I
was sitting on the train to Cumbres, between Francis Whitaker and his wife, Portia. I had already had a day with the

Whitakers, meeting them in Santa Fe, then driving to Chama early the next morning—the Whitakers get up at six. Now there were seven of us in the group that was to install the plaque. Besides the Whitakers and myself, there were two other people from New York, and a couple from California. We were all sitting in the lead car of a twelve-car train made up of eighty-year-old boxcars with windows chopped out of their wooden sides and comfortable-enough molded-plastic seats bolted to their floors. There were two hundred and fifty people on the train. Francis was wearing a Tyrolean hat and an old Burberry of his brother's—a coat Rogers had had with him for at least a million miles of his train travels. Francis had a picnic hamper on his lap. Portia was wearing a large straw hat and carrying a Polaroid. She told me the names of the wild flowers we were passing. The conductor, talking over a loudspeaker, told an unknown passenger to "put your child's legs back inside the train."

When no one else was talking, Francis, in a quiet, measured voice, told me about people who had climbed over Cumbres through the years. The mountain sun poured in the open windows on all aboard, and the mountain air swirled through the cars and set the coattails of Francis's Burberry flapping. I was very conscious of holding tightly to the plaque. Utes and Apaches, Francis began, were probably the first people to find Cumbres. After them came Spanish explorers from Mexico, who named both the mountains and the pass —"Cumbres" is Spanish for "summits," "highlights," "culminations." After them came mountain men and beaver trappers, and then Missouri soldiers hunting Indians, and then miners, and then homesteaders, with their cattle and covered wagons. But more memorable than any of these, to Francis' way of thinking, were the railroad builders, a gang of Irish and French-Canadian workers, who, using only dynamite and hand tools, graded the line, blasted a curving tunnel three hundred and sixty-six feet long out of solid rock, built two wooden trestles more than a hundred feet high, and then, skirting a six-hundred-foot drop into Toltec Gorge and cresting Cumbres itself, put down the sixty-four miles of track between Antonito and Chama—and did all this work in just one month more than a year. The first rails on the Chama side of Cumbres, along the grade we were now ascending, were spiked to hand-hewn ties during the snows of November and December 1880. "They were rugged men," Francis said. "Is their work still visible? Can we look at the track here now and see how much effort, how much ingenuity, how much firmness of purpose went into it? I often think if we could look at a house or a fence or a garden and see the presence of these things within, then there couldn't be any vandalism, because we would have too much respect."

While Francis Whitaker was passing on these stories and reflections, I found myself thinking, for the first time, of how this expedition had come about. Rogers Whitaker had traveled over every mile of passenger track in North America. But it was Francis Whitaker who had decided on this spot to remember him at. And it was Francis Whitaker who had made the plaque, who had arranged with officials in Colorado and New Mexico to let him place it on their railroad, and who had gathered our group together and put us on the train. I began by thinking, What a remarkable pair of brothers! And it also seemed to me—although I couldn't really explain it— that in getting to know Francis I was getting close to something in Frimbo himself that I hadn't known in all my years with him.

Francis Whitaker is seventy-six, and lives and works in

Aspen, Colorado, when he isn't out on the road. He moved to Aspen from Carmel, California, in 1963—even though he was a member of the Carmel City Council at the time—because he thought Carmel was getting too stodgy. He has his own forge, the Mountain Forge, in downtown Aspen, where, either alone or with a student, he hand-forges wrought-iron gates, ornamental fences, railings, tables, lamps, candlesticks, fireplace tools, and what is called door hardware, meaning latches, hinges, and handles. Wrought iron means worked iron, as distinguished from cast iron, which gets its shape in a mold. People who do this kind of handwork are nowadays often called artist-blacksmiths, to differentiate them from farriers—the blacksmiths who shoe horses—but Francis says he was always happy just to be known as a dirty old blacksmith. For fifty years, Francis has had as much work as he can handle, but he is also now in constant demand as a teacher, and he and Portia regularly travel to schools and forges all over the country, where Francis holds workshops for groups of up to twenty master and apprentice blacksmiths and also gives demonstrations for audiences of several hundred people. Every year, a couple of dozen of his students write him thank-you notes. A recent one said, "I find that your direct blacksmithing approach, supported by your highly developed skills, has proved to me that productivity lies in the hands of the smith, not in an arc welder or machine tools, etc."

The skills that Francis acquired as a young man—shaping and putting together pieces of iron by heating them, setting them on an anvil, and then striking them with a hammer while the iron is still hot—had been developed and improved by a succession of blacksmiths over the last four thousand years. A smith is a smiter, someone who knows how to hit metal; and iron is the black metal: blacksmith. Two thousand years before blacksmiths, there were redsmiths—people who shaped the soft red metal, copper. The techniques of the black-smiths, the product of perhaps a hundred and fifty generations of human effort, observation, and intelligence, almost dis-appeared in this country during the Second World War, with the adoption of two new tools that almost anyone could master in short order: the acetylene torch, which made cutting a piece of iron nearly as easy as cutting a piece of wood with a jigsaw, and the arc welder, which made sticking together two pieces of iron nearly as simple as gluing them together.

Francis Whitaker taught welding at a San Francisco ship-yard during the Second World War. Then he returned to his forge and went back to work with a hammer. In the late 1960's, there was a revival of interest in traditional black-smithing in this country, and, in March of 1973, twenty-seven smiths and would-be smiths attended a meeting in Lumpkin, Georgia, and formed an international organization, the Artist-Blacksmiths' Association of North America (ABANA)—some-thing blacksmiths in this country had never thought of doing before. Three years later, Francis, who had worked by himself since 1945, and had never exhibited his work except at county fairs, was discovered by ABANA, which by then had six hundred members, and he was invited to demonstrate his methods at an ABANA conference in Carbondale, Illinois. In 1978, Francis served a term as president of ABANA, and since then he has been founding president of the Southwest Artist Blacksmith Association and has been made an honorary life-member of the Upper Midwest Blacksmiths' Association, the California Blacksmiths Association, the Arizona Artist Blacksmith Association, the Southern Ohio Forge & Anvil, and the Appalachian chapter of ABANA. ABANA itself now has more than two thousand members, most of them under forty. ABANA, says Francis, "caught on like a combination of wildfire and snowballs."

Francis Whitaker today is the most sought-after teacher of blacksmithing in the country. His 1983 itinerary included workshops in New Mexico, Alabama, Illinois, Pennsylvania, and North Carolina, where he has helped the Campbell Folk School, in Brasstown, set up a forge with eleven hearths and eleven anvils. He was also head demonstrator at the ABANA tenth-anniversary conference, in Madison, Georgia. In between trips, he completed some thirty jobs at his forge, including a four-and-a-half-foot by six-and-a-half-foot gate, a railing to go around the forge, and a hundred and six door handles for a house in Breckenridge, Colorado.

In July of 1981, Francis and Portia added a three-day trip to Cumbres to their 1981 itinerary. They drove down to Chama through Cumbres, spent the night in a motel, and then got on a train for Cumbres the next morning. Francis had Rogers' ashes with him. He had decided to scatter them at Cumbres, but he wanted to bring them there on the train so he could add a final 37.92 miles to Frimbo's millions. Last year, Francis cut the plate for Frimbo's plaque, wrote out the inscription for it, and hammered in the words with letter punches at his forge. Then he set about getting permission from the Colorado and New Mexico authorities to add this piece of hardware to their railroad line and gathered the seven of us together to take the plaque to Cumbres on the train. He told us on the train that he'd had a good time making the plaque, because a brass plaque was one thing he had never made before, and that the timing of this train trip had worked out well for him, because he had been able to fit it in between holding a workshop near Santa Fe, where he had made a railing for a circular staircase, and finishing an ornamental fence for a new house in Aspen. (Aspen is by now something of a museum of Whitaker ironwork.) He had already arranged to have the workshop coincide with his annual trip to the Santa Fe Opera with Portia and some friends he has known for fifty years.

"My kid brother has a busy schedule" was what Rogers Whitaker usually said whenever he had a piece of news about Francis to pass on. As a result, when I finally met Francis—in 1981, when he was in New York to visit Rogers in the hospital—I already knew about many of the things he had done. I knew that three years after Francis moved to Aspen he became chairman of the Aspen Planning and Zoning Commission and persuaded the city to adopt a new master plan that put strict limits on future growth in central Aspen. And I knew that Francis had forged a set of iron gates for Leon Uris' house in Aspen, using a figure of a Haganah freedom fighter as the center of the design; that Francis had been elected and reelected to the Aspen City Council; that Leon Uris had modeled Conor Larkin, the blacksmith hero of *Trinity,* after Francis; that Francis had designed two fireplaces for John Denver's house in Aspen; that Francis had been awarded an honorary doctorate of humane letters by the University of Colorado; that Francis was known as the dean of American blacksmiths. After Frimbo's last visit to Francis and Portia in Aspen, he had reported that when Francis works in his forge he wears steel-rimmed spectacles and a flat black cloth cap; that Francis likes to get to work at seven or seven-thirty in the morning; that he likes to take a break at three in the afternoon and sit on a little bench in front of the forge and drink a can of Coors; that a friend of Francis' caught him

doing chores around the house and helping Portia in her garden, and accused him of being a "wife pleaser"; that when
Francis had been awarded his honorary degree and was seated
in academic robes among his fellow-honorees, including former mayor of Denver and the chief justice of the Supreme
Court of Colorado, he began waving his arms, trying to attract
the attention of his son, Dr. Stephen Whitaker, a professor of
chemical engineering at the University of California at Davis,
who was in the audience taking photographs and hadn't noticed that he had forgotten to remove his lens cap.

I also knew a few personal details about Francis and Portia. I knew that after Francis met Portia, who is his second
wife, seventeen years ago, they got married in two months.
(Portia was living in Sterling, Colorado, and Francis told her
they were going to get married because their phone bills were
higher than either one of them could afford.) That Portia's
mother was the first woman to graduate from North Carolina
Medical College, married a Russian agronomist, and went off
to Russia with him. That Portia was born in Turkestan and
that her family had to flee Russia during the Revolution. That
she wound up in Colorado, where she married a building
contractor, raised four sons, helped to run the contracting
business after her husband died, and learned to ski when she
was fifty (Francis can ski two miles down Aspen Mountain in
seven minutes flat). That when Francis and Portia got married
they didn't know if they wanted a honeymoon, because although they were sure they wanted to live together they
weren't sure whether they would make compatible traveling
companions. In the end, they went on a trial honeymoon,
driving to one state park, two national parks, and four national monuments in seven days; and when they found that
they liked this trip they chartered a sailboat with a captain

and a cook and a crew of deckhands for a week in the Grenadines, having first made sure that on their final night, when they planned to have steak and champagne in the Tobago keys, there would be a full moon. Francis is good at planning this kind of moment. He carries in his wallet a picture of himself and two friends taken one morning in California in 1963, at sunrise, on the top of Mt. Whitney, the highest peak in the lower forty-eight states. The three friends had climbed all night by moonlight in order to see the sun rise over the edge of the world.

When I first met Francis and Portia, he was busy dealing with Rogers' affairs, and I really had a chance for only a brief look at him. My first impression was of his *Whitakerness.* There was no doubt that he and Rogers were brothers—they had the same big frame and big head and high forehead and prominent nose. Francis is taller and leaner, but the impression was: so this is what Rogers would have looked like if he had spent more time outdoors, if he had spent more time standing up, if he had used a hammer instead of a pen. Francis wears glasses, whereas Rogers didn't, and he has a softer voice and a much milder look; but there was something familiar about the strength inside the voice and the attentiveness behind the look. After Rogers' death, Francis went back to Aspen before I had time to get to know him, and as the year went on my sense of Rogers himself—strengths and weaknesses both—seemed to be beginning to slip away.

That summer, Rogers' books and papers and personal effects were packed up and shipped to the American Heritage Center of the University of Wyoming, at Laramie, and most of his railroad-magazine subscriptions started to expire. It seemed as though I had just about finished saying good-by.

But it turned out that the good part of the good-by came a little later, when I began hearing unexpectedly from a few people who had decided to make some kind of memorial tribute to him. John L. Haber, a young New York theatre director who conceived and directed *Frimbo*, a musical that played in Grand Central Terminal in 1980, began preparing a documentary about Rogers' life. Haber videotaped interviews with forty-six of Frimbo's friends, including night-club singers, two Amtrak presidents, a couple of peers, and Harvard's football coach. Robert Lewis, who was the publisher of *Railway Age, Railway Track & Structures*, and *International Railway Journal*, and who had been a traveling companion of Frimbo's since the late 1930's, called up to say that he had somehow persuaded New Jersey Transit to put back in service, for one day only, an old, open-platform observation car that Frimbo had ridden in on its very first run, more than fifty-five years before, and that the car would be used for an E. M. Frimbo Memorial Trip. (Last August, twenty people, including a time-table publisher and the special-projects director of Amtrak, showed up for an early-evening run across New Jersey from Newark to Phillipsburg, on the Delaware River.) And Lewis said I might want to know how many things had been happening in passenger-train operations since Frimbo's last ride —things that showed that the world might be catching up with Frimbo, that Frimbo had been right never to lose interest in train travel. For one thing, Lewis said, Amtrak had scotched an attempt by the Reagan Administration to reduce it from a nationwide system to a short-haul corridor service between Boston, New York, and Washington. And Amtrak had turned itself into a good railroad, with very modern equipment, trains that ran on time, and a new president—W. Graham Claytor, Jr.—who promised to restore fresh food cooked on board to his dining cars and to replace the plastic knives and forks with stainless steel. (Claytor has fulfilled these promises, has added Häagen-Dazs ice cream to the menu, and has even restored overnight shoe-shine service to the sleeping cars of the Florida trains.) Overseas, Lewis continued, there were second-generation high-speed trains in France, the restoration of the Orient Express between London and Venice, and the inauguration of a touring train from Delhi, made up of twelve eighty-year-old state coaches, with chandeliers, carpets, separate dining cars for Continental and subcontinental cuisine, and an observation car with an open veranda and solid-brass pillars.

And I had a visit that fall from Dr. Gene M. Gressley, of the University of Wyoming, who is one of the country's great hunters of archival material, having in the last twenty-seven years obtained the books, papers, and files of eight thousand people for the university's American Heritage Center. It was Gressley who had arranged to have Frimbo's papers and effects from both his office and his apartment—they filled a truck—sent there, and he wanted to tell me that the material now formed the Rogers E. M. Whitaker Collection and would enrich the center's holdings in both transportation and journalism. A few months later, Gressley called me to say that a catalogue of the Whitaker Collection—running to three hundred and ninety-four pages—had been prepared, and that thousands of Frimbo's timetables, from six continents and many decades, and twenty thousand of his railroad postcards, together with his correspondence, fourteen bottles of wine, four Bobby Short albums, two homburgs, and a full-dress suit, are now available for scholarly inspection in the same building that houses the papers of Ada Louise Huxtable,

James Beard, Barbara Stanwyck, and Edward Everett Horton.

And then I heard from Francis Whitaker. Flying out to New Mexico to meet the Whitakers, I had a sudden sense that Frimbo's memory was being dispersed—to New Jersey, to Wyoming, to Colorado—and I was disheartened. It seemed to risk obliterating a man I had always felt to be all of a piece and one of a kind. The thought disappeared when I met the Whitakers, who gave me a Margarita; treated me to a Mexican dinner in a former convent; took me to the Santa Fe Opera; showed me, on the drive to Chama, one of the oldest irrigation ditches in the United States, which is half a mile long and was dug by Indians seven or eight hundred years ago and has been in continuous use ever since, having deposited many feet of topsoil on the otherwise barren land it waters; and introduced me to a rodeo cowboy who had constructed a machine that swung two drainpipes, like pendulums, in parallel arcs a few inches above the ground. The cowboy was lassoing the pipes in order to practice his steer roping—the pipes moving something like the hind legs of an escaping steer. The cowboy said he had broken his wrist and as a consequence had to relearn his throw, using different arm muscles. It took a lot of practice, because first he had to unlearn his old throw— he said that Pavlov had discovered that it takes twenty-nine times as long to break a habit as it does to inculcate one. Francis looked at the pipe-swinging machine and suggested that it would move more smoothly if he added a flywheel to his gear drive. "Oh, Portia," said Francis when we were all back in the car, "I'd forgotten what a beautiful ride this is."

It was on the train to Cumbres, as I said, that I first began to put the two brothers, Rogers and Francis, side by side in my mind. When I did this, instead of seeing two hard-working, strong-minded, unique, and unrepeatable people, I seemed to see the pair of them at once, moving in tandem across a long stretch of time. It was as if I had just doubled my memories of Rogers. When I thought of Rogers at his desk in his shirt-sleeves and braces, or at a football game with his enormous binoculars, or sitting on a train with his Burberry on his lap, the question came to me: And what was Francis doing then? After I had spent some time with Francis, he no longer looked to me extraordinarily like his brother, but in his company I felt the same quality of mind at work. I seemed to be noticing not the Whitakerness of Francis but the Frimboness of both Rogers and Francis. I seemed to be seeing, that is, not two sets of lifework but one worker making two different series of choices. Or maybe it was one endowment distributed between two different people. So the particular actions of Rogers were just Rogers' way of using something inside him. It seemed that such a something could appear in different people, and in people with different interests. But how was such an endowment formed?

The train reached Cumbres, but it was not time for installing the plaque. This was only a quick stop to take on water. The train was heading for a lunch stop at a station called Osier, twelve miles down the other side of the pass. There we would meet the daily train from Antonito, which would pull up alongside us on a short stretch of parallel track. A buffet lunch, choice of American (barbequed beef) or Mexican (enchilada and tamale), would be served to both sets of passengers. After lunch, the two trains would switch engines, and we would get on the Chama-bound train and come back up to Cumbres, where there would be a twenty-minute stop and time for the installation.

On the slight downgrade into Osier, the engine doesn't work so hard and puts out less smoke, and the trip is quieter, and talking is a simpler matter. I asked Francis if he knew what had led him to forge work, and he told me that the quick answer was his father, and the slow answer was both his parents. He said that his father, the first editor of the *Journal of the American Institute of Architects* in Washington, D.C., was always known in the family as the Skipper, and went on, "In 1922, when I was fifteen and at the end of my junior year of high school, at the School of Organic Education, in Fairhope, Alabama, I came home for the summer and told the Skipper, 'I can figure out how many yards of ditch a man can dig in a day if he can dig so many cubic feet an hour, but I know nothing about his experience, or his life.' The Skipper didn't necessarily see that I had a blacksmith in me, but he was wise enough to steer me in the direction of handwork; and because he knew everyone in the field of building he got me a place that fall as a helper under Samuel Yellin, of Philadelphia, who made great decorative ironworks for architects, and who was probably America's greatest smith. And the first time I got hold of a piece of hot iron and a hammer—and I have heard other smiths say the same thing—I knew this was for me. I never went back to school.

"The fascination was this, and remains this: iron has a strength no other material has, and yet it has in it at the same time a capacity for being light, graceful, and beautiful. It has this capacity—but no desire. It will do nothing by itself, except sit there and resist you. Even when it's heated, it remains stubborn and has, at best, the consistency of lead—sort of mushy and sticky or spongy. All the desire, and all the knowledge of how to impart this desire to the iron, must come from the smith. He needs quite a bit of strength, but not an abnormal amount. It is largely upper-body strength, and this is the only reason almost all smiths are men. He has about thirty seconds to work after each heating of the iron—time enough for forty or fifty swings of a two-and-a-half-pound hammer. Each blow is doubled, because the anvil underneath exerts an equal and opposite force, but each blow of the hammer affects only the area directly hit. So every blow must tell, and to make it do so a smith must concentrate all his attention, and be completely relaxed, and not think at all when he swings his hammer. When he swings, he will use his whole body and swing from his heels. And if he gets a drop of molten metal between his hammer handle and his palm while making a forge weld he must let it burn and dig it out afterward. The time to think and plan is while the metal is heating. When the iron comes out of the fire, the smith becomes deaf and dumb. Striking is executing what you've planned. I lose myself in my work and get a lot done. Because, when you know how to handle it, iron is very flexible: you can twist it, stretch it, bend it, split it, pierce it, or upset it—which means thicken it, swell it out. Nothing comes naturally with iron. But when a great smith like Samuel Yellin works it, the iron looks as if it could have taken that shape by itself.

"Forge work is a very good combination of the use of the eye, the hand, and the mind—and it's creative. And iron itself is an extremely educational material—it can teach you how to deal with resistant things in yourself, in architects and clients, in life. I think now that at fifteen I was starting late —that the human nervous system matures at a rate that makes ten to twelve the right time to begin learning eye-hand co-

ordination. The smiths of the old European workshops knew
this intuitively, which is why apprentices were started at this
age—to help them, not to exploit them. But even at fifteen I
could see that there was more than a lifetime of learning here,
and I still get such a kick out of it. In sixty years, I've mastered
practically every technique that has to do with working iron,
but my students teach me things I don't know, and some days
I'll figure out a new way of doing something and wonder: Why
didn't I think of that ten years ago?

"But I began to tell you how both my parents led me to
forge work. Before I went to Yellin's shop, I had learned from
them how to work. My mother taught us how to cook, darn
socks, wash dishes—skills she thought every human being
ought to have. She made most of our clothes—even after I
left home she made shirts for me for years. She was a dedicated
suffragette and got her head cracked once in Washington. Both
my parents were perfectionists, in a real way, as long as you
were working toward something that was attainable. I've
never quite got there with my work, but I can still keep trying,
and I have some reason for satisfaction. They gave both Rogers and me a tremendous vocabulary. I think of Rogers as an
example of a marvelously trained mind. Rogers always re-
sented the Skipper for yanking him out of Princeton at the
end of his sophomore year and sending him off to New York
with nothing more than three letters of introduction to New
York publishers, where he found his work. But my mother
and the Skipper really had already given us the same thing
—they made learning interesting for us, and they made work
a pleasure. And when I found my work I had good teachers;
in my contact with them I had enough real, thorough, basic
training to be able to go on and develop my skills. Personal
contact—that is the real requirement, the only way things get

passed on, whether you are an ironworker or a weaver or a storyteller. I did know a doctor once who taught himself to ski from a book, but when I see someone trying to master something without the benefit of personal instruction I think, Lord, he'll never make it. And sometimes I think, Lord pity us when we come to have an absolutely perfect substitute for that kind of experience. Then we'll have nothing and think we have everything, and that'll be the absolute end."

Francis's training was a seven-year apprenticeship that was compressed into three years. The first year was with Samuel Yellin, who had created a kind of university of black-smithing unlike anything else in the history of metalwork in this country. Yellin's name is becoming well known again in the early 1980's; Jack Andrews, a Philadelphia smith and writer, prepared a major retrospective of Yellin's work that was seen in four states, and also wrote a monograph on him. When Yellin, who was Polish, got to the United States, in 1906, he was already a master of both the techniques and the designs evolved by a hundred and fifty generations of black-smiths. The traditional designs of the craft are based not only on the smiths' discoveries of what iron can be made to look as if it wanted to do, but also on the shapes—usually bars, rods, or sheets—in which the metal came to the smiths from the ironmakers. The finished product often remains essentially bars, rods, and sheets, but if the smith knows how to bring out what is hidden inside these shapes, then his work looks alive. There is quite a lot of Yellin's work in New York City that anyone can go and see, and after I got back to the city from my trip to Colorado I went and looked at some of it. This was a very interesting thing to do at a moment when its creator was just being rediscovered. All the work I saw looked very much alive, and there are two pieces that even seem to be growing. A pair of massive tripartite lanterns flanking the front entrance of the Federal Reserve Bank, and decorated with leaves, spikes, acorns, and small dragons' heads with tongues or teeth, look like elegant, giant, triple-flowered plants that have just burst through the heavy stone blocks of the front wall. At the bank, a vice president showed me around and took me to the original banking hall, a two-story-high room on the executive floor, so that I could see the fireplace screen and hood that Yellin had forged for the huge stone fireplace, where a fire is lighted once a year for the bank's Christmas dinner. But while the Yellin work in that building is cared for with the respect we accord to a masterpiece, in a second building work just as good or better is treated like secondhand furniture. At the old Central Savings Bank building, at Broadway and Seventy-third Street, which in the 1980's became a branch of the Apple Bank for Savings, Yellin's work has had to take its chances. Bank employees say they love the ornamental-ironwork front of the hundred-foot-long tellers' cage, but much of it has been removed to give the banking lines a better look at the tellers; and (at least the day I was there) the delicate little iron roses and flower baskets on top of the cage are dusty and hung with cobwebs.

When Francis Whitaker went to work for Yellin, his shop had sixty forges and two hundred men. Yellin had been awarded the Federal Reserve Bank contract two years earlier; it called for a total of four hundred thousand pounds of wrought iron—the largest single order for ornamental ironwork ever placed with an American blacksmith. To fill his orders, Yellin had taken to meeting immigrant boats and hiring master smiths as they disembarked. He had more smiths than helpers, and their common language was work—eight hours a day, without coffee breaks. In a single year, which Francis says was the equivalent of three years' work nowadays, he worked with smiths from Italy, Germany, England, France, Spain, Poland, Switzerland, and the Virgin Islands. Many of them stayed with Yellin until his death in 1940. His big commissions had disappeared when construction stopped in the Depression, but he kept his men on salary, paying them with his own money, hoping to set up a permanent school of blacksmithing. He was never able to get this school started. Yellin had had a serious heart attack in 1930; he was fifty-five years old when he died.

In 1923, Francis went to Berlin and served a two-year apprenticeship with a German smith, Julius Schramm, who, like Yellin, was famous for his large ornamental pieces. Almost all of Schramm's work was destroyed by bombing during the Second World War. Francis worked nine hours a day, six days a week, at Schramm's forge. He says that two years with Schramm was the equivalent of four years' work nowadays. Francis went from Berlin to Carmel, where he worked for seven years for a contractor who needed a lot of ironwork because he was building in the Spanish Revival style, which had become popular during the rebuilding of Santa Barbara after an earthquake there in 1925.

In 1932, in the depths of the Depression, Francis decided to go into business for himself. For six months, he welded fenders, sharpened plows, and did whatever work came his way. But by the end of that time he had begun getting enough decorative ironwork commissions to see him through, and it's been that way ever since. It has always been his aim to be his own boss, so that he can meet the people who will be using what he creates; and he has always made it a point to live in a place where work, day-to-day living, and vacations are all a pleasure. He signs everything he makes:

This is an ironworker's design. Open up the diamond and it becomes:

Back on the train after lunch, I was again holding Frimbo's plaque on my lap, and we were slowing down—we were almost at Cumbres again. Then we stopped, and in the silence we heard cows and birds. We saw a cowboy on horseback rounding up seventeen head of Black Angus and also saw two finches chasing each other in front of the train. It was time to install the plaque. Our party of seven got off the train, and Francis found a brand-new tie about twenty-five yards in front of the engine, near the place where Frimbo's ashes had been scattered. A brand-new tie won't have to be replaced for some thirty years. Francis rolled up one leg of his pants above the knee, knelt down and took a small drill, eight screws, and a screwdriver out of his pocket, and drilled eight holes in the tie; and then we all gave the screwdriver a few turns. This was just for now; the railroad people had promised Francis that they would bolt the plaque down in a few days. Then we got back on the train, and Francis opened the picnic hamper he had had on his lap during the morning. Inside were plastic champagne glasses, ice cubes, a cocktail shaker, heavy cream, brandy, and crème de cacao. He and Portia had decided the day before that the only fitting way to close the ceremonies was to drink a toast to Rogers in his favorite cocktail—a brandy Alexander. So that's how the trip ended —with brandies Alexander.

It has been said that in the midst of all our confusion today Americans are trying to choose the best elements from our culture and set aside less useful things. If we still have a wide range of things to choose from, this is in part thanks to various Frimbos. In the case of the Whitakers, Rogers continued to ride trains and Francis continued to work iron long after most Americans considered both activities irrelevant. When another generation arrived, and wanted to know about such things, the information was still available. And so was the idea that learning can be interesting and work itself a pleasure.

Postscript from the Original Edition by E. M. Frimbo

Gentle Reader:

Should you, having finished this book, wish to say to me, "Gee, I wish I'd done that, too," my answer to you is: "For God's sake, go and do it, instead of joining the Catalpa Avenue Acey-Deucey Ladies' Whist Club. Get on a train!"

There are many of these adventures that you might duplicate, even yet. Here is one—I haven't even mentioned it before—just to get you started: A couple of times a week, from the city of Winnipeg, Manitoba, Canada (a town that is not inaccessible by passenger train, no matter what people tell you), a train with a sleeping car departs for Port Churchill, on Hudson's Bay. It's a whole new world: first take a look at the treeless tundra, the Eskimo settlements; then, practically from the railway station at the end of the run you can see the blue whales spouting in the bay.

Get on a train!

About the Authors

Rogers E. M. Whitaker was born in Arlington, Massachusetts, on January 15, 1900, and attended Princeton University. After working for the *New York Times,* Whitaker joined *The New Yorker* in 1926, where he mastered half a dozen trades, including sports reporting—a job about which he later remarked, "I became a sports writer . . . so that someone would pay me to go by train to universities in the eastern part of the United States and report on their winter sports." In 1945 he also became copy for *The New Yorker,* when the magazine first began publishing sparkling accounts of Frimbo's worldwide rail journeys. Mr. Whitaker was a director of the Valley Railroad of Connecticut, life member and honorary engine driver of the Festiniog Railway of Wales, and an honored member of many railway, historical, and preservation societies in the United States, Canada, and the British Isles. In 1991 Amtrak christened one of its inaugural trains the *E. M. Frimbo Special.* During Whitaker's many decades of travel he traversed nearly 3,000,000 railway miles. Following Mr. Whitaker's death on May 11, 1981, his ashes were scattered over Cumbres Pass on the tourist railway line that links Chama, New Mexico, and Antonito, Colorado, the highest elevation passenger railroad in the continental United States.

Tony Hiss became a staff writer at *The New Yorker* in 1963, soon after his graduation from Harvard University. During his thirty-three years with *The New Yorker,* he has published several hundred reports and profiles on a wide variety of topics, including urban planning, transportation, land use, social psychology, sports, and wildlife. In 1995 he also became a visiting scholar at New York University's Taub Urban Research Center. His 1990 book, *The Experience of Place,* won many awards and has been published in Germany and Japan. In 1994 Mr. Hiss received a Guggenheim Fellowship for his biography (in progress) of Frederick Law Olmsted. Mr. Hiss lives in New York City with his wife, the novelist Lois Metzger, and their son, Jacob.

ANSHA GLOBE

ational in scope, this series offers distinguished books that explore the customs, and mindsets of peoples and cultures around the world.

Other Kodansha Globe titles of interest

CHARTING THE SEA OF DARKNESS:
The Four Voyages of Henry Hudson
by Donald S. Johnson This fascinating book helps modern readers discover why whole societies were mesmerized by the voyages of heroic maritime figures like Henry Hudson. "Johnson . . . recounts Hudson's growing obsession with locating a northwest passage. . . . Fascinating."—Douglas A. Sylva, *The New York Times Book Review*
($14, 1-56836-105-X)

THE HEART OF THE SKY: *Travels Among the Maya*
by Peter Canby A writer finds a vital culture in the lands of the Maya, even while the modern world threatens to engulf it. "Canby makes an immensely appealing traveling companion. . . . He makes us feel that we have just begun to comprehend a rich, profoundly different and endangered culture." —Francine Prose, *The New York Times Book Review*
($13, 1-56836-026-6)

MY LIFE AS AN EXPLORER:
The Great Adventurer's Classic Memoir
by Sven Hedin Hedin traveled the ancient Silk Road, discovered long-lost cities, mapped previously uncharted rivers and deserts, and saw more of the "roof of the world" than any European before him. "An account of an astonishing number of adventures . . . and of perils, a tithe of which would satisfy most men."—*New York Tribune*
($16, 1-56836-142-4)

Please contact your local bookseller **KODANSHA AMERICA, INC.**
for these and other Kodansha titles, **Attn. Order Department**
or mail your order with payment to: **c/o Oxford University Press**
2001 Evans Road
Cary, North Carolina 27513

All orders must be accompanied by payment in full *(check or money order payable to KODANSHA, in U.S. funds only, no cash or C.O.D.s)*, including shipping & handling charges ($3.50 for the first book, $1.00 for each additional book). California and North Carolina residents please include applicable sales tax. Allow 3–6 weeks for delivery. Prices are subject to change without notice.

When ordering by credit card call **1-800-451-7556.**